The Cambridge Companion to the Rolling Stones

The Rolling Stones are one of the most influential, prolific, and enduring rock and roll bands in the history of music. This groundbreaking, specifically commissioned collection of essays provides the first dedicated academic overview of the music, career, influences, history, and cultural impact of the Rolling Stones. Shining a light on the many communities and sources of knowledge about the group, this *Companion* brings together essays by musicologists, ethnomusicologists, players, film scholars, and filmmakers into a single volume intended to stimulate fresh thinking about the group as they vault well over the mid-century of their career. Threaded throughout these essays are album- and song-oriented discussions of the landmark recordings of the group and their influence. Exploring new issues about sound, culture, media representation, the influence of world music, fan communities, group personnel, and the importance of their revival post-1989, this collection greatly expands our understanding of their music.

VICTOR COELHO is Professor of Music and Director of the Center for Early Music Studies at Boston University, as well as a lutenist and guitarist. His previous publications include *Instrumentalists and Renaissance Culture, 1420–1600* (with Keith Polk, Cambridge, 2016), *The Cambridge Companion to the Guitar* (2003), and *Performance on Lute, Guitar, and Vihuela* (Cambridge, 1997).

JOHN COVACH is Director of the University of Rochester Institute for Popular Music, Professor of Music in the College Music Department, and Professor of Theory at the Eastman School of Music. He is the principal author of the college textbook *What's That Sound? An Introduction to Rock Music* (2006) and has co-edited *Understanding Rock* (1998), *American Rock and the Classical Tradition* (2000), *Traditions, Institutions, and American Popular Music* (2000), and *Sounding Out Pop* (2010).

Cambridge Companions to Music

Topics

The Cambridge Companion to Ballet
Edited by Marion Kant

The Cambridge Companion to Blues and Gospel Music
Edited by Allan Moore

The Cambridge Companion to Choral Music
Edited by André de Quadros

The Cambridge Companion to the Concerto
Edited by Simon P. Keefe

The Cambridge Companion to Conducting
Edited by José Antonio Bowen

The Cambridge Companion to Eighteenth-Century Music
Edited by Anthony R. DelDonna and Pierpaolo Polzonetti

The Cambridge Companion to Electronic Music
Edited by Nick Collins and Julio D'Escriván

The Cambridge Companion to Film Music
Edited by Mervyn Cooke and Fiona Ford

The Cambridge Companion to French Music
Edited by Simon Trezise

The Cambridge Companion to Grand Opera
Edited by David Charlton

The Cambridge Companion to Hip-Hop
Edited by Justin A. Williams

The Cambridge Companion to Jazz
Edited by Mervyn Cooke and David Horn

The Cambridge Companion to Jewish Music
Edited by Joshua S. Walden

The Cambridge Companion to the Lied
Edited by James Parsons

The Cambridge Companion to Medieval Music
Edited by Mark Everist

The Cambridge Companion to Music in Digital Culture
Edited by Nicholas Cook, Monique Ingalls and David Trippett

The Cambridge Companion to the Musical, third edition
Edited by William Everett and Paul Laird

The Cambridge Companion to Opera Studies
Edited by Nicholas Till

The Cambridge Companion to the Orchestra
Edited by Colin Lawson

The Cambridge Companion to Percussion
Edited by Russell Hartenberger

The Cambridge Companion to Pop and Rock
Edited by Simon Frith, Will Straw and John Street

The Cambridge Companion to Recorded Music
Edited by Eric Clarke, Nicholas Cook, Daniel Leech-Wilkinson and John Rink

The Cambridge Companion to the Singer-Songwriter
Edited by Katherine Williams and Justin A. Williams

The Cambridge Companion to the String Quartet
Edited by Robin Stowell

The Cambridge Companion to Twentieth-Century Opera
Edited by Mervyn Cooke

Composers

The Cambridge Companion to Bach
Edited by John Butt

The Cambridge Companion to Bartók
Edited by Amanda Bayley

The Cambridge Companion to The Beatles
Edited by Kenneth Womack

The Cambridge Companion to Beethoven
Edited by Glenn Stanley

The Cambridge Companion to Berg
Edited by Anthony Pople

The Cambridge Companion to Berlioz
Edited by Peter Bloom

The Cambridge Companion to Brahms
Edited by Michael Musgrave

The Cambridge Companion to Benjamin Britten
Edited by Mervyn Cooke

The Cambridge Companion to Bruckner
Edited by John Williamson

The Cambridge Companion to John Cage
Edited by David Nicholls

The Cambridge Companion to Chopin
Edited by Jim Samson

The Cambridge Companion to Debussy
Edited by Simon Trezise

The Cambridge Companion to Elgar
Edited by Daniel M. Grimley and Julian Rushton

The Cambridge Companion to Duke Ellington
Edited by Edward Green

The Cambridge Companion to Gilbert and Sullivan
Edited by David Eden and Meinhard Saremba

The Cambridge Companion to Handel
Edited by Donald Burrows

The Cambridge Companion to Haydn
Edited by Caryl Clark

The Cambridge Companion to Liszt
Edited by Kenneth Hamilton

The Cambridge Companion to Mahler
Edited by Jeremy Barham

The Cambridge Companion to Mendelssohn
Edited by Peter Mercer-Taylor

The Cambridge Companion to Monteverdi
Edited by John Whenham and Richard Wistreich

The Cambridge Companion to Mozart
Edited by Simon P. Keefe

The Cambridge Companion to Arvo Pärt
Edited by Andrew Shenton

The Cambridge Companion to Ravel
Edited by Deborah Mawer

The Cambridge Companion to the Rolling Stones
Edited by Victor Coelho and John Covach

The Cambridge Companion to Rossini
Edited by Emanuele Senici

The Cambridge Companion to Schoenberg
Edited by Jennifer Shaw and Joseph Auner

The Cambridge Companion to Schubert
Edited by Christopher Gibbs

The Cambridge Companion to Schumann
Edited by Beate Perrey

The Cambridge Companion to Shostakovich
Edited by Pauline Fairclough and David Fanning

The Cambridge Companion to Sibelius
Edited by Daniel M. Grimley

The Cambridge Companion to Richard Strauss
Edited by Charles Youmans

The Cambridge Companion to Michael Tippett
Edited by Kenneth Gloag and Nicholas Jones

The Cambridge Companion to Vaughan Williams
Edited by Alain Frogley and Aiden J. Thomson

The Cambridge Companion to Verdi
Edited by Scott L. Balthazar

Instruments

The Cambridge Companion to Brass Instruments
Edited by Trevor Herbert and John Wallace

The Cambridge Companion to the Cello
Edited by Robin Stowell

The Cambridge Companion to the Clarinet
Edited by Colin Lawson

The Cambridge Companion to the Guitar
Edited by Victor Coelho

The Cambridge Companion to the Harpsichord
Edited by Mark Kroll

The Cambridge Companion to the Organ
Edited by Nicholas Thistlethwaite and Geoffrey Webber

The Cambridge Companion to the Piano
Edited by David Rowland

The Cambridge Companion to the Recorder
Edited by John Mansfield Thomson

The Cambridge Companion to the

ROLLING STONES

....

EDITED BY

Victor Coelho
Boston University

John Covach
University of Rochester, New York

CAMBRIDGE
UNIVERSITY PRESS

CAMBRIDGE
UNIVERSITY PRESS

University Printing House, Cambridge CB2 8BS, United Kingdom

One Liberty Plaza, 20th Floor, New York, NY 10006, USA

477 Williamstown Road, Port Melbourne, VIC 3207, Australia

314–321, 3rd Floor, Plot 3, Splendor Forum, Jasola District Centre, New Delhi – 110025, India

79 Anson Road, #06–04/06, Singapore 079906

Cambridge University Press is part of the University of Cambridge.

It furthers the University's mission by disseminating knowledge in the pursuit of
education, learning, and research at the highest international levels of excellence.

www.cambridge.org
Information on this title: www.cambridge.org/9781107030268
DOI: 10.1017/9781139343336

First published 2019

Printed in the United Kingdom by TJ International Ltd, Padstow, Cornwall

A catalogue record for this publication is available from the British Library.

Library of Congress Cataloging-in-Publication Data
Names: Coelho, Victor. | Covach, John Rudolph.
Title: The Cambridge companion to the Rolling Stones / edited by Victor Coelho, John
    Covach.
Description: Cambridge, United Kingdom ; New York, NY : Cambridge University Press,
    2019. | Includes bibliographical references and index.
Identifiers: LCCN 2019000406 | ISBN 9781107030268 (hardback : alk. paper)
    | ISBN 9781107651111 (pbk. : alk. paper)
Subjects: LCSH: Rolling Stones. | Rock musicians–England. | Rock music–History and
    criticism.
Classification: LCC ML421.R64 C25 2019 | DDC 782.42166092/2–dc23
LC record available at https://lccn.loc.gov/2019000406

ISBN 978-1-107-03026-8 Hardback
ISBN 978-1-107-65111-1 Paperback

For Arjun and Susie

Contents

Illustrations

Tables

Notes on Contributors

Michael Brendan Baker is Professor of Film Studies in the Faculty of Humanities & Social Sciences at Sheridan College in Ontario, Canada. He specializes in documentary film and video, music and the moving image, and film history. He is author of numerous book chapters and journal articles on a range of subjects including documentary, popular music and film, and new media.

Daniel Beller-McKenna is Associate Professor at the University of New Hampshire where he teaches courses in American popular music and the Western classical tradition. In addition to scholarship on Brahms, current projects include studies of Townes van Zandt and Johnny Paycheck, and an active avocation as a pedal steel guitarist.

Victor Coelho is Professor of Music and Director of the Center for Early Music Studies at Boston University. His publications include *Instrumentalists and Renaissance Culture, 1420–1600* (with Keith Polk, Cambridge), *The Cambridge Companion to the Guitar*, and *Performance for Lute, Guitar, and Vihuela* (Cambridge). As a lutenist he co-directs the group Il Furioso and records with Toccata Classics. As a guitarist he leads the Rooster Band, which for ten years toured with the Chicago bluesman, Lou Pride. people.bu.edu/blues/

John Covach is Director of the University of Rochester Institute for Popular Music, Professor of Music in the College Music Department, and Professor of Theory at the Eastman School of Music. He has published on popular music, twelve-tone music, and the philosophy and aesthetics of music. He is the principal author of the college textbook *What's That Sound? An Introduction to Rock Music* (2006) and has co-edited *Understanding Rock* (1998), *American Rock and the Classical Tradition* (2000), *Traditions, Institutions, and American Popular Music* (2000), and *Sounding Out Pop* (2010).

Paul Harris toured Canada as a guitarist in the late 1980s with the Calgary roots-rock band, the Burners, prior to studying historical musicology at the University of Calgary (MA) and the University of North Carolina at Chapel Hill (Ph.D.). Since 2008, he has taught at the University of Puget Sound.

Brita Renée Heimarck is Associate Professor of Music at Boston University. She has authored two books, *Balinese Discourses on Music and Modernization* (2003) and *Gender Wayang Music of Bapak I Wayan Loceng from Sukawati, Bali* (2015). She is currently working on an edited volume entitled *Yogic Traditions and Sacred Sound Practices in the United States.*

Bill Janovitz has appeared and published widely as a specialist on the Rolling Stones and is the author of *Exile on Main Street* for the 33⅓ series and *Rocks Off: 50 Tracks that Tell the Story of the Rolling Stones* (2013). He is also a singer, guitarist, and songwriter in the band Buffalo Tom.

Ralph Maier is on the faculty at the Mount Royal University Conservatory of Music, and at the University of Calgary where he teaches classical guitar, chamber music, and a wide range of musicology classes from Renaissance Print Culture to 1970s Progressive Rock. Recent projects include the recording, engineering and production of his most recent CD, *Variations*, with performances on vihuela, baroque guitar, romantic guitar, classical guitar, and electric guitars.

Philippe "Philfan" Puicouyoul is a French filmmaker at the Centre Pompidou in Paris. His work deals principally with fans, audiences, and the culture of music, and he has produced films dealing with the French punk scene (*Le brune et moi*, 1981) and fans of the Rolling Stones (*Vers l'Olympe: être fan des Rolling Stones*, 2008). He is the author of *Pop Fiction* (1991), about being a fan at rock shows.

Preface

The long and durable musical career of the Rolling Stones continues to span almost the entire history of rock and roll. Making their recording début in 1963 with their single "Come On," a Chuck Berry cover, the Stones were catalysts in the important British blues revival of the early 1960s, and along with the Beatles, Animals, Who, Kinks, and Yardbirds spearheaded the British pop music invasion of the 1960s. Appearing first on widely watched nationally televised variety shows, followed by regular tours, the group has now played more than 2,100 shows, reaching some 45 million fans.[1] For over 50 years, and with a body of music amounting to over 400 songs, they have sustained an impact that has been musically influential, culturally powerful, and economically crucial to the development of virtually all aspects of the massive rock music industry. Adapting to and in many cases anticipating new (or retro) trends in popular music during their long career – rock, folk, psychedelic, funk, punk, reggae, disco, and others – the Stones nevertheless remained true to the fundamental stylistic roots and sound of rock and roll: R&B, country, and most of all, the blues, to which their indebtedness is reverential. Their amalgamation of these styles into an individual, highly distinctive, roots- and riff-based sound, along with their trademark subversive attitude (no less influential than their music), skillfully mediated the commercial and poetic boundaries of popular music. As a result, the Stones are both a barometer of rock aesthetics and a guide to its culture over the last half-century.

Given their long career and vast musical production, the group has received prolonged attention through some excellent journalism, detailed reference works chronicling their tours, recordings, and gear, studies of specific albums, biographies, and key autobiographies by Bill Wyman, Keith Richards, Ron Wood, Marianne Faithfull, and Andrew Loog Oldham, all of this supplemented by extensive concert footage, interviews, film documentaries, and a – literally – weighty amount of large-format, glossy, but occasionally valuable books in the "coffee table" genre. The sum total of this body of work is massive, often guideless, of variable quality, and unfortunately fragmented among many fields, industries, and specialists. *The Cambridge Companion to the Rolling Stones* was conceived to "de-silo" the field and shine a light on the various communities of knowledge about the Rolling Stones. It brings musicologists, ethnomusicologists, players, Stones scholars, film scholars, and filmmakers into a single volume intended to stimulate fresh thinking about the group as they vault well over the mid-century of their career. It further broadens the approach to their music by considering new issues about sound, culture, media representation, the influence of world music, fan communities, group personnel, and the importance of their revival, post-1989. In addition, threaded throughout these essays are album- and song-oriented discussions of the landmark recordings of the group and their influences.

The present collection is cast in three parts. In Part I, "Albums, Songs, Players, and the Core Repertory of the Rolling Stones," John Covach traces the rapid evolution of the Stones through their recordings up to 1974, with particular emphasis on their early stylistic development and singles. Bill Janovitz looks at the relationship between the original composition of the band and the critical changes that take place musically through successive personnel changes and the eventual enlargement of the band's sound in the 1970s. In a further study, Covach revises the notion that the Stones' 1967 album *Their Satanic Majesties Request* is the end of the group's "Psychedelic" phase and shows instead traits of Psychedelia continuing in and influencing *Beggars Banquet*. Victor Coelho accepts the notion of the four albums from *Beggars* to *Exile* as the "core repertory" but places the texts and musical styles of these releases within the larger poetic and political dimension of exile, one that allows many vernacular, rural, and gospel styles to enter their sphere as another vocabulary. Paul Harris' essay follows the group from their "exilic" period to their unsure position in the mid- to late-seventies, in which a new urban sound is cultivated under the influences of punk, post-punk, and club culture.

Part II, "Sound, Roots, and Brian Jones," begins with Ralph Maier, who, drawing on gear, recording, and studio equipment, contributes an important study of the Stones' *sound*, an often neglected but critical topic whether discussing recorded or live performance. The deep influence of country – and of country records, players, and techniques – on the Stones is analyzed by Daniel Beller McKenna in his essay that draws on case studies of five songs and their roots backgrounds. Finally, ethnomusicologist Brita Heimarck takes a fresh approach to the influence of Brian Jones, perhaps the most mythologized and misunderstood member of the Rolling Stones, using Deleuze's theory of *assemblage* to explain his unusually wide influences and culturally diverse musical interests.

Finally, Part III, "Stones on Film, Revival, and Fans," begins with film scholar Michael Baker's study of the Stones as represented on film within the context of the "rockumentary" genre, from Whitehead to Scorsese. Coelho's essay on "Second Life" examines how the Stones at the end of the 1980s, corroded internally, marginalized by rap, and seemingly left with only their past history, triumphantly revived themselves, and in the process curated a lasting history of the band – on their own terms. Modern culture is full of "shrines" to the Rolling Stones – websites, fanzines, and a flourishing market for relics (bootlegs, outtakes, videos, and the like), which cry out for attention within the study of identity formation and the rituals of audiences. Filmmaker Philippe Puicouyoul's "fan memoir" that closes the volume gives us a close view of the global Stones fan community, and is a fitting conclusion underlining the main element common to those of us who listen to, play, study, and write about the Stones: we are all, in the end, fans.

We express gratitude here to a number of people who have contributed everything from crucial information and deep conversations about the Stones' music to small, but valuable pieces of knowledge, in particular: Peter Deacon, Tom Knowles, Kenton McDonald, Dave Morton, Larry Finn, Thomas Peattie, Marcie Cohen, Jason McCool, John Kmetz, David Campbell, Peter Whitehead, the Rev. Robert Hill, and David Dolata; and for granting many requests to visit the Rolling Stones Mobile Studio, Andrew Mosker, President and CEO of the National Music Centre in Calgary, Alberta, where the mobile resides. We also thank Vicky Cooper, former Commissioning Editor at Cambridge University Press, for helping us conceive of this *Companion*.

In addition, we acknowledge the digital repositories and archives that made their collections available and kindly assisted with the images used and cited in this book, in particular Art Resource of New York, Getty Images, the Howard Gotlieb Archive at Boston University, and the Library and Archives of the Rock and Roll Hall of Fame in Cleveland.

Finally, we thank Eilidh Burrett and Lisa Sinclair at Cambridge University Press, and the copy-editor Andrew Dawes, for their careful work on the manuscript, and of course Kate Brett, Publisher, Music and Theatre at the Press for her excellent suggestions, encouragement, and, above all, patience.

VC AND JC
Boston and Rochester

Note

1 Cited in the official program booklet for the Rolling Stones traveling exhibit, *Exhibitionism: The Rolling Stones* (n.p. [2016]).

Abbreviations

According	Dora Loewenstein and Philip Dodd, eds., *According to the Rolling Stones*. London, 2003.
Dalton*FTY*	David Dalton, ed. *The Rolling Stones: The First Twenty Years*. New York, 1981.
Dalton*RS*	David Dalton, ed. *Rolling Stones*. New York and London, 1972.
Faithfull	Marianne Faithfull (with David Dalton), *Faithfull: An Autobiography*. New York, 1994.
Janovitz*EMS*	Bill Janovitz, *Exile on Main Street*. New York, 2005.
Janovitz*RO*	Bill Janovitz, *Rocks Off*. New York, 2013.
Karnbach & Bernson	James Karnbach and Carol Bernson, *It's Only Rock 'n' Roll: The Ultimate Guide to the Rolling Stones*. New York, 1997.
Life	Keith Richards (with James Fox), *Life*. New York, 2010.
Margotin & Guesdon	Philippe Margotin and Jean-Michel Guesdon, *The Rolling Stones – All the Songs: The Story Behind Every Track*. New York, 2016.
MM	*Melody Maker*.
Rock Hall	Library and Archives, Rock and Roll Hall of Fame Museum.
RSCRS	Martin Elliott, *The Rolling Stones – Complete Recording Sessions 1962–2012: 50th Anniversary Edition*. London, 2012.
RSG	Andy Babiuk and Greg Prevost, *Rolling Stones Gear*. Milwaukee, 2013.
RSt	*Rolling Stone* (magazine).
Trynka	Paul Trynka, *Brian Jones: The Making of the Rolling Stones*. New York, 2014.
Wenner*MJR*	Jann Wenner, "Mick Jagger Remembers," *Rolling Stone* (December 14, 1995): https://www.rollingstone.com/music/music-news/mick-jagger-remembers-92946.
Wyman*RWTS*	Bill Wyman, *Rolling with the Stones*. New York, 2002.
Wyman*SA*	Bill Wyman, *Stone Alone: The Story of a Rock 'n' Roll Band*. New York, 1990.

PART I

Albums, Songs, Players, and the Core Repertory of the Rolling Stones

1 The Rolling Stones: Albums and Singles, 1963–1974

JOHN COVACH

The Rolling Stones are one of the most critically and commercially successful acts in rock music history. The band first rose to prominence during the mid-1960s in the UK, and in the USA as part of what Americans call the "British Invasion" – an explosion of British pop ignited by the UK success of the Beatles in 1963 and their storming of the American shores and charts in early 1964 (see Figure 1.1). The Beatles and the Stones were part of a fab new cohort of mop-topped combos that also included the Animals, the Dave Clark Five, Gerry and the Pacemakers, the Yardbirds, the Zombies, the Kinks, the Who, the Hollies, Herman's Hermits, and even Freddie and the Dreamers. However much comparisons between the Beatles and the Stones may irritate the faithful of both groups, the similarities and differences can nevertheless be useful. Place of origin matters: The Beatles were not the first pop act from Liverpool to hit it big in London, but they were perhaps the first not to hide their northern roots. Although Brian Jones was from Cheltenham (Gloucestershire), the Stones as a band were, by contrast, from London. Songwriting factors in: John Lennon and Paul McCartney were writing together even before the Beatles were a band, while Mick Jagger and Keith Richards did not start writing until after the Stones had already begun their careers together. Commercial success is also worth noting: The first Beatles No. 1 hit single in the UK was "Please Please Me," released in March 1963; the first Stones UK No. 1 was "It's All Over Now," released in August 1964. "I Want to Hold Your Hand" topped the American charts in late January and February 1964; the Stones' "(I Can't Get No) Satisfaction" hit the top of the US charts in the summer of 1965. The most important distinction between the two bands – and the one that probably tells us the most about the stylistic distance between them – has to do with early influences. The Beatles were very much a "song band," focused mostly on pop songs and their vocal delivery. And while Jagger and Richards were fans of the 1950s rock and roll of Chuck Berry and Buddy Holly, they were also students (along with Brian Jones) of American blues. As a result, the Stones' music is often more "rootsy," at times placing more emphasis on expression than on polish.

Figure 1.1 The Rolling Stones in Paris, 1964 (Charlie Watts is absent from the photo). Courtesy HIP/Art Resource, NY.

This chapter provides a broad survey of the Stones' music over their first dozen years, beginning with the band's earliest recordings in 1963 and extending to *It's Only Rock 'n Roll* of 1974.[1] Its purpose is to provide a historical context for several of the chapters that follow and to sketch an outline of the band's releases and stylistic development over this period. As we shall see, the Stones emerged out of a small London blues scene to explore many styles over these twelve years. The period from 1963 through the end of 1967 – from "Come On" to *Their Satanic Majesties Request* – finds the Stones becoming increasingly ambitious musically, relying more and more on their own songwriting while following, and at times fueling, a practice among rock bands during the mid-1960s that emphasized innovation and experimentation. If *Their Satanic Majesties Request* represents the culmination of these early years of stylistic development, *Beggars Banquet* of 1968 marks the beginning of what would become the band's most productive years, as the Stones balance the musical ambition and accomplishment of their previous music with a return to blues, country, and rhythm and blues influences, producing a series of albums and singles that have come to define – for fans and critics alike – the classic Stones sound. The first dozen years of the band's history can thus be divided into two arcs of stylistic development: the period from 1963 to 1967, which is driven by increasing musical and artistic ambition; and the period from 1968 to 1974, which is characterized by striking a distinctive balance between musical ambition and stylistic tradition.[2]

Students of the Blues and Early Singles, 1962–63

What would become some of the most internationally celebrated music in rock history, performed in stadiums and arenas around the world, started from a desire to recreate American blues in a few small London clubs in the early 1960s. The Beatles spent their early years performing in Liverpool and Hamburg, often playing long hours and performing sets filled with their versions of American hits.[3] The Stones, by contrast, developed their musical skills in the London blues revival scene of the early 1960s, far from the center of UK pop and mostly off the commercial radar. Since the mid-1940s, there had been a significant British interest in markedly American styles such as jazz, folk, and blues. By the late 1950s, the "trad" jazz scene had developed in the UK, led by performers such as Acker Bilk, Kenny Ball, and Chris Barber – the "three Bs."[4] Grounded more in Dixieland jazz than in the American bebop of the time, these British musicians were often dedicated students of American recordings. In the second half of the 1950s, a skiffle craze hit the UK, led by guitarist/vocalist Lonnie Donegan, whose "Rock Island Line" added a big beat to an American folk classic and became a hit not only in the UK but also in the USA. Like many other British musicians interested in American music, Donegan developed into an expert on American folk, reportedly scouring every possible source for information and recordings, including the library in the American Embassy in London.[5] British enthusiasm for the blues on the London scene was led by guitarist Alexis Korner and harmonica player Cyril Davies.[6] Their band, Blues Incorporated, began playing Sunday nights at the Ealing Club in March 1962 and in May took over Thursdays at the Marquee Club.[7] Both Korner and Davies were at least ten years older than most of the young musicians they would influence, including not only Jagger, Richards, Jones, and Watts, but also Jack Bruce, Eric Clapton, Ginger Baker, Paul Jones, Eric Burdon, John Mayall, and Jimmy Page.[8] The musical approach of Blues Incorporated is accurately represented on the band's *R & B at the Marquee* album, recorded in June 1962 and released in November.[9] This recording features a mix of originals with versions of blues classics based on recordings by Muddy Waters, Howlin'

Wolf, and Lead Belly. Blues Incorporated plays faithfully in the late 1950s American electric blues style without being slavish imitators, turning in a series of convincing performances that might easily be mistaken for authentic Chicago blues tracks.[10]

The Rolling Stones began, at least as far as Brian Jones was concerned, as a band very much in the mold of Blues Incorporated.[11] The band's first gig was at the Marquee, filling in for Blues Incorporated on the bill also featuring a band quickly formed by singer Long John Baldry.[12] Bassist Bill Wyman joined the Stones in December 1962, with Charlie Watts (who had played drums with Blues Incorporated but quit to return to school) joining in January 1963. In February the Stones began their residency at the Crawdaddy Club, initially managed by Giorgio Gomelsky. In April, just two months into those gigs, a young Andrew Loog Oldham heard the band for the first time at the Crawdaddy, and by May he and senior partner Eric Easton had signed the Stones to both a management deal and a recording contract with Decca.[13] The Rolling Stones' first single, a version of Chuck Berry's "Come On" (Chess Records, 1961) was released in the UK in June 1963 – less than a year after the band had played their first gig at the Marquee. That début single, which rose only as high as No. 38 in the UK, featured a version of Willie Dixon's "I Want to Be Loved" on the B side – a song that had been recorded by Muddy Waters (Chess, 1955). The two sides of this first single clearly announce who the Stones will be over the next few years: a band pursuing pop appeal while also retaining a strong blues sensibility.

The path to the Stones' second single perhaps reveals more about their aspirations for commercial success than about their blues roots. In July 1963, the band recorded Jerry Leiber and Mike Stoller's "Poison Ivy" (originally released by the Coasters on Atlantic Records in 1959), which was to be issued as the follow-up to "Come On" in August.[14] But Oldham felt the track was not strong enough; he withdrew plans for its release and drafted Lennon and McCartney to write "I Wanna Be Your Man" for the Stones. Released in November 1963, this second single rose to a promising No. 12 in the UK, establishing the Stones as rising stars on the British pop scene. The Beatles also released a version of this song on *With the Beatles*, with Ringo singing lead. The contrast between the blues-driven, rootsy intensity of the Stones version and the commercial polish of the Beatles track provides a succinct measure of the stylistic distance between these two groups. The record also provides, on its B side "Stoned," an early instance of the band recording its own original material. This mostly instrumental track is based loosely on "Green Onions," a 1962 hit for Booker T. and the MGs. The Stones, however, credit songwriting to Nanker Phelge – a pen name given to songs "written" by all of the band members.[15] Subsequent early Stones releases would include additional Nanker Phelge songs, which were often based on specific tracks written by others.

Singles and Albums, 1964–65

In January 1964 the Rolling Stones had their first success on the top of the charts: The EP *The Rolling Stones* (containing four tracks, including the previously withdrawn "Poison Ivy") topped the UK charts. This was followed by the British release in February of "Not Fade Away," a Buddy Holly/Norman Petty song from 1957. The B side was "Little by Little," another Nanker Phelge song, this time based on Jimmy Reed's "Shame, Shame, Shame" (Vee-Jay Records, 1963). This third single went to No. 3 in the UK, and when released in the USA in March with "I Wanna Be Your Man" as the B side, rose to No. 48 – the Stones' first chart appearance in the States.[16] Aside from the songs attributed to Nanker Phelge – which, as already noted, were not particularly original – the first three singles and first EP featured no songs written by Jagger and Richards. Table 1.1 lists the Rolling Stones' singles from 1963 to 1965. Note that it is with the fourth single (not counting the aborted release of "Poison Ivy") that a Jagger/Richards song, "Good Times, Bad Times," is included, though as a B side. "Tell Me" marks the first Jagger/Richards song to appear as the

Table 1.1 *Rolling Stones singles, 1963–65*

"Come On" (Chuck Berry) b/w "I Want to Be Loved" (Muddy Waters), June 1963, uk21, UK only
"Poison Ivy" (Coasters) b/w "Fortune Teller" (Benny Spellman), withdrawn
"I Wanna Be Your Man" (Lennon/McCartney) b/w "Stoned" (Booker T. and the MGs/Nanker Phelge), November 1963, uk12, US release did not chart
"Not Fade Away" (Buddy Holly) b/w "Little by Little" (Jimmy Reed/Nanker Phelge), February 1964, uk3; US release b/w "I Wanna Be Your Man," March 1964, us48
"It's All Over Now" (Valentinos) b/w "Good Times, Bad Times" (Jagger/Richards), June (uk1), August (us26) 1964
"Tell Me" (Jagger/Richards) b/w "I Just Want To Make Love To You" (Muddy Waters), June 1964, us24, US only
"Time Is on My Side" (Irma Thomas) b/w "Congratulations" (Jagger/Richards), September 1964, us6, US only
"Little Red Rooster" (Howlin' Wolf) b/w "Off the Hook" (Willie Dixon/Nanker Phelge), November 1964, uk1, UK only
"Heart of Stone" b/w "What a Shame" (both Jagger/Richards), December 1964, us19, US only
"The Last Time" b/w "Play with Fire" (both Jagger/Richards), February (uk1), March (us9) 1965
"(I Can't Get No) Satisfaction" (Jagger/Richards), b/w "The Under Assistant West Coast Promotion Man" (Nanker Phelge); UK release b/w "The Spider and the Fly" (Jagger/Richards), May (us1), August (uk1) 1965
"Get Off Of My Cloud" b/w "I'm Free," September 1965, us1; UK release b/w "The Singer, Not The Song" (all Jagger/Richards), October 1965, uk1
"As Tears Go By" b/w "Gotta Get Away" (both Jagger/Richards), December 1965, us6, US only

Note: Chart numbers refer to A side of each single release (first-listed song). Names in parentheses indicate original artist recording that song, except in the case of "Jagger/Richards," which indicate the songwriters. Parentheses marked "Nanker Phelge" also include the original recording artist who provided a model for that song.

A side of a single, though it was released in this way only in the USA. After this, with only one exception, the remainder of the singles listed in Table 1.1 feature at least one, and sometimes two, songs written by Jagger and Richards. Note also that in the fall of 1964 the band released "Time Is on My Side" in the USA (going to No. 6), but released "Little Red Rooster" in the UK. "Rooster" had been released by Howlin' Wolf on Chess in 1961, and the release of this slow blues number as a pop single was a risky move – though it paid off with a No. 1 hit. It seems likely that with the clear pop emphasis of the previous singles, the band was eager to reestablish its blues-revival bona fides with "Rooster," especially at home in the UK.[17] Table 1.1 provides a good picture of how, over the period 1963–65, the Stones moved from versions of songs previously recorded by others to Jagger/Richards originals.

The absence of Jagger/Richards songs in the first batch of singles, as well as on the first EP, might suggest that Jagger and Richards were either not writing much or were unwilling to release what they may have been writing.[18] As can be seen in Table 1.2, however, Jagger and Richards were indeed writing during this period, though these songs were released by other artists, two as early as January 1964. Among these songs, the most interesting is Marianne Faithfull's recording of "As Tears Go By," which (as seen in Table 1.1) the Stones released in their own version in late 1965. The use of chamber strings in the Stones version seems to be influenced by the Beatles' "Yesterday," but the philosophical quality of the song's lyrics actually predates McCartney's "Yesterday" lyrics by a year. Still, the character of these Jagger/Richards songs recorded by others suggests that the Stones believed that material to be too pop-oriented for the band. And the timing of those first songs, released in early 1964, suggests that the October 1963 meeting with Lennon and McCartney that produced

Table 1.2 *Early Jagger/Richards songs*

"That Girl Belongs to Yesterday," Gene Pitney, January 1964 (uk7, us49)
"Will You Be My Lover Tonight," George Bean, January 1964
"Each and Every Day," Bobby Jameson, February 1964 (B side)
"Shang a Doo Lang," Adrienne Posta, March 1964
"Tell Me," the Rolling Stones, June 1964 (us24) (April 1964 LP)
"Good Times, Bad Times," the Rolling Stones, June 1964 (B side, "It's All Over Now")
"As Tears Go By," Marianne Faithfull, June 1964 (uk9, us22) (later released in Stones version)
"So Much in Love," the Mighty Avengers, August 1964
"Congratulations," the Rolling Stones, September 1964 (B side, "Time Is on My Side")
"Grown Up Wrong," the Rolling Stones, September 1964 (not a single, album track, *12 × 5*)
"Blue Turns to Grey," the Mighty Avengers, February 1965 (later released in Stones version)

Note: Indented singles are Rolling Stones releases.

Table 1.3 *Rolling Stones album projects, 1964–68*

The Rolling Stones (April 1964, uk1)/*England's Newest Hit Makers – The Rolling Stones* (June 1964, us11), prod. by A. Oldham [10v 2np 1jr]

12 × 5 (November 1964, us3), prod. by A. Oldham [7v 2np 3jr]

Rolling Stones 2 (January 1965, uk1)/*Now!* (February 1965, us5), prod. by A. Oldham [13v 4jr]

Out of Our Heads (July 1965, us1; September 1965, uk2), prod. by A. Oldham [8v 10jr]

Aftermath (April 1966, uk1; June 1966, us2), prod. by A. Oldham [0v 15jr]

Between the Buttons (January 1967, uk3; February 1967, us2), prod. by A. Oldham [0v 14jr]*

Their Satanic Majesties Request (December 1967, us2, uk3), prod. by the Rolling Stones [0v 9jr + 1Wyman]

Beggars Banquet (December 1968, uk5, us3), prod. by J. Miller [1v 9jr]

Note: UK release date is listed first, with US release listed second.

v = version of a song previously recorded by another artist.

np = song attributed to Nanker Phelge.

jr = song written by Mick Jagger and Keith Richards.

* According to Bill Wyman, the first album to be conceived as an album and not simply as a collection of singles.

"I Wanna Be Your Man" helped prod Jagger and Richards into writing their own music.[19]

As Table 1.1 suggests, the differences in UK and US releases can make the chronological organization of the Stones' singles difficult – or at least complicated. The problem is even more pronounced when it comes to the Stones' albums, at least up to *Their Satanic Majesties Request* of December 1967. Albums with the same name, for instance, will contain a different collection of songs, while albums (or EPs) that appeared on one side of the Atlantic were never released on the other. Table 1.3 lists eight "album projects," with each album project representing the combination of all songs that appeared on the US or UK versions of a given album. For example, the début LPs in the USA and UK together include thirteen tracks; eleven appear on both albums, while one appears on the US version only ("Not Fade Away") and another appears on the UK version only ("Mona (I Need You Baby)"). The combination of the UK and US versions of *Out of Our Heads* totals eighteen tracks, with six held in common and six appearing only on one or the other. This approach to organizing the Stones' releases has the advantage of grouping together tracks that were recorded at about the same time, allowing the development of the band's style to be tracked from one album project to the next.[20] There are some songs along the way that get left out using this general organizational scheme, but these are few. There are also albums such as *December's Children* (December 1965, USA only), *Big Hits (High Tides and Green Grass)* (March 1966, USA; November 1966, UK), and *Flowers* (June 1967, USA only) that are left out of this listing; such albums are primarily compilations that introduce only a few new tracks, with these new recordings placed side by side with ones recorded much earlier and thus blurring the band's stylistic development.[21]

In addition to identifying the eight Stones album projects from 1964 to 1968, Table 1.3 provides the number of songs written by Nanker Phelge and Jagger/Richards on each of these. Note that the first four album projects are dominated by Stones versions of music written by others.[22] The first album project contains ten versions, two Nanker Phelge tracks (based, as noted above, on the music of others but not versions, strictly speaking), and one Jagger/Richards song. While the number of Jagger/Richards songs increases with each subsequent album project, the fourth, *Out of Our Heads*, still contains eight versions of songs previously recorded by others. A dramatic and important change occurs with the fifth album project, *Aftermath*, which contains Jagger/Richards songs exclusively – a feature continued in the sixth album project, *Between the Buttons*. Their *Satanic Majesties Request* includes one song by Bill Wyman but is otherwise all Jagger and Richards. *Beggars Banquet* settles into what will become the model for the Stones – one version among otherwise exclusively Jagger/Richards material. Viewed against the rest of the Stones recordings through the years, the first four albums stand out for their dependence on the music of others.

Table 1.4 lists the original artists who previously recorded the songs appearing on the first four album projects. These album versions provide us with a general sense of the music the Stones seem to have enjoyed most during these years and the names listed are almost entirely those of American rhythm and blues artists.[23] Two of the hit singles from 1965 (see Table 1.1), while credited to Jagger and Richards, also reinforce this strong American R&B influence. "The Last Time" is heavily indebted to the Staple Singers' 1954 single "This May Be the Last Time," while "(I Can't Get No) Satisfaction" draws on Martha and the Vandellas'

Table 1.4 *Versions on the first four album projects (original artists)*

The Rolling Stones/England's Newest Hit Makers – The Rolling Stones (April/June 1964) [10v 2np 1jr]
Buddy Holly, Chuck Berry, Muddy Waters, Jimmy Reed, Bo Diddley, Slim Harpo, Marvin Gaye, Solomon
  Burke, Rufus Thomas
12 × 5 (November 1964) [7v 2np 3jr]
Chuck Berry, Little Walter, Irma Thomas, the Drifters, Solomon Burke, Dale Hawkins
Rolling Stones 2/Now! (January/February 1965) [13v 4jr]
Solomon Burke, Alvin Robinson, Chuck Berry, Otis Redding, Bo Diddley, Howlin' Wolf, Irma Thomas,
  Barbara Lynn Ozen*, the Drifters, Muddy Waters
Out of Our Heads (September/July 1965) [8v 10jr]
Don Covay, Marvin Gaye, Otis Redding, Sam Cooke, Solomon Burke, Larry Williams, Chuck Berry,
  Barbara Lynn Ozen*

---

* The Stones' version of Barbara Lynn Ozen's "Oh Baby (We Got a Good Thing Going)" appeared on *Now!*
in the USA and on *Out of Our Heads* in the UK.

Table 1.5 *Rolling Stones singles, 1966–67*

"19th Nervous Breakdown" (us2, uk1) b/w "Sad Day"; UK release b/w "As Tears Go By," February 1966
"Paint It, Black" (us1, uk1) b/w "Stupid Girl"; UK release b/w "Long Long While," May 1966
"Mother's Little Helper" (us8) b/w "Lady Jane" (us24), July 1966, US only
"Have You Seen Your Mother Baby" (us9, uk5) b/w "Who's Driving Your Plane?," September 1966
"Let's Spend the Night Together" (us55, uk3) b/w "Ruby Tuesday" (us1), January 1967
"We Love You" (uk8, us50) b/w "Dandelion," August 1967 (UK), September 1967 (US)
"In Another Land" (Wyman, us87) b/w "The Lantern," December 1967, US only
"She's a Rainbow" (us25) b/w "2000 Light Years From Home," December 1967, US only

Note: Chart numbers refer to song they immediately follow.
All songs written by Jagger and Richards except where noted.

"Nowhere to Run," released in early 1965.[24] With these songs, the Nanker-Phelge practice of adapting the music of others seeps from B sides and album tracks into Jagger and Richards A sides, and suggests that the many versions that appear on Stones albums and singles through 1965 played an important role in the band's stylistic development. The complete turn away from versions that first occurs in 1966 with *Aftermath* thus marks an important shift that divides the 1963–67 period roughly into two parts: 1963–65 and 1966–67.

Singles and Albums, 1966–67

The practice of abandoning versions of songs recorded by others that marks *Aftermath* and the album projects that follow can also be seen clearly in the singles released by the Stones in 1966–67 (see Table 1.5); all but one of the songs appearing on these releases is written by Jagger and Richards, and that one song not credited to Jagger and Richards was written by Bill Wyman. These singles mostly rose into at least the top ten in the USA and UK, though the second half of 1967 finds the band struggling somewhat in the US charts due to the relatively poor showing of "We Love You" (No. 50) and "She's a Rainbow" (No. 25), while Wyman's "In Another Land" (No. 87) barely made a dent. The three Stones album projects during the same period, however, were strong commercial successes (see Table 1.3). The summer of 1967 was marked by legal and business problems for the band. At various points Jagger, Richards, and Jones all faced drug charges, while simultaneously the band's relationship with manager and producer Oldham was deteriorating. While some critics believe these events took a heavy toll on the band's music, at the very least they were a distraction that might partly explain the temporary dip in the group's success.[25]

In my chapter focused on *Beggars Banquet*, I detail the band's increased musical ambition in the period from about 1965 to the release of *Their*

Satanic Majesties Request in late 1967. During these years we find the Stones employing novel instrumentation (sitar, dulcimer, Mellotron, and more) and moving away from the two guitars, bass, drums, and vocals combo approach characteristic of the music from the 1963–64 period. They blend aspects of classical music into their style, by both the use of instruments associated with it (harpsichord, strings) and employment of harmonic and melodic materials that reference classical practice ("Ruby Tuesday," "She's a Rainbow"). The lyrics are at times philosophical and often contain evocative imagery. During the same time, it must be noted, the band also produced driving rock tracks such as "19th Nervous Breakdown," "Mother's Little Helper," and "Let's Spend the Night Together." Thus, the overall arc from 1963 is first marked by a decisive shift towards Jagger/Richards songs, and then by a tendency to explore a variety of styles and instrumental combinations. *Their Satanic Majesties Request* is a point of arrival that prepares the way for *Beggars Banquet* and the Stones music that follows.

Singles and Albums, 1968–74

The Stones' move towards increasingly ambitious approaches to their music leading to 1967 was not unusual in rock music of the mid-1960s. The Beatles' album releases of 1967, *Sgt. Pepper's Lonely Hearts Club Band* and *Magical Mystery Tour*, combined with the singles "Penny Lane" and "Strawberry Fields," marked a high point of musical ambition for them, as had the Beach Boys' *Pet Sounds* and "Good Vibrations" of 1966.[26] At about this same time, significant changes were afoot in the music business, especially in the United States. The emergence of psychedelic culture into American mainstream culture during 1967's Summer of Love brought with it an emphasis on albums rather than singles: Singles would come to be the format for AM radio – devoted to hit records in much the same way pop radio had been earlier in the decade – while the burgeoning FM band, freer in approach and at least initially less driven by advertising, would be the home for album tracks. FM radio and album-oriented rock became the music of college-age fans; pop singles on the AM band were targeted at teens and pre-teens. This change in the American music business impacted the Rolling Stones, who began to think more in terms of albums than singles.[27]

Table 1.6 provides a listing of Stones singles from the 1968–74 period, while Table 1.7 lists the albums from the same years. A comparison with Tables 1.1, 1.3, and 1.5 above reveals how the pace of these later releases slowed during the late 1960s and into the 1970s. In the 1963–67 period, for instance, the band released three or four singles a year and usually two

Table 1.6 *Rolling Stones singles, 1968–74*

"Jumpin' Jack Flash"* (uk1, us3) b/w "Child of the Moon,"* May 1968 (UK), June 1968 (US)
"Street Fighting Man" (us48) b/w "No Expectations," August 1968, US only
"Street Fighting Man"*/"Surprise, Surprise,"* July 1971 (uk21) (released earlier in US)
"Honky Tonk Women"* (uk1, us1) b/w "You Can't Always Get What You Want," July 1969
"Brown Sugar" (us 1, uk2) b/w "Bitch," May 1971; UK release b/w "Bitch" and "Let It Rock"*
    (Chuck Berry), April 1971
"Wild Horses" (us28) b/w "Sway," June 1971, US only
"Tumbling Dice" (us7, uk5) b/w "Sweet Black Angel," April 1972
"Happy" (us22) b/w "All Down the Line," July 1972, US only
"Angie" (us1, uk5) b/w "Silver Train," August 1973
"Doo Doo Doo Doo Doo (Heartbreaker)" (us15) b/w "Dancing with Mr. D," December 1973
"It's Only Rock 'n Roll" (us16, uk10) b/w "Through the Lonely Nights,"* July 1974

Note: Chart numbers refer to song they immediately follow.
All songs written by Jagger/Richards except where noted.
* Indicates track that did not appear on studio album at approximate time of release.

Table 1.7 *Rolling Stones albums, 1968–74*

Beggars Banquet, December 1968 (us5, uk3), prod. by J. Miller [1v 9jr]
    Robert Wilkins, "Prodigal Son"
Let It Bleed, November 1969 (us3), December 1969 (uk1), prod. by J. Miller [1v 8jr]
    Robert Johnson, "Love in Vain"
Sticky Fingers, April 1971 (us1, uk1), prod. by J. Miller [1v 9jr*]
    Fred McDowell, "You Gotta Move"
Exile on Main Street, May 1972 (us1, uk1), prod. by J. Miller [2v 16jr†]
    Slim Harpo, "Shake Your Hips," and Robert Johnson, "Stop Breaking Down"
Goats Head Soup, August 1973 (us1, uk1), prod. by J. Miller [0v 10jr]
It's Only Rock 'n Roll, October 1974 (us1, uk2), prod. by the Glimmer Twins (Jagger/Richards) [1v 9jr]
    The Temptations, "Ain't Too Proud to Beg"

* Marianne Faithfull is credited along with Jagger and Richards on "Sister Morphine."
† Mick Taylor is credited along with Jagger and Richards on "Ventilator Blues."
Versions found on each album are listed, providing recording artist and song title.

albums (not counting compilation albums). Table 1.6 shows that this rate slowed to about two releases a year for singles, and Table 1.7 lists roughly one album per year (with no album released in 1970). This pattern conforms to a general practice among other bands during the same period, as groups took longer to record albums. It is also worth noting that for these years there is no need to invoke the album project scheme to organize the album content, since UK and US albums were identical in terms of tracks included, perhaps owing to this new focus on the album as a whole. Table 1.6 also indicates that Stones singles in the first half of the 1970s were all tracks contained on the albums released during the same general period, another indicator that singles were no longer the band's primary focus.

As noted in the discussion of the Stones' album projects during the 1964–68 period (and shown in Table 1.3), *Beggars Banquet* contains one version of a song previously recorded by another artist, Robert Wilkins'

"Prodigal Son." Table 1.7 extends the listing of Stones albums to 1974. Note that each album contains one version with the remaining tracks being Jagger/Richards songs (except where indicated). The exceptions are *Exile on Main Street*, a double album that includes two versions, and *Goats Head Soup*, which includes none. The songs the band rework clearly gravitate toward the American rhythm and blues tradition (the songs and artists are listed in Table 1.7). While the first four album projects had included significantly more versions than these later albums, the relatively consistent practice found on these releases beginning in 1968 shows a significant return to roots for the band, especially considering the absence of such versions on the 1966–67 albums. A comparison between Tables 1.3 and 1.7 also reveals that the albums from the 1964–67 period were almost all produced by Oldham, while those from the 1968–74 period were mostly produced by Jimmy Miller.[28] The exceptions come at the end of each period, as *Their Satanic Majesties Request* is recorded during the break-up with Oldham (production credit is given to the band and Oldham's name is excluded), and *It's Only Rock 'n Roll* is produced by Jagger and Richards. And while production during the period up through 1967 was marked by increasing experimentation, often fueled by Jones' introduction of instruments new to the band's sound and novel in a pop and rock context, Miller's productions more often exploited the virtuosic playing of Taylor, as well as that of other musicians such as saxophonist Bobby Keys.[29]

As mentioned at the beginning of this chapter, the Stones albums from the 1968–74 period strike a balance between the version-heavy releases of 1963–64, the musical ambition of 1965–67, and a return to a distinctive directness of expression that reaffirms their roots in rock and roll, rhythm and blues, and country music. Indeed, each of the six albums from *Beggars Banquet* to *It's Only Rock 'n Roll* includes a relatively broad stylistic range of material, from acoustic ballads to blues-based rockers, from ambitious tracks that employ aspects of classical or psychedelia to those that highlight instrumental virtuosity, and from tracks that display a folk influence to those that engage the gospel tradition. It is also worth noting that while the Beatles began to come into their own, each as solo artists, during *The White Album* (1968), at about the same time the Stones developed a band sound that broke free of the influence of the Beatles, and ironically right after the most seemingly imitative album (*Majesties*).[30] Other chapters in this collection delve into these Stones albums in more detail; it is nevertheless worth emphasizing here how significant this series of albums from the 1968–74 period are in securing the Stones' prominent place in the history of rock music. They are a logical point of stylistic arrival considering the music from 1963–67 that preceded them. And they are the musical points of reference for all of the band's music that followed.

Notes

1 Paul Harris' Chapter 5 in this volume (see 75–97) traces the band's development during the subsequent, 1975–83 period, while Victor Coelho's Chapter 10 picks up in 1989 and tracks the later releases (see 184–93).

2 This division into two arcs, which are organized according to the tenures of Brian Jones and Mick Taylor, follows the grouping employed by Bill Janovitz in his chapter (see 18–39); the first of my arcs corresponds roughly with the time Jones was in the band, while the second generally covers Taylor's tenure. The alignment with Janovitz's scheme is not exact, since Jones remained in the group (though often on the periphery) throughout 1968 and into the summer of 1969, at which point Taylor began working with the band and stayed through 1974. Janovitz's third era begins in 1975 when Ronnie Wood joined the Stones.

3 See Walter Everett, *The Beatles as Musicians: The Quarry Men through* Rubber Soul (New York, 2001), esp. 86–90, 96–7, 115, 138–41. Everett notes the particular emphasis on versions of girl-group hits on the first Beatles albums.

4 Wyman*SA*, 87, remarks that Barber was also "a pivotal force in championing blues music in Britain. His importance for providing source material for Britain's emerging musicians has been criminally unrecognized. By providing a base first for skiffle and then for the blues, he was virtually a founding father for what came next: a British rock scene."

5 For an extended consideration of Donegan in the context of musical culture in post-war Britain, see Patrick Humphries, *Lonnie Donegan and the Birth of British Rock & Roll* (London, 2012). See also Chas McDevitt, *Skiffle: The Definitive Inside Story* (London, 2012); and Michael Brocken, *The British Folk Revival, 1944–2002* (Farnham, Surrey and Burlington, VT, 2003).

6 Wyman*SA*, 86, describes Korner as "a French-born blues fan who was one of the pioneers of that music in Britain," and "one of the great characters of the contemporary-music scene in Britain in the early 1960s." According to Richards (*Life*, 88), "Alexis Korner was the daddy of the London blues scene" and "something of an intellectual in the musical world ... He knew his stuff backwards; he knew every player who was worth his salt." Watts (*According*, 29) remarks, "Alexis was a musicologist. Alexis knew everything about music."

7 For a personal account of the rise of British blues, see Dick Heckstall-Smith and Pete Grant, *Blowin' the Blues: Fifty Years of Playing the British Blues* (Bath, 2004). See also Harry Shapiro, *Alexis Korner: The Biography* (London, 1997); and Paul Myers, *It Ain't Easy: Long John Baldry and the Birth of the British Blues* (Vancouver, 2007).

8 Korner was born in 1928 and Davies in 1932. Jagger and Richards, by contrast, were both born in 1943. John Mayall (b. 1933) and Bill Wyman (b. 1936) were closer in age to Korner and Davies. For accounts of the influence of Blues Incorporated, see *Life*, 87–9.

9 *R & B at the Marquee* is probably the first UK electric blues recording released there. Korner's modest ambition was to use the album as a kind of business card in the service of getting more and better gigs. The album uses different backing musicians from the usual band, but it can nevertheless be considered a faithful representation of the group's sound and approach.

10 Korner and Davies had different approaches to the blues tradition: Korner's was looser while Davies' was more traditional. This led to an eventual split, with Davies going on to form the Cyril Davies All Stars, recording for Pye Records, but passing away in January 1964. See Shapiro, *Alexis Korner*, 117.

11 Bill Wyman writes as follows on Jones: "the love of music that grew inside him was by far the most important force in the Stones's story. A rebel with a cause, he nursed an absolute fervor for true American blues. This obsession created the Stones, made them what they were – totally different from every other group. His knowledge of the origins of our music, and the translation of it into a British sound, was our blueprint." See Wyman*SA*, 77.

12 This gig took place on July 12, 1962, and the band consisted of Jones (Elmo Lewis), Jagger, Richards, Ian Stewart (piano), Dick Taylor (bass), and Mick Avory (drums). See *Life*, 97 and *RSG*, 28. Blues Incorporated performed that night on BBC Radio's 'Jazz Club' program. Baldry, who was a regular singer with Blues Incorporated and appears on the *R & B at the Marquee* album, helped to cover the evening at the Marquee, naming his hastily assembled group Long John Baldry and His Kansas City Blues Men. See Myers, *It Ain't Easy*, 47.

13 Oldham was forced to enlist the older Easton as a partner, since at the time Oldham was too young (19) to hold a license as a manager. Dick Rowe at Decca signed the Stones, having famously declined on the Beatles. After losing management of the Stones to Oldham and Easton, Gomelski did not make the same mistake with his next band, the Yardbirds. See Andrew Loog

Oldham, *Stoned: A Memoir of London in the 1960s* (New York, 2000) for an extended account of these events; and Jim McCarty with Dave Thompson, *Nobody Told Me! The Yardbirds, Renaissance, and Other Stories* (n.p., 2018), 67 *et passim* for an account of how the Yardbirds were signed by Gomelski.

14 "Fortune Teller" (written by Allen Toussaint under the pen name Naomi Neville) was the planned B side. This song had previously been the B side to "Lipstick Traces (on a Cigarette)," a 1962 No. 28 R&B hit for Benny Spellman in the USA.

15 Nanker Phelge is derived from a combination of "nanker" (pulling a face) and the last name of band friend Jimmy Phelge, designating a group composition (Jagger, Richards, Jones, Wyman, Watts, and Stewart). See Philip Norman, *The Stones* (London, 1993), 90.

16 This was not the first appearance on the US charts for Jagger and Richards, however. Their song "That Girl Belongs to Yesterday" was released by Gene Pitney in January 1964, rising to No. 49. See Table 1.2 and discussion below.

17 Richards writes: "When we put out 'Little Red Rooster,' a raw Willie Dixon blues with slide guitar and all, it was a daring move at the time, November 1964. We were getting no-no's from the record company, management, everyone else. But we felt we were on the crest of a wave and we could push it. It was almost in defiance of pop." See *Life*, 160–1. Jagger remarked likewise: "We had been going on and on about blues, so we thought it was about time we stopped talking and did something about it" (quoted in Wyman*SA*, 281).

18 The Stones' second EP, *Five by Five*, was released in the UK only in August 1964 and contained two Nanker Phelge songs along with three versions of songs by other artists.

19 In a discussion of how "As Tears Go By" was written, Richards remarks: "After that we wrote lots of airy-fairy silly love songs for chicks and stuff that didn't take off. We'd give them to Andrew and, amazing to us, he got most of them recorded by other artists. Mick and I refused to put this crap we were writing with the Stones. We'd have been laughed out of the goddamn room" (*Life*, 143). Oldham's account of his efforts to force Jagger and Richards to write is recounted in his autobiography *Stoned*, 250–2.

20 This method of organizing the Stones' music follows the standard practice in Beatles scholarship, which prioritizes the UK albums and singles on Parlophone over the American releases on Capitol. The UK albums contain music from the same sessions, while the American releases frequently mix sessions separated by several months and sometimes even by a year or more, obscuring stylistic change and development. Of course, a reception history of the music of either band would necessarily include consideration even of the most hodge-podge of collections, and any obscuring of stylistic development arising as a result would be part of the story.

21 The combined US and UK versions of *Big Hits* includes seventeen tracks, all of which had been previously released.

22 The term "version" is used here rather than the more generally (and too loosely) used term "cover." The use of "version" refers to a long-standing music-business practice of multiple artists recording the same song without there being any significant intertextual reference between versions. "Cover" tends to imply that there is some original version that provides a basis for a subsequent version and that this relationship is important in how a listener understands the later version. "Copies" are those versions that are very similar to some prior recording and do not engage intertextuality. During the 1963–65 period, for instance, most Beatles versions are very close to being copies of the prior recordings, while Stones versions tend to be looser treatments of the song. In neither case would it have been expected that the listener might know the prior recording and thus be equipped to detect an interaction between the two recordings. The Stones' version of "Ain't Too Proud to Beg" (*It's Only Rock 'n Roll*) is an instance in which the term "cover" is appropriate, however, since most listeners in 1974 could be expected to know the Temptations original from 1966. For a fuller discussion of these terms and the issues involved, see my "Yes, the Psychedelic-Symphonic Cover, and 'Every Little Thing'," in *The Routledge Companion to Popular Music Analysis: Expanding Approaches*, ed. Ciro Scotto, Kenneth Smith, and John Brackett (New York, 2018), 279–92.

23 Daniel Beller-McKenna's chapter in this volume (see 121–41) focuses on the influence of country music on the Stones and it is worth noting in the current context that the Stones single that precedes "The Last Time," "Heart of Stone," displays marked country features. Indeed, the original demo for the track included pedal steel guitar, though the steel guitar was ultimately nixed in the final arrangement.

24 Richards has remarked that the opening riff to "Satisfaction" is based on a horn line in Martha and the Vandellas' "Dancing in the Street" (*RSCRS*, 59). But "Nowhere to Run" was the hit

for Martha and the Vandellas during the time in May, 1965 when the Stones were recording "Satisfaction." The horn line from "Nowhere to Run" is much more similar to the guitar riff in "Satisfaction" than the line that opens "Dancing in the Street," and the harmonic movement in "Nowhere to Run" and "Satisfaction" are almost identical. In addition to the Martha and the Vandellas influence (whichever song it may have been), Richards has also admitted that he had Chuck Berry's "Thirty Days" in mind, and even the opening riff from Roy Orbison's "Pretty Woman." See Margotin & Guesdon, 120; and *RSG*, 169–71.

25 For accounts of these 1967 events, see Wyman*SA*, 404ff; *Life*, 225–30; and Andrew Loog Oldham, *2Stoned* (London, 2003), 352ff.

26 The Beach Boys' aborted *Smile* album would have continued in this direction. See Dan Harrison, "After Sundown: The Beach Boys' Experimental Music," in *Understanding Rock: Essays in Musical Analysis*, ed. John Covach and Graeme Boone (New York, 1997), 33–57. For a chronicle of the Beatles' increased ambition across the 1960s, see my "From Craft to Art: Formal Structure in the Music of the Beatles," in *Reading the Beatles: Cultural Studies, Literary Criticism, and the Fab Four*, ed. Kenneth Womack and Todd K. Davis (Albany, NY, 2006), 37–53.

27 *Between the Buttons* was the first album that the band recorded with an eye toward the album as a whole. Wyman writes that it was "the first studio session at which we concentrated on an album as a finished product . . ." See Wyman*SA*, 399.

28 This production credit also extends to the singles recorded during these two periods, as listed in Tables 1.1, 1.5, and 1.6.

29 Janovitz details the role of these musicians in his chapter in this volume (see 18–39), while Brita Heimarck's chapter (see 142–61) provides a detailed and focused account of Jones' contributions.

30 For a fuller discussion of the emergence of each of the Beatles as a solo artist on *The White Album*, see my "George Harrison, Songwriter" and "Afterword," in Mark Osteen, ed., *Part of Everything: The Beatles' White Album at Fifty* (Ann Arbor, 2019), 177–96 and 263–9, respectively.

2 Guitar Slingers and Hired Guns: The Musicians of the Rolling Stones

BILL JANOVITZ

Fifty-seven years together is a remarkable achievement for any combination of humans – in marriage; siblings; a company; not least an artistic collaboration with a core of three men, together from the fresh optimism of their twenties to the deep-lined wisdom of their seventies. It is only natural to divide such an eon into more manageable eras and chapters in order to discuss the results of such a collective. This is the organization I adopted in my most recent book about the Rolling Stones, *Rocks Off: 50 Tracks that Tell the Story of the Rolling Stones* (New York, 2013), in which discussions of the songs are grouped into three large sections corresponding to the band's three guitar players who served as Keith Richards' counterpoints over the band's history: Brian Jones, Mick Taylor, and finally, Ron Wood. Each of these guitarists had a significant impact on the sound of the Stones, and most longtime fans view the history of the group as divided along these lines. Though there have been many other people contributing to over a half-century of Stones recordings and tours, I will be concentrating here on the musicians who made indelible impacts on Stones records, especially those who were with the band for multiple years and albums.

Guitar Slinger One: Brian Jones

For many of the original Stones fans, nothing beats the Brian Jones years, and a number who hold this opinion stopped paying attention to the band around the time of the 1969 Hyde Park Concert, which served as the coming-out party for the twenty-year-old Taylor. This type of fan values the blues purism of the early Stones and their rock and roll roots in Chuck Berry the most, while other fans of this period emphasize the sonic textures and diverse musical styles that the multi-instrumentalist Jones brought to the records of the mid-sixties. In the early days of the band, Richards and Jones spent hours trying to discern the various parts played by the musicians in their pooled record collection, but what really excited them was the overall sound of the music, the effect of the whole (ensembles and vocalists) that was greater than the sum of the individual parts. This is the direction that the Stones themselves followed on their own earliest recordings. The twin guitars of Richards and Jones are intertwined and almost indistinguishable from each other on 1964–66 albums like *The Rolling Stones* (UK, 1964), *England's Newest Hit Makers* (USA, 1964), *12 × 5* (1964), *Out of Our Heads* (separate UK and US versions, both 1965), and *December's Children* (1965). Their producer for these records was the inexperienced Andrew Loog Oldham, who was deeply under the influence of his mentor, Phil Spector. The Stones began to achieve more clarity in their recordings at Chess Studios in Chicago and RCA Studios in Hollywood, though Oldham's production tastes leaned towards large amounts of reverb. So the Stones' records of this period are generally awash in echo, and tend to have a dark and murky wall of sound, while Jagger's vocals struggle to climb above it all to be heard.

The listening experience, however, is exhilarating. A prime example of the Jones and Richards guitar interplay can be heard on the original up-tempo blues, "Little by Little." We know Richards is playing the brighter of the two electric guitars, because it is the one that slips into a solo at the beseeching of Jagger, who yells, "All right, Keith, come on!" During this solo, we can more clearly discern that Jones is playing the roots of the chords and some fine blues riffs. It is as if the two divide up the frequency range of the electric guitar, with Jones taking the low notes and Richards taking the high strings, instead of more clearly delineated rhythm and lead guitar parts.

The Stones, alongside the Beatles, set the template for the two-electric-guitar model for rock and roll bands. For most prior combos, a guitar was backed by drums, a bass, and maybe a piano. Or if there were two guitars, one was generally an acoustic strumming the rhythm with a lead player on electric (or in country and western, electric lap steel or pedal steel). A classic example would be the early Elvis Presley band with Scotty Moore playing single-note lines on his electric while Elvis strummed an acoustic. And with the Beatles, it was George Harrison who usually played the solos and riffs, while John Lennon was busying himself with strumming and singing. The Stones, though, were all about two guitarists playing interlocking rhythms and riffs, what Richards would later often refer to as "the ancient form of weaving." It was a dynamic that he felt went missing for much of the Mick Taylor era, at least in live performances.[1] But it clicked back into place in full force with Ron Wood joining the band.

Another early recording at Regent Sound Studios was the Stones' version of Slim Harpo's "I'm A King Bee," which offers a more delineated rhythm/lead guitar split. Here is Richards strumming an acoustic bed over the sturdy laid-back groove set down by Charlie Watts and Bill Wyman, who slides his note up to replicate the buzz of a bee. Jones breaks out of his low-note riffing with a bottleneck slide, stinging us with his high notes. With one fewer electric guitar competing for space and a relatively slower song, the track is one of the crisper mixes from the band's early period: the drums cut through, the acoustic guitar is clear, and the vocal is heard up front and present. The bass and Jones' riffs weave around each other in the same frequency range.

A more plaintive version of his slide guitar work is on "No Expectations," from *Beggars Banquet* (1968), in which Jones offers a mournful, bottleneck part on an acoustic guitar. While Jagger's vocal is sublimely doleful and heavy with emotion, Jones does more than merely underscore the melancholy; his opening guitar lines set the tone of the song more than words themselves could. Though Richards described Jones' minimal contributions to *Let It Bleed* (1969) – a percussion part on "Midnight Rambler" and autoharp on "You Got the Silver" – as "a last flare from the shipwreck," it is really this single slide part that was Jones' last cry.[2]

These two trademark slide guitar parts are bookends to a rich palette of colors that Jones brought to the Stones' recordings of the 1960s. He was easily bored, did not write music for the band, and did not sing. On each successive record, Richards increasingly overdubbed multiple guitar parts while Jones explored different instruments. His sense of wonder was piqued when the band was let loose at the RCA Studios in Hollywood, with huge rooms full of exotic instruments, leading to his playing sitar on "Paint It, Black," dulcimer on "Lady Jane" and "I Am Waiting," marimba on "Under My Thumb," and harpsichord and koto on "Ride on Baby."[3] Though he has no songwriting credits on *Aftermath* (1966), it's as much a Brian Jones record as one by Jagger/Richards.

Jones' spirit of experimentation mirrored what was occurring across town at Abbey Road Studios on Beatles recordings. We must also point to such indelible parts as his woody recorder on "Ruby Tuesday," use of organ on "Let's Spend the Night Together," and of Mellotron (a keyboard that plays tape loops, like an early analog sampler) on "2000 Light Years From Home" and "She's a Rainbow." Of course, this experimentation went hand in hand with drug use, and, like many of his colleagues, Jones slid from experimentation to drug abuse, falling into a downward spiral of paranoia and self-medication. He was officially fired in 1969 while the Stones were hard at work on *Let It Bleed*, and in a matter of days was found dead, his drug-addled body drowned in the swimming pool of his home.

Guitar Slinger Two: Mick Taylor

With most of *Let It Bleed* completed, the band searched for a suitable replacement. On the recommendation of the Bluesbreakers' bandleader, John Mayall, the Stones invited twenty-year-old Mick Taylor down for a session. The first track he played on was "Live With Me," on which he traded licks with Richards in real time at Olympic Studios during the actual tracking. Taylor said that he and Richards clicked immediately on the session, and according to Taylor, they would alternate playing rhythm and lead, but live there was more lead playing, which was given to Taylor.

Thus, the Stones' sound was changed the instant Taylor was introduced to the band. Richards had played a few concise solos on the late 1960s sessions. One thinks of the memorable cutting solo on "Sympathy for the Devil" and the slowhand blues solo on "Gimme Shelter." Taylor was already known among guitar fans as a virtuoso blues soloist of the B.B. King, Freddie King, Eric Clapton, and Jeff Beck lineage. The first time the public heard Taylor on a Stones recording, though, was the twangy country bends that introduce the chorus of the "Honky Tonk Women" single. The solo on that track is trademark Richards, with an unhurried pace and economical note choice. While known as a lead player, Taylor also relished the chance to lay down rhythm parts and riffs to suit and support the songs.

It was rather in the live arena that Taylor particularly shone. A lot had changed on the road during the years the Stones had not toured, and by 1969, live sound technology had grown exponentially. Sound systems now could fill arenas with relatively decent sound, with each instrument mic'd up, amplified, and mixed along with the vocals through the large PA speaker stacks that typically flanked the stage. Touring became a big business in and of itself, not just a way to promote records. Bands were now playing "concerts" with sets an hour plus in length. The influence of drugs and musical experimentation was now being played out in live performances as well, from Jimi Hendrix's incendiary performances at Monterey Pop Festival in 1967 (literally setting his guitar on fire) and Woodstock in 1969, to the Who's high-volume, instrument-wrecking affairs, and the Grateful Dead's long jamming takes on psychedelic Americana. Now, the Stones were retooled for this new terrain, with long-form jams like "Midnight Rambler" and the usual encore "Street Fighting Man," the mini-epic "You Can't Always Get What You Want," and "Sympathy for the Devil," which could be stretched out for extended guitar solos. Such songs were reinterpreted each night. On the studio recording of "Sympathy for the Devil," for example, the only guitar is Richards' solos. The rest is piano driven. But on the live versions, Richards would generally start a chord progression with Watts tumbling in with a drum fill, Wyman falling in behind, and Taylor playing lead lines when Jagger was not singing.

"Midnight Rambler" provides an interesting case study as a song that Richards labored over in the studio, weaving together a couple of compelling rhythm parts on his own. He perfected the slide part alone over five nights, erasing each previous take and starting anew. Taylor was already playing torrid slide guitar solos in his début performance of the song at his coming-out party, the concert in Hyde Park in the summer of 1969. On the 1969 live album, *Get Yer Ya-Ya's Out!*, Richards starts the song at a faster, galloping pace. Taylor joins him in playing a similar rhythm part, but swinging a bit from the relentlessly steady Richards part. It is the sort of tack that Brian Jones might have taken. The soloing is left for Jagger on the harp over the arrangement's chugging parts. When the song breaks down in the middle, we can hear Taylor playing tastefully reined-in blues bends, freeing himself a bit more during the crescendo build-up in the final two minutes of the song. But "Midnight Rambler" took on almost operatic proportions over the next few years, so that by 1972 (as seen in the concert film, *Ladies and Gentlemen: The Rolling Stones*) and 1973 (as heard on the *Brussels Affair* live album) the song reached lengths of ten to fifteen minutes. As experienced via those recordings, the guitar interplay epitomizes the particular strength of the Richards-Taylor tandem when it was working on all cylinders. Richards launches into some of his Chuck Berry-inspired two-note solos, while Taylor eases back and forth from bluesy single-note hammerings, picked flurries, and bends, into variations of the rhythm parts.

The sustained level of excellence from *Sticky Fingers* (1971) through *Exile on Main Street* (1972) offers myriad examples of why the Mick Taylor era is so highly regarded. We get early glimpses of Taylor's versatility on *Sticky Fingers*, where at the end of "Can't You Hear Me Knocking" he evokes Carlos Santana with a serendipitously recorded, impromptu, Latin-tinged jam as a coda. We also hear Taylor's poignant slide and electric riffs interacting with Jagger's gentle acoustic licks on "Moonlight Mile," one of the Stones' most sublimely beautiful ballads. It is a song without a Richards guitar track; Jagger and Taylor handled all the guitar work at the session for the song. As the recording reaches its conclusion, we hear Taylor playing an ascending and descending pentatonic figure that gets picked up and elaborated upon by the string arranger on the recording, Paul Buckminster. It has been argued that Taylor should have received some writing credit for his contributions. What constitutes songwriting as opposed to arranging is a controversial topic among collaborative bands and it was seemingly a sore point for Mick Taylor, an official member of the band. It is easier for session players to accept that their contributions to a song's arrangement, as hired guns, will not receive songwriting credit. For example, Nicky Hopkins was an almost constant presence on Stones recordings and live performances from 1966 through 1974. His contribution in arranging "Sympathy for the Devil," transforming it from an ambling folk song into a raging samba, is accurately documented in Jean-Luc Godard's film *One Plus One* (later retitled *Sympathy for the Devil*). In the end, all guitars except Richards' lacerating solo are stripped away and the song is propelled by Hopkins' piano and the rhythm section. But Jagger had the chord progressions and seemingly much of the lyric content written before they started. What we witness in the film is how significantly an arrangement can affect the end result of a song. In this case, the final product is about 180 degrees different from how it was originally presented to the group. The case can be made that such substantial arranging warrants writing credit, and over the years Bill Wyman, Mick Taylor, and Brian Jones could have laid claim to such credit, but very few songwriters would agree.

Taylor may actually have added more than arrangement ideas. Such contributions are difficult to extricate and measure when so much of the band's writing came out of organic jamming. In the end, Taylor's feelings on the subject were apparently one of the main reasons he decided to leave the Stones. "I'd seen him a few days earlier and he'd spoken excitedly about some songs he'd written with Jagger and Richards that were to appear on *It's Only Rock 'n Roll*," writes Nick Kent referring to the 1974 album. "When I told him that I'd seen the finished sleeve with the song-writing credits and that his name wasn't featured, he went silent for a second before muttering a curt 'We'll see about that!' almost under his breath. Actually, he sounded more resigned than anything else . . ."[4]

Some of Taylor's final tracks before he left the group are among his finest recorded moments. He did not get many big, soaring opportunities on *Exile on Main Street*. Most of his work on that record is confined to second rhythm parts and concise solos mixed relatively low dynamically as part of the whole *Exile* gumbo. But he did receive a writing credit on the smoldering "Ventilator Blues," which likely means he came up with the song's insistent main riff, as the song sprung from one of the jams the band had in the basement of Richards' rented Nellcôte villa on the French Riviera. We also heard Taylor spread his wings on recordings from the subsequent live tour. But on the next two records, *Goats Head Soup* (1973) and *It's Only Rock 'n Roll* (1974), we are treated to heart-melting solos on the songs "Winter," and "Time Waits for No One," respectively. On the latter recording, Taylor got to stretch out for more time than was typically budgeted for on Stones studio recordings. For a band that would marinate song ideas in meandering, often directionless jams, the final products tended toward the succinct and economical, in service of the songs themselves. The first song recorded for the *It's Only Rock 'n Roll* sessions, "Time Waits for No One," is the final song on side one of the LP. "There was going to be a space for a guitar solo, it was a first take," Taylor recalled. "I mean the backing track and the guitar solo is the first or second time we actually ran through the song, so the guitar solo was done live. It's got a long sort of extended guitar solo at the end, which is because it was a good solo and it's peaking. That's how long the track goes on for."[5] The song would serve as the perfect swan song for Taylor, if the last song to actually feature him had not been the even more fitting "Till the Next Goodbye."

Guitar Slinger Three: Ron Wood

Ron Wood had showed up in Munich to help out on the 1975 *Black and Blue* sessions, unaware that the Stones were holding auditions for a permanent replacement guitarist to fill the shoes of Taylor. When he arrived, he saw Eric Clapton, who was one of an impressive list of hotshots who had been called into the sessions in Munich (and other dates in Rotterdam). Names commonly associated with these sessions include Irish blues sensation Rory Gallagher, Humble Pie's Steve Marriott (also famous as singer of the Small Faces), Peter Frampton (formerly of Humble Pie and now a rising solo artist), Muscle Shoals session guitarist Wayne Perkins, Canned Heat's Harvey Mandel, and Jeff Beck, who claimed he was tricked into auditioning.

It seems that Beck was not the only one unaware of the audition nature of the session. Despite his ties to the Faces, Wood had showed up as if the gig were his to take if he wanted it, knowing that the Faces were floundering while their singer, Rod Stewart, was enjoying superstardom as a solo artist. "Clapton said to me in Munich, 'I'm a much better guitarist than you,'" writes Wood. "I responded, 'I know that, but you gotta live with these guys as well as play with them. There's no way you can do that.' Which is true. He could never have survived life with the Stones."[6]

One of the main criticisms of Ron Wood from his detractors among Stones fans is that he is too much like Keith Richards and does not bring the musicality of Brian Jones or the virtuosity of Mick Taylor. But this misses the point. Wood has shown a significantly wide versatility, able to approximate the 1960s sounds that Jones brought to the table, the bluesy slides and bends that Taylor tracked, while offering distinctive contributions of his own, such as the unexpected pedal steel guitar parts on "Shattered" and other *Some Girls* songs, and the authentic American funk sounds he brought to the late-1970s Stones. In fact, prior to the Faces, Wood played bass in the Jeff Beck Group (in which Rod Stewart was the lead singer), and his funky/heavy blues-rock playing on that band's version of "I Ain't Superstitious" on the 1968 *Truth* LP was an early indication of his inventiveness. It is, in fact, the funk element that Wood brought in on his first session for *Black and Blue*. "Hey Negrita" was a funky riff with a reggae upstroke rhythm that he had been kicking around. "So all of us, independently and together, were into reggae, and it was also a mood of the time," said Wood.[7]

Charlie Watts' recollection about Wood confidently showing up with his own idea reveals the comfort level within the group and why he immediately fitted in.[8] Watts had played in a band with Wood's brother, Art, before the Stones. Ron Wood was more like family. When Rod Stewart left the Faces in 1975, the Stones hired Wood, though he did not become a permanent member of the band until 1976, and was not a full equal partner in the band until 1990.

Wood's impact was felt immediately. While not on the level of Mick Taylor, he ripped out great solos, such as those heard on the 1975–76 *Love You Live* versions of "You Can't Always Get What You Want," "Sympathy for the Devil," and "You Gotta Move." While Wood's strident tone and style is not as distinctive as that of Taylor, whose parts were almost always immediately identifiable, his solos have often been deeply soulful, with an effortless-sounding fluidity that belied his ability. His parts generally fit in with the band's overall sound. But his approach was not always at the expense of pyrotechnics, as the torrid ending of his solo on the live "You Can't Always Get What You Want" demonstrates. But the most satisfying moments in Wood's tenure have generally been the intertwining parts he played with Richards, picking up the "ancient form of weaving" that Richards and Jones had practiced. The two in each case made no clear distinction between "lead" and "rhythm" roles. If there is an analogy, the Stones of the Wood era are more like a dinner conversation in a big family, with people talking to, over, and around each other. As with those Chess records they cherished early on, it was more about the ensemble sound.

This is what we hear perfectly on Wood's first start-to-finish album project with the Stones, *Some Girls* (1978). The Stones had weathered deaths, perilous financial straits, drug addictions, and arrests, including, with Richards, a charge of trafficking for the amount of heroin he tried to smuggle into Toronto while the band was rehearsing for a tour there. And while some critics had been writing them off since 1967, by 1977 the Stones did seem musically adrift and at times directionless. Whether or not listeners consider *Sticky Fingers* or *Exile on Main Street* to be the apex of the band's catalog, most agree that the material started to fall off in quality thereafter. Many of us who came of age during the mid-1970s feel *Goats Head Soup*, *It's Only Rock 'n Roll*, and *Black and Blue* to be fine, and even underrated records. And in hindsight, even some older fellow fans have warmed up to a number of those songs. It is clear that the group continued to push itself, mainly under the guidance of Jagger, to remain artistically and commercially relevant.

Jagger, rock and roll's Peter Pan, was not about to go gracefully into that good night, or to accept middling reviews and sales for the band's records while some young upstarts playing punk rock, which was just a garage variation of the sort of two-guitar, attitude-heavy, back-to-basics attack that the Stones made famous. "No Elvis, Beatles, or the Rolling Stones in 1977," sang Joe Strummer of the Clash. While Strummer no doubt felt as let down by his boyhood heroes as anyone – watching rock and roll morph into heavy and self-important "rock" made by bloated, jet-setting junkies and coke fiends – the Clash, Sex Pistols, and others merely understood marketing and the importance of distinguishing your generation's music from the previous one's.

But no musician has understood branding and marketing better than Mick Jagger. He embraced many of the surface elements of mid-to-late 1970s punk and so-called new wave. More significantly, he thrived on the energy of the music, and of disco and funk, as he trolled the clubs of New York, London, and Paris. When the band was gathering for rehearsals outside of Paris for the *Some Girls* sessions, he strapped on a Strat, plugged into a loud Mesa Boogie amp, and joined Richards and Wood in a three-guitar front line and kicked out the jams on the 1978 album. The sustained excellence of *Some Girls* proved the band remained a major cultural force, and could still make an album with not even so much as an ounce of fat on its lean twelve inches of vinyl.

And while Jagger kicked them into gear, Wood was a significant contributing force of new energy to the group. He found the space between rock and roll's finest rhythm section and its most identifiable rhythm guitarist, a trio of musicians who had developed their own sense of timing and groove-making over the course of fifteen years of constantly playing together. And Wood managed this while Jagger relentlessly pounded away on his own guitar throughout an album's worth of material, for the first time in the band's career. "Mick was bringing songs in and wanted to play the electric guitar," said Chris Kimsey, the engineer and co-producer of *Some Girls* and a few subsequent albums. "His energy is very different than that of Keith or Ronnie in playing guitar. It is more, I suppose you could say punk rock. It's just a very animalistic, basic way of bashing out the chord sequence ... which kind of fits with his energy as a person, the way he moves and sings anyway."[9]

Listening to the conversation between the guitars on *Some Girls* is a treat. While Jagger pumps up the adrenaline, Wood and Richards hang their loosely woven guitar parts around the tense core of the fast songs. But it is on the slower numbers, such as the ballad "Beast of Burden," that a listener can really soak in the pleasure of interlocking guitar parts. Not coincidentally, it is one of the few without Jagger on guitar. There is plenty of space left and Wood and Richards use it well, rarely strumming a steady pattern. Instead, you hear the two listening to and answering each other, neither one anticipating their time to shine in a solo moment.

Versatility, and not virtuosity, has been the calling card of Wood. He had been used to playing with another great soul-influenced rhythm section in the Faces, Kenney Jones (one of rock and roll's least-appreciated drummers) and Ronnie Lane. And here he is bringing that looseness of the Faces to the Stones – rather than resulting in redundancy, the Stones settled into its strength as a groove machine, which is how the band has remained for thirty-plus years.

Hired Guns: Key Contributors to Rolling Stones Recordings

While the changing three guitarists – all official members of the group – resulted in easily recognizable shifts in the sound of the decidedly guitar-driven band, each of the Stones' hired keyboardists brought relatively less obvious, but nevertheless essential, personality and color to the group's recordings and performances. Al Kooper brought a distinct and indispensable gospel flavor on piano and organ to his one-off contribution, "You Can't Always Get What You Want." And former Faces keyboardist, Ian McLagan, sat in with the Stones from *Some Girls* (1978) through their early-1980s touring. But for the purposes of this essay, we will concentrate on the four long-term contributors on piano and organ. As with Brian Jones, Mick Taylor, and Ron Wood, the band's keyboardists correspond respectively with the Stones' early, middle, and late periods. Ian Stewart was a constant presence in the band until his death in 1985, due to his role as a founding member of the group and his running of its stage management, touring details, and equipment inventory. But his playing is mostly associated with the Brian Jones early years. Nicky Hopkins entered the fray as the band transitioned through their brief flirtation with psychedelia and stayed right through the most classic recordings and tours of their golden era (1968–72). Billy Preston started working with the Stones on *Goats Head Soup* (1973) and continued through *Black and Blue* (1976). And Chuck Leavell joined them for the early 1980s and has remained with them since.

Piano Pounder One: Ian Stewart

As a founding member who was jettisoned from the band, Stewart is thought of as a main character in Stones lore, as well as a pianist. His death from a heart attack in 1985 was a stunning blow to the group.

Stewart was a relatively clean-living regular bloke who eschewed drugs. His meat-and-potatoes lifestyle was reflected in his straightforward playing, informed by boogie-woogie jazz and its Johnnie Johnson/Jerry Lee Lewis rock and roll variations. Though closely linked to their early days, Stewart periodically played with the band on record and in concert until his death. He chose his spots, and there is no greater example of Stewart's strengths and limitations than the 1969 recording session in Muscle Shoals, Alabama, at the tail end of the band's American tour. The Stones were not yet touring with Hopkins, their regular session player at that point, and Stewart would sit in on live performances of "Honky Tonk Women" and the Chuck Berry covers "Little Queenie" and "Carol" (as heard on the 1969 live album from the tour, *Get Yer Ya-Ya's Out!*). The three-day session in Alabama produced "Brown Sugar," "Wild Horses," and "You Gotta Move."

Stewart begged off of "Wild Horses," later explaining, "I don't play minor chords," which he also mocked as "Chinese chords." "When I'm playing on stage with the Stones and a minor chord comes along, I lift me hands in protest."[10] Jim Dickinson, who became a legendary producer but was only at this session as a young fan, got to sit at the upright tack piano (a piano with tacks punched into the hammers to produce a honky-tonk sound) and contribute to the beautiful ballad. However, the famously bawdy "Brown Sugar," a classic R&B-based number, was right up Stewart's alley. He is heard entering on the choruses, helping to build the arrangement. Stewart pounds in with upper-register right-hand figures on the first chorus, adding a few boogie trills before ducking back out. He re-enters on the second chorus with a steadier pattern that plays off the rhythm guitars. After Bobby Keys' overdubbed sax solo, the band slips back into the chorus again, with Stewart coming in playing a quarter-note on the same one or two keys, using the piano as a percussion instrument, sounding almost like a cowbell. As the band starts to vamp out with the repeated final chorus and "Yeah, yeah, yeah, woo!" parts, we can hear Stewart at his best, slowly adding ascending right-hand riffs and trills. When the vocals end and the sax and guitar lock into the repeated ending riff, Stewart plays off of the figure. It is the sort of part for which Stewart had been known since the Stones' first gigs and recordings.

Listen, for example, to the band's take on Chuck Berry's "Around and Around," which served as the lead-off track to the *12 × 5* US LP and *Five by Five* UK EP (both 1964). It is one of the clearest and dynamically loudest examples of Stewart on the early Stones sides, cutting through the middle frequency range taken up by Richards' and Jones' guitars by playing in the higher registers. It is clear he was a disciple of Berry's pianist, Johnnie Johnson, both of them masters of rhythm, sliding in and over the guitars with a mix of percussive hammering and triplets, weaving in and out like tinsel garland around a Christmas tree.

Piano Pounder Two: Nicky Hopkins

In 1966, the Stones brought in Nicky Hopkins – they had known him since the early days of the London blues scene – to start playing the kind of material that was not Stewart's forté. The band had already gravitated away from the straight R&B-based rock and roll they had been playing, broadening their palette with the *Aftermath* LP (1966). Jimmy Page, who was a well-known session musician before his Yardbirds stardom, recommended Hopkins to Brian Jones, who hired Hopkins for work on the soundtrack to the film *A Degree of Murder* (1967).[11] Hopkins first appeared on a Stones album in a few of the tracks on *Between the Buttons* (1967). However, one of the most famous Stones piano-driven songs from that album, "Let's Spend the Night Together," was played by Richards and Jack Nitzsche, an LA-based arranger for Phil Spector who worked with the Stones on most of their mid-to-late 1960s records and played keyboards on a few tracks.

The boundaries of pop music were being stretched into experimental psychedelia, heavy rock, orchestral elements, English music hall traditions, satire, and more. Hopkins had already played with the Who, for example somehow managing to play a compelling piano part to cut through the raucous din of the 1965 single "Anyway, Anyhow, Anywhere." And he would soon go on to be a member of the heavy blues Jeff Beck Group with Wood (and Rod Stewart), and San Francisco's psychedelic Quicksilver Messenger Service. In that sense, Hopkins, who could roll with anything, was right for the Stones as they wandered off into the psychedelia of *Their Satanic Majesties Request* (1967). But, as with the Stones themselves, Hopkins' main interest was American roots music like blues and country. So when the band got back to their roots, taking a step back and two steps forward with *Beggars Banquet* (1968), the first record of their golden period, Hopkins was their man. He plays on almost all of the tracks and Stewart is not on any, even though much of the material is blues based (there is also gospel, country, country-blues, and straight-up rock, all of the essential ingredients of the Stones sound). Piano plays a big part in the natural sound of the album, which contains one of Hopkins' signature moments, "Sympathy for the Devil," which is driven by his samba-like part and the highly percussive rhythm section. No guitar other than Richards' solo remains on the finished recording.

The *Sympathy for the Devil* Godard film, which intersperses didactic staged pieces with filmed scenes of the Stones hard at work on the song at Olympic Studios, is extremely useful for fans. We get to see how the band worked, coming in with the germ of an idea and collaborating for hours (in this case, days) as they hashed out a final master recording. We also see the diligent Hopkins, head down in the corner of the studio, switching from organ to piano as the band ever so slowly starts to settle into the groove that culminated in the song. As Bill Wyman recounted:

> All Stones stuff came from jamming in the studios. A riff or a few lyrics would be built on, sometimes for days and days, but you could always say "Ere Nicky, can you try something completely different, something much more off the wall" and he'd do it. He wasn't bogged down in a particular way of playing like I might have been; if I couldn't get some bass line idea out of my head then someone else, like Keith, would try, just to get a different feel, but Nicky could change totally from one style to another.[12]

In fact, in the film we see Wyman starting in his usual position on a stool with the bass guitar, trying along with the others to find the right arrangement. By the time Hopkins has switched to piano, Richards has taken over the bass, playing a far busier part than Wyman likely would have. As with other sidemen, Hopkins didn't receive songwriting credit on Stones tracks, no matter how big a part he played. The song "We Love You" from *Satanic Majesties*, for example, was based on a riff that Hopkins had been working on for weeks, but like everything else, it is attributed to Jagger/Richards.

Relegating Stewart as a salaried employee and Hopkins as a freelance sideman (though the latter's family maintains he was offered a full-time spot in the band) allowed the group more flexibility to vary their sound. After all, it would be difficult for a collective band to simply leave out one of its permanent members in order to hire an outside musician to play on a particular track. By contracting a side or session musician, a group can instantly add a dimension not being fulfilled by one of the main players. But with the unpredictability of the Stones' schedule, coupled with a lack of songwriting royalties or even a place on the permanent payroll, Hopkins had to look in other places to help pay the bills, and he continued to get pulled into other sessions, including a steady spot with Quicksilver Messenger Service, as well as sessions for Jefferson Airplane and the Steve Miller Band. Hopkins' work is all over the Stones' next masterpiece, *Let It Bleed* (1969), but was absent for "You Can't Always Get What You Want," and his piano/organ spot was occupied with aplomb by Al Kooper, who just happened to be in London for a vacation. Hopkins was also unavailable for the 1969 tour. But once Quicksilver broke up, Hopkins had more time to spare and, though he only plays on one song, "Sway," on *Sticky Fingers* (1971) (which had a total of seven people playing keyboards), he was with the band on their 1971 tour and then joined them in France for the recording of much of *Exile on Main Street* (1972).

While many highlights of Hopkins' tenure with the Stones can be heard on *Beggars Banquet* and *Let It Bleed*, it can be argued that his work on *Exile on Main Street* sets a high-water mark. Hopkins is back at the piano for most of the tracks. The first time we hear him enter is on the first pre-chorus of the lead-off track, "Rocks Off," and right away we can tell why he is held in such great esteem. He almost builds the arrangement himself, varying each section to distinguish it from the others, not only the verse from the chorus, but each verse from the other verses, and each chorus contains its own exuberant pattern and ad-libs.

It is the sort of rock and roll number that Stewart would have generally also handled. But now Hopkins was around the Stones full time – literally, in this case, living with them on the French Riviera as they recorded in Richards' rented basement. Stewart was in charge of the Rolling Stones Mobile Unit, a truck fitted out with a recording studio control room, and by all accounts, challenging to keep powered up and running. Given that his responsibilities included keeping the band's equipment and instruments functioning in the extremely humid basement of the villa, Stewart was likely too busy to sit in often on piano, especially when they had Hopkins there all the time. Stewart does, however, play on three central tracks: "Shake Your Hips," "Sweet Virginia," and "Stop Breaking Down." But if "Rocks Off" was right in Hopkins' wheelhouse, then "Rip This Joint" could have been tailor-made for Stewart. Yet the barrelhouse boogie-woogie we hear on that track is Hopkins again. He tears up the track with nimble fingerwork. The torrid tempo is the fastest of any Rolling Stones track and the wall-to-wall part that Hopkins plays seems to accelerate the breathless speed of the recording.

The intensity and heat gets turned up later on during the album, on another highlight, "Ventilator Blues." Somehow, Hopkins finds a counter-rhythm to play off the stop-and-start groove of the slide guitar and drums. "Bobby Keys wrote the rhythm part, which is the clever part of the song," said Charlie Watts. "Bobby said, 'Why don't you do this?' and I said, 'I can't play that,' so Bobby stood next to me clapping the thing and I just followed his timing."[13] Hopkins keeps it funky and restrained until he lets loose at the end, peppering it with Otis Spann-inspired sprays of high notes. Spann, a member of Muddy Waters' band, is a sensible reference point, as the menacing, claustrophobic atmosphere of the song itself was ripped from the Waters playbook.[14]

While Hopkins could keep pace with the most intense, the loudest, and the fastest of them, his most rewarding work tended toward the elegiac and pastoral. For pure piano goodness, one need not look any further than the creamy opening chords of *Exile*'s "Loving Cup." The entire first verse is backed only by Hopkins' piano and Richards' acoustic guitar. While Jagger and Richards pop in with a two-part harmony to open the song, the piano remains high in the mix. In fact, the vocals are low relative to how most of us are accustomed to hearing popular music. The effect, as with all of *Exile*, is exhilaration as the vocals strain to be heard. Hopkins was also strongly influenced by Floyd Cramer, a Nashville legend who played his slip-note riffs (playing a chord where one quickly slides or hammers the "wrong" note into the "correct" note for a bending feel) on records in the 1950s and 1960s by everyone from Elvis Presley and the Everly Brothers to Patsy Cline and Don Gibson. Cramer's honky-tonk fingerprints can be heard on the parts Hopkins adds to the countrified "Torn and Frayed" and even on the gospel-informed "Let It Loose."

What makes the latter such an original Stones song, as opposed to a straight gospel homage, are the twists that the band bring to it. Instead of, say, a Hammond B-3 organ opening the song as in a traditional gospel number, Richards begins with a guitar amplified via a revolving Leslie organ speaker to achieve a sound similar to that of an organ. When Hopkins enters introducing the second verse, it is not what one would immediately associate with gospel piano playing. Instead, his is a country part, which he starts to mix together with some gospel riffs and chord suspensions. The song is exemplary of the instincts Hopkins had for slipping in and out of an arrangement and for the laid-back feel for the beat that he possessed. Listen, for example, how he drops out for the vocal breakdown at about the 2:00 mark. He enters after the third line, like wisteria weaving around a trellis, dipping behind the music and then coming out to blossom at the right spot.

Piano Pounder Three: Billy Preston
– and Bobby Keys, Jim Price, and Merry Clayton

While Hopkins was conversant in gospel piano, Billy Preston was the real deal (see Figure 2.1). He played organ with Mahalia Jackson and James Cleveland, gospel royalty, at the tender age of ten. From there, he hooked up with Little Richard's band, eventually touring England, and meeting the Beatles in the process. Preston went on to play with Ray Charles and returned to England in 1968–69 to sit in with the Beatles on *Let It Be* (1970). The Beatles also signed Preston as a solo artist to their Apple label. He nurtured his successful solo career concurrent with making stellar guest appearances with other artists, such as Aretha Franklin, Bob Dylan, Delaney and Bonnie, and, of course, the Rolling Stones, as is discussed later in this chapter.

Bobby Keys (saxophone) and Jim Price (trumpet) had also played in the Delaney and Bonnie & Friends band and came over to the UK at the request of George Harrison to work on his masterpiece, *All Things Must Pass* (1970).

Figure 2.1 Mick Jagger with Billy Preston, Plaza Monumental, Barcelona, 1976. Album/Francesc Fàbregas/Art Resource, NY.

Keys met Jagger while in London and soon he and Price became the horn section for the Stones. Starting with the appearance of Keys on "Live With Me" (from *Let It Bleed*) in 1969, the horns added an indelible dimension to *Sticky Fingers* (1971) and *Exile on Main Street* (1972), as well as the tours supporting those records. The interaction between all of these musicians on the records and tours of Harrison, Joe Cocker, Eric Clapton, and the Stones was indicative of an overall back to roots movement heard in the immediate post-psychedelia late 1960s on such records as the Band's *Music from Big Pink* (1968), Dylan's *John Wesley Harding* (1967), the Stones' *Beggars Banquet* (1968), and the Beatles' *White Album* (1968). But with added horn sections and backing singers, some rock shows were resembling the soul revue-type ensembles of Ike & Tina Turner, Stax, and Motown. Jim Price eventually left the fold, becoming a producer, but Keys remained a loyal sideman to the Stones for decades, falling out for a few years due to drug abuse, but back in the fold from the 1980s to his death in 2014. His brassy sax solos are inextricable from such songs as "Live With Me," "Can't You Hear Me Knocking," and "Sweet Virginia," and, of course, there is his signature solo in "Brown Sugar."

The Stones had famously covered songs by soul artists such as Otis Redding, Don Covay, Sam Cooke, Marvin Gaye, and Solomon Burke, just to name a significant few. These influences crept back as the Stones entered the seventies. "Through that whole period, there wasn't a whole lot going on in terms of saxophones and horns," Keys told me, discussing the time period surrounding the Summer of Love. "Except for the soul thing: Stax,

Otis Redding, Wilson Pickett, and that whole bunch from Memphis. I really loved that stuff. But up until then, most bands were guitar oriented, except for a few. We were hearing some of the first Stax stuff up at Leon Russell's house. Steve Cropper and Duck Dunn had come from Memphis to Los Angeles to do some overdubs. So I heard some of that stuff before it came out. And I was thinking this is definitely the wave of the future. It has all of these wonderful horns in it. So hell, I guess I am in good shape here."[15]

The brassy element of this period is essential to the gospel-soul sound of the early-1970s Rolling Stones. Indeed, it seems that Jagger was influenced to write such songs as the Otis Redding-inspired "I Got the Blues" by his time spent enjoying Redding and other Stax records with Keys in the early days of their budding friendship, and, of course, the group had covered some of Redding's songs on their early albums. There was an overall revival of the African-American influence – specifically gospel and its secularized offspring, soul – on rock and roll. I suggested to Keys that the horns were inspiring the Stones' songwriting itself, with songs such as "Let It Loose" and "Shine a Light." "Right, and Billy Preston brought a lot of that influence too," he said.

Preston's first appearance on a Stones record was on "Can't You Hear Me Knocking," followed by a searing, emotional Hammond organ solo on "I Got the Blues," both from *Sticky Fingers*. As great as Hopkins, Stewart, Nitzsche, and the Stones themselves were at adding piano and organ, it is hard to imagine any of them ripping out something as authentically gospel as this concise solo. Preston only makes one appearance on *Exile on Main Street*, on "Shine a Light," but it is another soul-stirring performance on both piano and organ, adding percussive and sweeping fills on each instrument during the transitions for verse to chorus. The difference in the individual styles that Preston and Hopkins brought to the Stones is obvious. Preston was also the organizing force behind the backing vocalists and the arrangements for vocal ensemble.

The Stones started adding extra voices to their records in earnest with "Salt of the Earth" from *Beggars Banquet*, specifically with a gospel feel in mind. Despite the addition of the Los Angeles-based Watts Street Gospel Choir, it does not come off as a gospel number, *per se*. But one can see the beginnings of the genre's influence on the Stones, so that for the next album, *Let It Bleed*, the band took another swing and ended up with the epic "You Can't Always Get What You Want," a song that begins as a folk-rock song but quickly becomes so full-on gospel that the group apparently felt it would be advantageous to undercut it with some irony. Instead of having the typical African-American Baptist choir, the Stones brought in the London Bach Choir:

"I'd ... had this idea of having a choir, probably a gospel choir, on the track," said Jagger, "but there wasn't one around at that point. Jack Nitzsche, or somebody, said that we could get the London Bach Choir and we said, that will be a laugh."[16] [Richards explains the use of the choir]: "Let's put on a straight chorus. In other words, let's try to reach the people up there as well. It was a dare, kind of ... And then, what if we got one of the best choirs in England, all these white, lovely singers, and do it that way? ... It was a beautiful juxtaposition."[17]

Also on *Let It Bleed* is the legendary star vocal turn from Merry Clayton, who gives a spine-chilling solo performance on "Gimme Shelter" – the first from a non-Rolling Stone on one of their recordings. Having written about this in detail elsewhere, suffice it to say her high-register attack, during which her voice buckles and then cracks as she soulfully pushes it even harder, is one of rock music's greatest moments.[18] It added a brand-new texture into a band which had been around for six years. On the scale of contender for greatest rock song of all time, the energy injected by Clayton's performance tipped "Gimme Shelter" from competitor to grand champion.

As the Stones increasingly brought outside contributors to their recording sessions, they also grew more comfortable with expanding their core band into a touring ensemble that continues to characterize their live performances today, augmented by regular sidemen and women, and sharing the spotlight with guest stars. In addition to his appearances on *Sticky Fingers* and *Exile*, Preston was the mainstay keyboardist on the three albums that followed – *Goats Head Soup*, *It's Only Rock 'n Roll*, and *Black and Blue* – and attendant mid-1970s tours. In fact, he was more than a mere sideman, sometimes sharing the microphone with Jagger on prominent vocal parts, and even a few turns singing one or two of his own songs.

Preston was still with the Stones in 1977, when they played the small Toronto El Mocambo Club (some of this gig is heard on *Love You Live* [1977]), and it was apparently there that he demonstrated the four-on-the-floor beat that formed the backbone of disco music.[19] So while he is not present on the Stones' next LP, *Some Girls* (1978), his influence carried through in Watts' playing on the song "Miss You," a smash single for the band at a crucial point.

Piano Pounder Four: Chuck Leavell

Alabama-born Chuck Leavell joined the band's 1981 European tour on the recommendation of Stewart. Leavell had played with the Allman Brothers (that's him with a virtuoso part on "Jessica"), among others, and grew up as a fan of both the Stones and Nicky Hopkins. "The fact is that Stu and I hit it off right away," said Leavell.

> I think he and the rest of the band liked that I am from the South. They have a deep affinity for Southern music of all kinds. From my perspective, I felt very comfortable from the first note I played with them at my audition. My attitude was, "Hey, I played all this stuff when I was a kid in my first bands back in Tuscaloosa, Alabama," and that seemed to serve me well. I just came as myself, with no pretension and (pardon the pun) no expectations. In the end it all worked out, thank heaven.[20]

Leavell started appearing with the Stones on recordings during the *Undercover* sessions, which meant getting used to the instrument *du jour* of the era, the digital synthesizer. Analog synths such as those pioneered by Robert Moog in the late 1960s had been responsible for some pleasantly thick textures on albums appearing soon after and in the early 1970s, such as the Beatles' *Abbey Road*, the Stones' *Satanic Majesties*, and Stevie Wonder's *Music of My Mind*. But the early digital versions could generate an unpleasant, thin, grating buzz: "I'm not a big fan of synth stuff," Leavell admitted.[21] Jagger in particular has always remained concerned with sounding contemporary and keeping the band current. In the 1980s that meant embracing the sonic textures of digital recording, sampled sounds, and the synthetic sounds of synthesizers. Nevertheless, the Stones always kept guitars at the forefront.

The relationship, musical and personal, between Richards and Jagger was strained for most of the 1980s, and the songwriting suffered as a result. *Tattoo You* (1981) was arguably the last solid Stones album, and that was put together from outtakes compiled and polished off by Jagger with engineer/producer Chris Kimsey. *Undercover* (1983) had some fine moments, including the blues-based "Tie You Up (The Pain of Love)" and "Feel On Baby," with Leavell playing Wurlitzer electric piano and Hammond organ, the organic-sounding tools of the trade since the 1960s. Stewart even makes appearances on a few tracks. But there is little in the way of distinctive keyboard work on the album.

Dirty Work (1986) is often cited as the nadir of the band. All one has to do is listen to "Winning Ugly" to hear ugly sounds indeed. Until Jagger comes in with the faux tough-guy growl he appropriated for the whole album, the backing track, with horrendous synth "horns," simply sounds like a movie theater jingle advertising its concession stand. Leavell provides a tasteful, prominent piano backing for the Richards-sung ballad that closes the album, "Sleep Tonight," though the synth strings pop out here and there.

Leavell has mostly played respectful and tasteful parts throughout the Stones albums and tours to which he has contributed. One cannot point to him as being as distinctive a stylist as Stewart, Hopkins, or Preston. He certainly subscribed to the "diamond tiaras" style, which is how Stewart referred to the high-register piano work that Nicky Hopkins often employed to cut through the mid-range guitars and vocals on Stones recordings.

***

The Stones remained off of the road for most of the 1980s, but came roaring back with the return-to-form *Steel Wheels* (1989) record and subsequent tours. The songwriting was still mostly sub-par, but at least the band returned to its rock and roll sound, with a two-guitar attack, organic keys, real brass, and unfussy production from Kimsey. The personal tensions might not have disappeared, but the hatchets were buried and Jagger and Richards managed to move on into their most lucrative period when records became calling cards for massive worldwide tours.

The band has struggled with the tension between their hefty legacy and the desire to remain vital artistically and commercially. One of Leavell's most significant roles has been as *de facto* music director on tours, helping to select a master list of songs to consider rehearsing and, once whittled down, working into set lists. It is like having an ombudsman or fan spokesman within the band itself, pointing out some deeper-cut gems that the diehard Stones fans might want to hear.

In 1989, Bill Wyman was the oldest member of the group at fifty-four. I was as guilty as anyone for underappreciating his legacy in the overall sound of the band. Replacement bassist Darryl Jones, an undisputed virtuoso who plays a critical role in keeping the sound vital, is not the swinging, old-school rock and roll player that Wyman is. Jones is a young player primarily raised on jazz and funk, whose performance credits include recordings with Miles Davis and Sting. Wyman's style was that of a musician who was raised on the upright bass of early rock and roll combos and the left hand of boogie-woogie pianists. His later style was informed by American soul and R&B electric bass players like Donald "Duck" Dunn and James Jamerson.

Though an unabashed lover of early rock and roll and a devotee of blues, Wyman adapted to the many stylistic changes taken on by the Stones, starting with the blues that was obscure to even him. But a fear of flying, a lack of creative input – either by choice or by discouragement, depending on which person is talking – and a general desire to move on to other things finally added up to his decision to leave the band in 1993, much to the dismay of Richards. Wyman walked away knowing he was leaving his share of a $41 million deal with Virgin Records on the table.

The choice (apparently left for Watts to make) of Darryl Jones was an interesting one. If the Stones had been looking for someone in the same vein as Wyman, Joey Spampinato, a real swinging traditional bass player from the band NRBQ, would have been a natural choice. Spampinato had just worked on two projects with Richards, the *Hail! Hail! Rock 'n' Roll* (1987) Chuck Berry tribute documentary film, and Richards' first solo LP, *Talk is Cheap* (1988). He was said to have the inside track on the position, but it would be reasonable to believe the rumors that Jagger was wary of his coziness within the Richards camp. It was also a period when Jagger felt like he was up against the weight of the Stones' past when trying to push the band forward, as producers like Don Was, who had grown up as fans of the band, entered the fray. Under such circumstances, one could also assume that Jagger did not want a replacement who was too traditional in style. Jagger saw himself as another of those impressive icons Jones had played with, while Spampinato was part of what many refer to as the greatest bar band of all time.

Despite his bluster about Wyman leaving, even Richards was guilty of taking the original bassist for granted. "You know, I'll tell you what, I was with Keith at his house in Turks and Caicos . . . a couple of years ago," said Bobby Keys. "And he had been listening to a lot of the outtakes from that [*Exile*] period, and he said to me, 'Man, Bobby, I never realized that Bill was such a motherfucker of a bass player!' he said. 'That sonofabitch was really good!'"[22]

Indeed he was. The Stones lost half of one of popular music's greatest rhythm sections and another original member. Their original piano player, Stewart, had passed away, and their almost-permanent sideman, Hopkins, died in 1994. The loss of Wyman was the one that most altered the sound of the band. But Jones is an extremely well-rounded, accomplished, and funky player. Leavell has now been with the Stones longer than any keyboardist. And with Jagger, Richards, and Watts continuing, it seems impossible to irreparably change the core sound of the band. All of these contributors I have discussed have colored the band's recordings and performances, nudged it into different directions than it might have taken without them, but the vital heart and soul of the Rolling Stones can still be heard in the personal and musical chemistry these musicians discovered almost sixty years ago.

Notes

1 According to Richards (*Life*, 372), "[Wood] was perfectly adapted to the ancient form of weaving, where you can't tell rhythm from lead guitar, the style I'd developed with Brian, the old bedrock of the Rolling Stones sound. The division between guitar players, rhythm and lead, that we had with Mick Taylor melted away."
2 *Life*, 270.
3 *RSG*, 204.
4 Nick Kent, "Mick Taylor: But I Still Love Him . . .", *NME* (October 12, 1974).
5 See the interview of Mick Taylor by Dave Schulps, "The Unknown Stone: Four and a Half Years Later, Mick Taylor Makes his Move," *Trouser Press* 41 (August 4, 1979). For a full analysis of Taylor's contribution to this song, see Janovitz*RO*, 269–74.
6 Ronnie Wood, *Ronnie: The Autobiography* (New York, 2007), 111.
7 *According*, 201.
8 In his autobiography (*Ronnie*, 112), Wood quotes Watts as saying: "He's only just walked in and he's bossing us around already."
9 Janovitz*RO*, 297.
10 Wyman*RWTS*, 482.
11 Hopkins later turned down an invitation from Page to join the New Yardbirds, who soon became known as Led Zeppelin. Robert Plant said they invited him twice, in fact; see Julian Dawson, *And On Piano . . . Nicky Hopkins: The Extraordinary Life of Rock's Greatest Session Man* (San Francisco, 2011), 97. For a chronicle of Hopkins' playing with the Stones, see *ibid.*, 88–96.
12 *Ibid.*, 90.
13 *According*, 159.
14 A good comparison is Waters' "When I Get To Thinking," from *Muddy Waters Sings "Big Bill"* (Chess LP 1444, 1960).
15 Phone interview between the author and Bobby Keys, July 23, 2012.
16 *According*, 125.
17 *Life*, 268.
18 Janovitz*RO*, 177–9.
19 *RSCRS*, 198.
20 Email interview between the author and Chuck Leavell, July 6, 2012.
21 *Ibid*.
22 Phone interview between the author and Bobby Keys, July 23, 2012.

3 The Rolling Stones in 1968:
In Defense of Lingering Psychedelia

JOHN COVACH

Recorded in March of 1968 and released in May, the Rolling Stones' "Jumpin' Jack Flash" quickly rose to the top of the charts in the USA and UK. Its driving guitar riff and straight-ahead rock feel seemed to signal to many that the band had emerged from the psychedelic meanderings of late 1967's *Their Satanic Majesties Request*, and the release of *Beggars Banquet* in December 1968 – the album "Jumpin' Jack" was originally intended for – served to reinforce the idea that the Stones had made a strong return to their musical roots. Brian Jones was reportedly so excited about the track that "as soon as the session finished he contacted a friend, Ronny Money – wife of musician Zoot Money – and told her that 'the Stones had returned to rock and roll with this thing called "Jumpin' Jack Flash," it's a gas.'"[1] Many writers have emphasized the band's seemingly new sound in 1968. Philippe Margotin and Jean-Michel Guesdon, for instance write that "the music ... represents a radical departure from *Between the Buttons* and *Their Satanic Majesties Request*," and Steve Appleford declares that "The Rolling Stones found their moment of absolute clarity in 1968, after a season of drug busts, bad press, and that swirl of forced experimentation called *Their Satanic Majesties Request*. Confusion was replaced by a new sense of purpose, where passing psychedelic fashion was cast aside in favour of the blues and rock roots that had first inspired them."[2]

While the rootsy dimensions of the band's music in 1968 indeed mark an important stylistic shift, that shift was not accompanied – as many have suggested – by a rejection of the psychedelic elements. This chapter will argue that features of the band's psychedelic experimentations constitute a significant part of the Stones' new approach to their music and presentation (including album art, performance, and video). Indeed, psychedelic elements linger in the band's music well into the 1970s. Though some might argue that *Their Satanic Majesties Request* was a wrong turn on the road leading from *Between the Buttons* to *Beggars Banquet* and beyond, this chapter will instead posit that the psychedelic music of 1967 was a necessary and logical stylistic precursor to 1968's recordings. Without majesties, there are no beggars. Finally, as noted earlier in this volume (see 4–5), *Their Satanic Majesties Request* is part of a general change in practice beginning in the mid-1960s in which bands explored new stylistic elements and novel sounds in the studio, exploiting a wave of technological development that made the recording studio into more than a place for documenting performances: The studio became a kind of sketchpad for sounds and combinations that had never been heard previously. The Stones' movement from covers to originals, and the accompanying and increasing attention to exploring new sounds in the studio, was thus securely in step with the times.[3]

Elsewhere I have discussed what I call the "hippie aesthetic," a formulation that attempts to account for this rise of rock ambition and the musical practices it produced.[4] There are five general ways in which rock poetics made the shift from something that might be thought of as craftsman-like to an approach that aspired to art: (1) the appropriation of classical music, a highbrow marker employed in earnest and with no sense of irony or critique; (2) the embrace of technology, including multi-track recording and the use of synthesized or electronically processed sounds and timbres; (3) increased instrumental virtuosity and a "musicianly" attitude and approach to playing; (4) lyrics that reject teenage love and strive to explore more adult approaches to relationships or other big ideas in culture, politics, religion, and literature; and (5) an emphasis on concepts, both in the rise of the concept album (or simply thinking in terms of albums rather than singles) and in the packaging of albums, as well as in theatrical approaches to performance. One can observe a gradual but continuous adoption of key elements of the hippie aesthetic in the Stones' music. The most obvious and heightened expression of the hippie aesthetic occurs with *Their Satanic Majesties Request* and the singles of that year. Psychedelia can thus be thought of – among all of the groups that engaged it and not only the Rolling Stones – as a particular and intense expression of the hippie aesthetic. The group's move in the direction that leads to the psychedelic 1967 recordings is in evidence at least as far back as 1964, though in 1965 this trajectory becomes clear. In order to track the band's development toward and engagement with psychedelia specifically, it is crucial to explore how this aesthetic and poetic shift occurs within the context of their embrace of the hippie aesthetic more generally.

"Play with Fire," a song recorded and released in early 1965 as the B side to "The Last Time," illustrates an early instance of the Stones engaging the hippie aesthetic, though not yet psychedelia. The lyrics deal with a complicated relationship, moving well beyond teen romance, and the music is set in an acoustic folk style, perhaps suggesting Dylan's influence.[5] The song is in a simple verse form, with four verses of twelve measures consisting of three four-bar phrases, the last of which is a refrain.[6] While the first eight measures of each verse employ a backing of acoustic guitar, bass, and tambourine, the refrains add harpsichord.[7] Since the lyrics deal with aristocracy, it is possible to view the harpsichord as a timbral reference to high society, but it is not used here in an ironic or critical manner; it is employed rather as a text-painting device. "As Tears Go By" offers another interesting early example. This song had been written by Jagger and Richards (with some help from Oldham and perhaps Lionel Bart) in early 1964 and given to Marianne Faithfull to record, whose version was released in mid-1964 and enjoyed chart success, especially in the UK. While orchestral instruments are employed on Faithfull's version of this song, their use does not especially suggest classical music and the musical ambition that might be associated with it. The strings instead provide the kind of soft pop orchestral backing so prevalent in early 1960s pop.[8] In late 1965, the Stones recorded their own version of "As Tears Go By," very much under the influence of the Beatles' "Yesterday" (which had been released and become a hit that fall) and employing a much more classically inflected string arrangement.[9] Referring to Jagger's lyrics, Marianne Faithfull has remarked that "it's an absolutely astonishing thing for a boy of twenty to have written – a song about a woman looking back nostalgically on her life."[10] The lyrics in the sixteen-bar verses of this simple verse form (with refrain) certainly move beyond teen romance and provide one of the earliest instances of a British Invasion song that engages a philosophical topic.[11] The band's use of classical music along with more ambitious lyrics in these two tracks, at a time when the Stones were still recording a lot of versions, signals the band's early steps on the way to psychedelia. According to Charlie Watts, "that music was the very, very beginning of flower power."[12]

As the Rolling Stones move from late 1965 into 1966 and the release of *Aftermath* in the summer, their music continues to grow in musical and artistic ambition. "Paint It, Black" explores new instrumental sounds, featuring Brian Jones on the sitar, while the lyrics engage the existential topic of death and loss – the singer's heart, a red door, is painted black. The song concludes in a bombastic frenzy, evoking a sense of ritual. Like "Play with Fire," this song employs a simple verse form, though here without a refrain, and presents five consecutive sixteen-bar verses before relaxing somewhat into a chanted section that then leads to the frantic coda. While the stylistic references here are not to classical music but rather to something vaguely exotic, the use of a non-rock instrument in an earnest manner – as with the harpsichord in "Play with Fire" – privileges the artist approach over the craftsmanly one.[13] "Lady Jane" also employs simple verse form, and its four sixteen-bar verses (with refrain) are set in what Keith Richards has described as "'Elizabethan' style."[14] Aside from the quasi-Shakespearian character of its lyrics, however, "Lady Jane" is a traditional love song, with the singer pledging his romantic fidelity. The accompaniment features acoustic guitar and bass, but also the dulcimer, played by Brian Jones. After an introduction that evokes traditional folk music in general and Simon and Garfunkel's "The Sound of Silence" (which had been a hit in late 1965/early 1966) in particular, the melody, harmony, and arrangement also make strong references to classical music. Jones' dulcimer lines echo Jagger's vocal phrases in the first half of the verses and the use of first-inversion harmonies in the second half creates a markedly "learned" reference. The entrance of Jack Nitzsche on the harpsichord during the instrumental third verse further reinforces the classical references.

Recorded during the second half of 1966 and released in early 1967, *Between the Buttons* further extends the band's engagement with the hippie aesthetic. Bill Wyman has remarked that this album "was the first studio session at which we concentrated on an album as a finished product."[15] "Cool, Calm and Collected" finds the Stones exploring approaches to musical form. While the song is in contrasting verse-chorus form, the verse and chorus contrast especially strongly, making this song distinctive in this regard.[16] The verse employs an energetic music-hall style, while the chorus is much calmer, with Brian Jones once again playing the dulcimer, but here in a very sitar-like manner. The revved-up bacchanal finale is reminiscent of the end of "Paint It, Black," though the addition of studio reverb and echo create a sense that the track does not so much conclude but rather implodes. Another album track, "Yesterday's Papers," is noteworthy as well for its use of vibraphone, played by Brian Jones, further suggesting that Jones was a driving force in the band's cultivation of new instrumental combinations. The arrangement also includes harpsichord, played once again by Jack Nitzsche. The innovative approach to form, the reference to Indian music, and the use of classical harpsichord all mark the Stones' continued push towards what would become psychedelia.

"Ruby Tuesday," a song largely composed by Brian Jones, was recorded during the same period as the *Between the Buttons* album tracks but was released as a single. The song is cast in contrasting verse-chorus form, combining a sixteen-bar verse with an eight-measure chorus. The verses once again make strong references to classical music – Jagger suggested that it sounded "like Chopin in parts" – with Brian Jones playing a melodic accompaniment to Jagger's vocal on the recorder.[17] Jack Nitzsche is now on piano, Keith Richards on acoustic guitar, Bill Wyman plays bowed upright bass on the verses (with occasional buzzes that are reminiscent of the sitar) and electric bass on the choruses, while Charlie Watts backs it all up on drums. The lyrics describe a free-spirited young woman and though they might represent any number of women the Stones had known, Keith Richards claims the woman he had in mind was ex-girlfriend Linda Keith.[18] The four-bar coda that ends this track may be the most classical ending the Stones ever recorded. The flipside of this single was "Let's Spend the Night Together," a track driven by an energetic piano lick. The song employs a compound AABA design, with the A sections based loosely on a contrasting sixteen-bar verse and eight-bar chorus pair. The contrasting B section, however, features a Beach Boys-inspired contrapuntal vocal arrangement, making it a Stones blues rocker with a bit of "Good Vibrations" for contrast.[19] My discussion will return to this blend of lick-driven rock with more ambitious musical features in the consideration of "Jumpin' Jack Flash" below. The examples presented thus far, however, support the idea that the Stones' music became gradually and increasingly ambitious as they approached 1967. The band's music is not yet psychedelic but can be seen to progressively engage aspects of the hippie aesthetic. The Stones' subsequent turn to psychedelia, understood in the context of their stylistic development in the years preceding *Their Satanic Majesties Request*, constitutes a next logical step.

Psychedelia, 1967, and *Their Satanic Majesties Request*

After the release of *Between the Buttons* in early 1967, the Stones devoted the rest of the year to recording their next album and a handful of singles. As mentioned briefly above, the band's work during the year was disrupted by serious brushes with the law that saw Jagger, Richards, and Jones arrested and convicted on drug charges. In the summer of 1967, while the Stones were trying to record amid legal proceedings, psychedelia arose out of underground scenes in San Francisco and London and into mainstream culture, most visibly represented by the Monterey Pop Festival in June, which was attended by Brian Jones. Flower Power, it suddenly seemed, was everywhere and the Summer of Love was in full bloom.[20] While psychedelia manifested itself in lifestyle (fashion, language, behavior, and attitudes), it is worth considering how the music itself – thought of apart from these other aspects of culture – participated in this cultural shift. Elsewhere I have discussed how music can be psychedelic, placing emphasis not only on aspects of the hippie aesthetic (especially musical ambition) but also on the influence of drug use.[21] Certain sonic features are clear markers of the psychedelic style, such as reversed tape effects, drones (heard most often in the bass) that underpin the music, melodic figures that evoke Indian music, and lyrics that engage philosophical, transcendental, spiritual, or political issues. These elements, however, are only part of psychedelia, though in some ways they are the most obvious features. At its core, psychedelic music is about the trip. Psychedelic music can either enhance a drug trip (and be designed to do so, as in the case of Country Joe and the Fish's *Electric Music for the Mind and Body*), or it can itself provide a kind of trip (as the concept album was thought to do).[22] In musical terms, this focus on the trip reinforces and fuels the hippie aesthetic, as bands work to create music that transports their listeners to new places using novel sounds, innovative recording techniques, and a broad range of musical styles.

Released in December 1967, *Their Satanic Majesties Request* is the Rolling Stones' most pronounced engagement with psychedelia. The elaborate cover, featuring the band dressed as colorful wizards and troubadours, is clearly inspired by the Beatles' *Sgt. Pepper's Lonely Hearts Club Band* cover.[23] This emphasis on album packaging is not new with either album, however. One can trace an attention to album art in the Beatles' music back at least as far as *Rubber Soul*, and in the Stones' releases as far back as the *12 × 5* cover and subsequent ones shot by both David Bailey and Gered Mankowitz. But both *Pepper* and *Majesties* especially draw attention to their packaging. Both albums also use reprise to organize the tracks into a larger whole. With *Pepper*, the opening title track returns just before the end of side two, announcing the end of the "show" and leading to "A Day in the Life." *Majesties* begins side one with "Sing This All Together," which then returns to close that side of the album. Both albums suggest a kind of musical trip, enhanced by the segue of certain tracks and very much in keeping with psychedelic practice.

The individual *Majesties* tracks continue to extend the musical ambition and innovation of the band's previous work. "She's a Rainbow," for instance, picks up once more with the use of classical idioms.[24] The song employs a contrasting verse-chorus form, but in a very interesting and novel way. The first three times the eight-bar verse occurs it is played instrumentally, with emphasis on a classical piano figuration (here played by Nicky Hopkins); it is thus not clear initially that this section is functioning as a verse in the form. A ten-bar sung chorus then follows each instrumental verse except the third (where the chorus is also instrumental), and it is not until Jagger enters singing this verse on its fourth appearance that the listener understands that what might have been heard previously as an interlude has actually been a verse all along. The use of chamber strings and harpsichord further reinforce the reference to classical music established by the piano part.[25] If "She's a Rainbow" invokes eighteenth- and nineteenth-century classical music, "2000 Light Years From Home" draws more on avant-garde classical elements. Beginning with an eerie introduction making use of electronic sounds and atonal, atmospheric piano and then a menacing guitar riff accompanied by Brian Jones' mysterious lines on the Mellotron, the track sets the stage for lyrics describing a space journey that ultimately arrives on the distant star Aldebaran – the singer's space journey takes him 100, 600, 1,000, and finally 2,000 light years from home.[26] The Stones may have been inspired in this instance by Pink Floyd's "Interstellar Overdrive" or "Astronomy Domine," which were staples of the Floyd's live show and appeared on their album *The Piper at the Gates of Dawn* in the late summer of 1967 (a live version of "Astronomy Domine" appears on the group's 1969 double LP *Ummagumma*). But the electronic sounds on "2000 Light Years From Home" are perhaps also reminiscent of an EP released in 1960 by legendary British producer Joe Meek entitled *I Hear a New World: An Outer Space Music Fantasy*. Meek's EP is filled with otherworldly electronic "space" sounds.[27] In any case, the Stones, the Pink Floyd, and Joe Meek were all engaging practices that were current in the avant-garde electronic and tape music of the time.

"We Love You," a single recorded during the *Majesties* sessions, perhaps provides the best example of the psychedelic peace-and-love ethos influencing Stones lyrics. The tune was recorded at the height of the Jagger and Richards legal proceedings during the summer of 1967; correspondingly, the song opens with the sound of a prison door slamming before introducing a driving piano figure played by Nicky Hopkins. Featuring help on background vocals from John Lennon and Paul McCartney, the song declares love in the face of persecution. Employing AABA form without reprise, the track ends with an extended coda, blending various music-textural layers together into a sonic collage reminiscent of "All You Need Is Love," though "We Love You" is more menacing than the Beatles' single. These kinds of sonic collages were made possible to a significant degree by advances in recording technology, which allowed for parts to be layered over one another. With "We Love You," one can see the Stones taking full advantage of this technology. "Dandelion" appeared as the flipside to "We Love You" and, like the choral interlude in "Let's Spend the Night Together," suggests a Beach Boys influence. The harpsichord once more appears on this Stones track, while Brian Jones plays both Mellotron and saxophone.[28] The lyrics are inspired by nursery rhymes and seem to suggest that when one gets hung up on the pressures of adult life, remember the dandelion, which is able to go wherever the breeze takes it with seeming unconcern. The song's compound AABA form employs a verse-chorus pair, each eight measures in length. The contrasting B section, however is seven bars, making for an interesting though not uncommon asymmetry. "We Love You" and "Dandelion" provide distinct examples of the whimsical elements of psychedelia that the Stones would soon reject, while also including important elements that would remain in the group's music for years to come.

Promotional videos directed by Peter Whitehead were made for "Let's Spend the Night Together" and "We Love You." Whitehead's engagement with the band began with his film of the group's first tour to Ireland in 1965, *Charlie Is My Darling*, and he also directed videos for "Have You Seen Your Mother, Baby, Standing in the Shadow," and "Lady Jane." Michael Lindsay-Hogg directed videos of "2000 Light Years From Home" and "She's a Rainbow."[29] Whitehead's video for "We Love You" is at least partially conceptual: Making reference to the Jagger and Richards trials, it casts band members and Marianne Faithfull as figures in the famous indecency trial of Oscar Wilde, and was subsequently banned from viewing by *Top of the Pops*.[30] Of the videos by Lindsay-Hogg, only the one for "2000 Light Years From Home" is available. The Stones appear performing the tune in psychedelic garb, with Jagger in a hood and wearing face make-up. The use of images nicely captures the mysterious and otherworldly atmosphere of the song without adding any additional narrative. Along with the album art, these videos underscore the growing importance to musicians concerning how the music is presented. Rock musicians increasingly began to think of their music as including more than just the recording: The music began to become conceptual in its various modes of presentation.

Surveying the *Majesties* period, it is clear that the hippie aesthetic is in full force for the Stones in 1967 (see Figure 3.1). The album art and video presentations expand our understanding of the music beyond the actual recordings themselves, the lyrics and music are ambitious, there is increasing use of non-rock instrumentation as well as studio effects and sonic experimentation, and there are numerous and substantial earnest references to classical music, a characteristic that – in the 1960s at least – increases the sense of artistic seriousness of the music. It is also clear that the album is meant to produce a kind of musical trip (though it is equally obvious that many fans may have used it to enhance a trip). The psychedelic aspect of this music is difficult to separate from its engagement with – and even extension of – the hippie aesthetic, and especially since that engagement begins with music by the Stones that is not generally considered to be psychedelic. The *Majesties* music is a logical progression according to a stylistic trajectory the Stones had followed since 1964. The album itself is psychedelic, but the hippie aesthetic is a constant element present both before and after *Majesties*.

Figure 3.1 The Rolling Stones, 1967. Courtesy HIP/Art Resource, NY.

The New Sound, "Jumpin' Jack," and *Beggars Banquet*

We can now return to "Jumpin' Jack Flash" and the important shift this track signaled in rejecting the psychedelia of *Majesties* and marking a new way forward.[31] Clearly the opening guitar riff drives "Jumpin' Jack" in a visceral way, and as the drums, bass, and additional guitars enter, the song rocks forward in a manner more grounded in the band's blues-rock roots than in their recent ambitious experimentation.[32] There are two aspects of this track, however, that continue the band's psychedelic practice. The first is the way that "Jumpin' Jack" ends: After the compound AABA form of the main song is presented, a longish coda occurs. These last forty-five seconds of the song feature a harmonically static texture made up of layers of music: guitar lines, organ chords and then melody, bass, drums – all combining into a kaleidoscopic swirl of sound that recalls the last ninety seconds of "We Love You" (or "All You Need Is Love"). Of course, the Stones had retained the long ending of "Goin' Home" on *Aftermath*, but these later psychedelic endings are of a different kind – they do not dramatically drive the song forward so much as simply float, encouraging the listener to relish an expanded moment of musical stasis. A second psychedelic aspect of "Jumpin' Jack Flash" concerns certain elements in one of the two promotional videos made for this track; for clarity, these are sometimes distinguished as the "make-up" and "no make-up" videos.[33] In the "make-up" version, the band performs on a dimly lit stage, with a barefoot Jagger wearing a sort of "war paint" on his face while sporting a circular watch medallion painted on his bare chest and stomach. Watts and Wyman also wear make-up, though theirs seems more androgynous, perhaps recalling the cover photo for "Have You Seen Your Mother, Baby, Standing in the Shadow." Jones wears bright green sunglasses and orange lipstick, while Richards wears dark glasses and a richly embroidered tunic. The overall look of this video is not as markedly psychedelic as the one for "2000 Light Years From Home," but it is also clear that director Michael Lindsay-Hogg has not rejected the psychedelic elements of the *Majesties* video in this one for "Jumpin' Jack Flash." While the static quality of the song's ending employs a psychedelic musical texture, the video retains psychedelic images and fashion.

"Child of the Moon" appears on the flipside of the "Jumpin' Jack Flash" single and it has its beginnings in the recording sessions for *Majesties*. It is perhaps not surprising, then, that "Child of the Moon" also retains elements from the band's most psychedelic LP. In fact, the static nature of the harmony and vocal harmonies of its verses is not only reminiscent of "We Love You," but also of the Beatles' "Rain," making this song seem perhaps more indebted to 1966 than 1967. As he has done before, Brian Jones performs on a new instrument, this time the soprano saxophone. The lyrics once again describe a free-spirited woman, as in "Ruby Tuesday" (Richards' lyric) or "She's a Rainbow." The Lindsay-Hogg directed video, like the one Whitehead directed for "We Love You," is conceptual – even if the exact concept is difficult to discern. The video opens with Jagger perched in a tree, as other band members stand along a country road. Later Jones will be shown peering out from behind another tree. Three women in turn approach the spot where the rather menacing-looking band is positioned along the road: a young girl (holding an apple), who stops and seems unafraid, but scurries back into the bushes; a young woman, who stops and turns back; and an elderly woman, who stops for a moment but then walks directly past the men. The theme of the video suggests that there are different choices one makes (or perhaps threats one perceives) at various stages of life, though a more precise meaning would be difficult to support. The precise interpretation of the video, however, is not important in this case; it is far more significant that the video seeks to explore a serious and philosophical question: in so doing it directly engages the hippie aesthetic.[34]

Like "Child of the Moon," the genesis of "Street Fighting Man" reaches back to 1967, perhaps even to late 1966. According to Richards, he had the music for the song but not the lyrics; these would be supplied by Jagger and prove to be quite controversial.[35] The track employs a contrasting verse-chorus form. Each ten-bar verse is driven by Richards' layers of guitars and keeps squarely within the blues-rock style. The choruses, however, open onto a slightly more exotic soundscape, as Brian Jones enters with the drone of the Indian tambura and Nicky Hopkins' acoustic piano helps push the song forward.[36] When the chorus appears a third time, the tambura is absent, though it reappears in the coda that follows, along with a sitar (also played by Jones) and an Indian horn called the shehnai, played in this instance by guitarist Dave Mason. The result is an expansion of the chorus that results in forty seconds of the same kind of static, psychedelic swirl that appears at the end of "Jumpin' Jack Flash" and "We Love You." Jagger's provocative lyrics arose from his political feelings of the time: He had attended an anti-Vietnam War rally in London's Grosvenor Square in March 1968 and was inspired to make his own statement, placing special emphasis on the idea of revolution. Released as a single in the USA at the end of the turbulent summer of 1968, the song was banned by some radio stations, who worried it might incite even more political violence.[37] "Street Fighting Man," therefore, brings together lyrics on a serious theme with extended moments of psychedelic music-textural stasis.

"Sympathy for the Devil" was perhaps the most ambitious track the Stones had recorded thus far and much of the ambition of the song is centered on the lyrics. Jagger assumes the persona of Lucifer as he moves through two thousand years of history, from the crucifixion of Jesus and the Hundred Years War to the Russian Revolution and the assassinations of John and Robert Kennedy. Jagger's devil is a wealthy and refined man; and the key to this master of deception's diabolical success is the obscuring of right and wrong, making one seem like the other and driving human-kind to evil, history-defining deeds. Jagger seems to have crafted his particular angle on Satan after reading Mikhail Bulgakov's novel *The Master and Margarita*, and the idea of creating an extended track (more than six minutes) based on history, religion, and literature is deeply sympathetic with the hippie aesthetic.[38] The actual recording of the track in May, 1968 was captured by director Jean-Luc Godard as part of a film engaging revolutionary politics. Ultimately released under the title *Sympathy for the Devil* (1970/2003), the film provides a rare glimpse into the transformation that can occur as a song is developed from its incipient creative idea into the finished product. The recorded version is in contrasting verse-chorus form, with five appearances of the seventeen-bar verses, each followed by an eight-bar chorus.[39] The accompaniment to Jagger's vocal is fairly straightforward, with Richards once again on bass, as well as lead guitar, Hopkins at the piano, Watts on the drums, and Wyman on the shekere, a West African percussion instrument. Rocky Dijon provides the distinctive conga part, while the Stones, three of their girlfriends (including Marianne Faithfull), and engineer Glyn Johns sing the back-up "devil's chorus" ("woo-woo") beginning with the third verse.[40] The track ends with almost two minutes of coda, but this is not the static psychedelic swirl found in "We Love You," "Jumpin' Jack Flash," or "Street Fighting Man." Instead, "Sympathy for the Devil" employs the kind of rhythm and blues extensions that can be found on Stones versions such as Otis Redding's "That's How Strong My Love Is" from *Out of Our Heads*. About the only aspect of the accompaniment to Jagger's lead vocals on this track that resonates with psychedelia is the persistence of the music: The repetitive forward push of the rhythm suggests a ritual, with the group chant of the back-up vocals supporting the voice of the devil as he sings.

In terms of the music alone, "Sympathy for the Devil" – aside from its ambitious lyrics – does not suggest much lingering psychedelia. The performance of this track, however, brings with it a new dimension. In late 1968, the Stones filmed a television broadcast entitled *The Rolling Stones Rock and Roll Circus*.[41] This project was a continuation of the band's previous work with director Michael Lindsay-Hogg and featured a line-up including the Stones, the Who, Jethro Tull, Marianne Faithfull, Taj Mahal, and the Dirty Mac (John Lennon, Eric Clapton, Mitch Mitchell, Keith Richards, and Yoko Ono). The Stones' set consists of "Jumpin' Jack Flash," "Parachute Woman," "No Expectations," "You Can't Always Get What You Want" (without choir), and finally "Sympathy for the Devil" as the set closer.[42] Throughout the performance Jagger has been clad in maroon pants and a red shirt and this is how he performs most of "Devil." When the band gets to the song's extended coda, here lengthened to four minutes in comparison with the album version, Jagger goes down on his stomach and then to his knees facing the crowd, placing the microphone between his legs and bending down to the floor to sing improvised phrases. He then bends his head all the way down to the floor and begins to remove his shirt. The crowd reacts, expecting that he will emerge shirtless. When he does stand up, it is immediately clear that this is not merely a gesture of rock and roll sexuality: Perhaps shockingly, he has tattoos of Lucifer painted on each arm and across his chest.[43] This dramatic bit of theater, intimately bound up with the theme of the lyrics, is a clear extension into the live performance realm of the conceptual approach that had previously been a key element in the "We Love You," "2000 Light Years From Home," and "Jumpin' Jack Flash" videos. While this performance is not in itself psychedelic, it extends an approach to performance developed in the band's psychedelic music. Of course, the circus setting of this television program already leans in the direction of psychedelia; there is, after all, a circus parade, trapeze artists, and a fire eater, and plenty of bright hippie clothing. The Stones' performance of the "Sympathy for the Devil" finale further reinforces that psychedelic inclination while simultaneously extending the band's own engagement with its recent psychedelic past.[44]

As mentioned above, the album cover design for *Majesties* had been markedly psychedelic. The initial design for the *Beggars* cover, by contrast, was thoroughly existential and transparently provocative.[45] When the record company rejected the initial images of a filthy toilet and graffiti-filled walls, the replacement design was one imitating an invitation to a formal banquet. The black-and-white simplicity of the replacement *Beggars* cover, like the original restroom design, might seem a rejection of the excessively colorful sleeve for *Majesties*. As a consequence, the *Beggars* cover might constitute a rejection of psychedelia in general. But both designs for the *Beggars* cover, in fact, are markedly conceptual, and their content is much more integrated with the music on the album than is the case with *Majesties*. The *Beggars* cover, then, is actually more faithful to the hippie aesthetic than the cover for *Majesties*, even if it is less psychedelic in its use of color and image.

Surveying these examples from *Beggars Banquet*, it is clear that there is a much more pronounced aspect of continuity with *Majesties* (and the band's earlier music) than is often acknowledged. That continuity is primarily driven by the hippie aesthetic, which as we have seen can be traced back to 1964 and finds its most obvious expression in the psychedelia of 1967. But it is not only the hippie aesthetic that continues to play a role in the band's "new sound." Specific psychedelic features recur in the band's music from 1968: the static endings of "Jumpin' Jack Flash" and "Street Fighting Man," the sitar, tambura, and shehnai of "Street Fighting Man," the trippiness of the "Child of the Moon" video, the performances of

"Jumpin' Jack Flash" and "Sympathy for the Devil" – all of these suggest that psychedelia, while no longer the focus of the band's music, remained within its stylistic palette.

Psychedelia Continues to Linger

Elements of the hippie aesthetic – and thus, in a certain sense, psychedelic elements – also recur in the albums that follow *Beggars Banquet*. In some ways "Gimme Shelter," from *Let It Bleed*, is a reworking of "Sympathy for the Devil," though this time constituting an ambitious track originating from Keith Richards.[46] "You Can't Always Get What You Want," from the same album, employs a concert choir, continuing the use of classical features in Stones music.[47] The extended jam that makes up the second half of "Can't You Hear Me Knocking" – with virtuosic solos from Bobby Keys and Mick Taylor – shows that as late as *Sticky Fingers* aspects of the hippie aesthetic were still a part of the band's musical approach. The strings on "Moonlight Mile" add a classical touch, and the last ninety seconds are static, atmospheric, and trippy, perhaps meant to suggest the quiet of a late-night bus or train ride to the next show (and perhaps even recalling the quiet sections of "Cool, Calm and Collected").

The recurrence of some aspects of the hippie aesthetic in the Rolling Stones' music after *Beggars Banquet* further reinforces the idea that, while 1968 saw a significant change in the band's stylistic emphases, it did not mark a rejection of the group's previous work, nor all aspects of *Their Satanic Majesties Request*. In retrospect, there is more continuity in the band's development than discontinuity. *Majesties* may have been a moment of maximum experimentation and experimental looseness, but it was only one stop on a road that led forward to the band's music in the 1970s and beyond. Elements of psychedelia indeed lingered long after the wizard and troubadour costumes had been discarded.

Notes

1 *RSCRS*, 99.

2 See Margotin & Guesdon, 250, and Steve Appleford, *The Rolling Stones – It's Only Rock and Roll: Song by Song* (New York, 1997), 69.

3 See John Covach, "From Craft to Art: Formal Structure in the Music of the Beatles," in *Reading the Beatles: Cultural Studies, Literary Criticism, and the Fab Four*, ed. Kenneth Womack and Todd Davis (Albany, NY, 2006), 37–53, for the ways in which the Beatles' music grew in musical ambition over the course of the 1960s; and Daniel Harrison, "After Sundown: The Beach Boys' Experimental Music," in *Understanding Rock: Essays in Musical Analysis*, ed. John Covach and Graeme Boone (New York, 1997), 33–57 for a similar study of the Beach Boys' music.

4 John Covach, "The Hippie Aesthetic: Cultural Positioning and Musical Ambition in Early Progressive Rock," in *Composition and Experimentation in British Rock 1966–1976*, a special issue of *Philomusica Online* (2007). Reprinted in *The Ashgate Library of Essays on Popular Music: Rock*, ed. Mark Spicer (Burlington, VT, 2012), 65–75.

5 Authorship of the song is credited to Nanker-Phelge, though Elliott (*RSCRS*, 53) writes that this is mostly a Keith Richards song; Babiuk and Prevost (*RSG*, 157) quote Richards attributing the writing to both him and Jagger.

6 The refrain is repeated instrumentally after verse two, and with singing to create a coda after verse four.

7 *RSCRS*, 53, Margotin & Guesdon, 112, and Richards (*Life*, 129) all report that Jack Nitzsche played harpsichord while Phil Spector played bass on a tuned-down guitar.

8 For accounts of the genesis of the song and the Faithfull recording, see *Faithfull*, 20–5, and Oldham, *Stoned*, 317–23.

9 Mike Leander composed the arrangements for both the Faithfull and Stones versions. A busy arranger in London at the time, he would also provide the arrangement for the Beatles' "She's Leaving Home."

10 *Faithfull*, 24.

11 While the Stones' version of "As Tears Go By" is clearly influenced by the Beatles' "Yesterday," it may be that McCartney's lyrics for "Yesterday" were influenced by "As Tears Go By," which he would have known in Faithfull's version. Note as well that the lyrics to "Play with Fire" clearly anticipate some of the increasingly mature Beatles lyrics that would appear on *Help!* later in 1965.

12 *According*, 85.

13 Richards has referred to this track as "Gypsy," while Jagger dubs it "Turkish." See Margotin & Guesdon, 168; and *According*, 100. While the use of sitar on this track seems influenced by the use of that instrument on the Beatles' "Norwegian Wood," the existential tone of the lyrics predates that of McCartney's "Eleanor Rigby," which was recorded a month after "Paint It, Black."

14 *According*, 146.

15 Wyman*SA*, 399.

16 Another song that employs this kind of strong contrast between verse and chorus is George Harrison's "I Me Mine," though it was written years later.

17 Jagger confirmed, however, that he had nothing to do with the writing of the song. See Wyman*RWTS*, 255.

18 *Life*, 187. On Jones' authorship and the song's background influences, see the chapter by Heimarck in this volume, 153, n. 44.

19 *Faithfull*, 88, credits the composition of this track to Jagger; Margotin & Guesdon, 239 and *RSCRS*, 86, however, attribute the music to Richards, who they report composed it at the piano (though Jack Nitzsche played the piano part on the recording).

20 See James Henke and Parke Puterbaugh, *I Want to Take You Higher: The Psychedelic Era, 1965–1969* (San Francisco, 1997), for a masterful chronicle of the rise of psychedelia during this time. See also Russell Reising and Jim LeBlanc, "Within and Without: *Sgt. Pepper's Lonely Hearts Club Band* and Psychedelic Insight," in *Sgt. Pepper and the Beatles: It Was Forty Years Ago Today*, ed. Olivier Julien (New York, 2016), 103–20; and Sarah Hill, *San Francisco and the Long 60s* (London, 2016).

21 John Covach, *What's That Sound? An Introduction to Rock and its History* (New York, 2006), 255–99.

22 See also Jim DeRogotis, *Turn On Your Mind: Four Decades of Great Psychedelic Rock* (Milwaukee, WI, 2003); and William Echard, *Psychedelic Popular Music: A History through Musical Topic Theory* (Bloomington, IN, 2017).

23 The covers for both albums were shot by Michael Cooper. The 3-D effect of the Stones cover is created by a process called "lenticular printing." See Margotin & Guesdon, 219.

24 In the period preceding *Majesties*, Oldham is credited as producer on Stones recordings. Oldham begins to separate from the band in 1967 and *Majesties* becomes the first album crediting production simply to the Rolling Stones.

25 The string arrangement on this track is by John Paul Jones, who would later be a member of Led Zeppelin.

26 See *RSG*, 267, for a detailed description of the instruments used on this track. The authors also report that Jagger began the lyrics to this song while sitting in prison after his drug conviction.

27　For a fuller discussion of Joe Meek and his role in British pop during the 1960s, see John Repsch, *The Legendary Joe Meek: The Telstar Man* (London, 2000); and Barry Cleveland, *Joe Meek's Bold Techniques* (Los Angeles, 2011).

28　Margotin & Guesdon, 244, suggest that Lennon and McCartney provide back-up vocals on this track as well, and that this accounts for the Beatles-esque flavor of the vocals. While Lennon and McCartney are likely singing on this track, the music itself could easily have fitted right into the Beach Boys' aborted *SMiLE* album of 1967. Interestingly, "Dandelion" originated during the sessions for *Between the Buttons* in late 1966 (see *RSCRS*, 84). Presumably because of this track's origins in this earlier session, Elliott (*ibid.*) suggests that Jack Nitzsche may be playing harpsichord on this track, if it is not Brian Jones.

29　See Karnbach & Bernson for a comprehensive list of Rolling Stones promotional videos. A promotional video was also made for "Dandelion," but the authors do not list a specific director, indicating simply "union." For a study of *Charlie Is My Darling* and Whitehead's relationship to the Stones, see Victor Coelho, "Through the Lens, Darkly: Peter Whitehead and the Rolling Stones," *Framework: The Journal of Cinema and Media* 52 (2011), 174–91. For a discussion of these videos in the broader context of the Stones' television and radio performances in the 1960s, see Richard Havers, *Rolling Stones On Air in the Sixties: TV and Radio History As It Happened* (New York, 2017).

30　See Coelho, "Through the Lens, Darkly," 184.

31　Jimmy Miller begins producing the Stones with these 1968 sessions.

32　Richards (*Life*, 238–41) discusses his use of cassette player to achieve the specific guitar tone used on "Jumpin' Jack Flash" and "Street Fighting Man" (discussed below). He refers to the opening lick from "Flash" as "basically 'Satisfaction' in reverse" (*ibid.*, 240). A quick comparison of the two reveals they share a distinctly similar rhythmic profile. For Wyman's claims on the authorship of the "Flash" riff, see Wyman*SA*, 482–3; see also *RSG*, 280–2.

33　See Karnbach & Bernson, 384–5.

34　Alan Clayson writes that this track "bridged a gap between psychedelia and the pastoral element embraced on *Beggars Banquet*, albeit with a hint that someone had skip-read black magician Aleister Crowley's *Moonchild*." See his *The Rolling Stones – Beggars Banquet* (New York, 2008), 174.

35　Richards made these remarks in an interview that appeared in the *Wall Street Journal*, quoted in Margotin & Guesdon, 267.

36　Each of the three verses is made up of two five-bar phrases while the chorus is eleven measures in length the first and third time, but fifteen bars on its second appearance allowing Richards, who plays bass on this track, to add melodic work in these four additional measures.

37　For accounts of the genesis of this song, along with the cultural and political context of the lyrics, see Philip Norman, *Mick Jagger* (New York, 2012), 285–9; and Marc Spitz, *Jagger: Rebel, Rock Star, Rambler, Rogue* (New York, 2011), 105–17. It is interesting to note that the sessions for "Street Fighting Man" predate those for the Beatles' "Revolution" – a John Lennon song – by a few weeks. Paul McCartney's "Blackbird," a song inspired by the civil rights movement in the USA, was recorded two weeks after Lennon's track. See *RSCRS*, 97–8 and 101–2, for information on the Stones sessions, including the session for "Pay Your Dues," an early version of "Street Fighting Man." For information on the Beatles' session, see Mark Lewisohn, *The Beatles – Recording Sessions* (New York, 1988), 135, 137.

38　See Norman, *Mick Jagger*, 290–2, for a comparison of the Bulgakov novel with Jagger's lyrics. Norman cites Jagger as having some reservations about the lyric for fear it might be viewed as too pretentious (291). See also Spitz, *Jagger*, 112–16.

39　The phrases each fall into a four-bar pattern except for the last in each verse, which is five bars. The reader may recall that the verses of "Street Fighting Man" were made up of two five-bar phrases.

40　Dijon contributed to many of the *Beggars Banquet* tracks. The tasteful use of percussion is an important aspect of Jimmy Miller's production approach. While percussion had occurred on previous Stones albums, Miller's use – perhaps because he was himself a drummer – adds a new dimension to these recordings.

41　*The Rolling Stones Rock and Roll Circus*, directed by Michael Lindsay-Hogg (DVD ABKCO Films, DVD 1003-9, 2004). See Norman, *Mick Jagger*, 312–17, for an account of the genesis and shooting of the film.

42　*Rock and Roll Circus* closes with the Stones performing "Salt of the Earth" with the other acts and audience after the band completes their set.

43 Wyman*RWTS*, 316–17, reveals that the band did six takes of "Sympathy for the Devil" and multiple takes of the other tunes. Norman (*Mick Jagger*, 321), relying on Lindsay-Hogg's recollection, reports that there were only three takes of "Sympathy."

44 *Circus* was never broadcast in December, 1968 as planned, and even after attempts to revive the project in early 1969, it was shelved. See Norman, *Mick Jagger*, 331–2.

45 See Margotin & Guesdon, 252–3, for a succinct summary of the struggle over the original cover. See also Clayson, *The Rolling Stones*, 154–6.

46 Richards (*Life*, 256–7) provides an account of the genesis of this song.

47 Margotin & Guesdon, 304–7, provide a useful account of how the London Bach Choir and Al Kooper ended up performing on this song.

4 Exile, America, and the Theater of the Rolling Stones, 1968–1972

VICTOR COELHO

I have wandered through almost every region to which this tongue of ours extends, a stranger, almost a beggar ... DANTE, *IL CONVIVIO*, I, 3

The lyrics range from scriptural verses about Lucifer and the Prodigal Son to stories of beggars, sinners, prowlers, addicts, transients, outcasts, Black militants, groupies, and road-weary troubadours; the web of musical influences is spun with multi-colored threads of urban and rural blues, country, calypso, R&B, rock and roll, folk, gospel, and even the English choral tradition. The four albums released by the Rolling Stones between 1968 and 1972 – *Beggars Banquet, Let It Bleed, Sticky Fingers*, and *Exile on Main Street* – constitute for critics, fans, and historians the core identity of the group and the lasting, canonical repertory that has defined the Stones' musical, historical, and cultural legacy.[1] As Jack Hamilton has written in a recent study of the group, the band's years from 1968 to *Exile* amount to "one of the great sustained creative peaks in all of popular music."[2] An insider's perspective on the moment when the Rolling Stones were guaranteed a place of distinction in the history of music is offered by *Rolling Stone* founder Jann Wenner. As the group finally extricated itself from the management of Allen Klein and ABKCO in 1970, Wenner implored Mo Ostin of Warner Bros to sign the group without delay:

> Dear Mo, The Rolling Stones contract with London/Decca is now up, or shortly about to be. They are not renewing. They are looking for a new label and company in the USA, but not their own label. They have two LP's now in the can almost ready for release: Live in the USA [*Get Yer Ya-Ya's Out!*], and the one they are [finishing] or have finished from Muscle Shoals [*Sticky Fingers*].
>
> Mick Jagger is the one who will make the decision on who is their new label. It's worth everything you've got to get this contract, even to lose money on it. The label that gets the Stones will be one of the winners in the 70's.
>   Contact Mick directly in London at MAY 5856, 46A Maddox Street, W1. [followed by in red pen] NOW.[3]

The critical reception of these albums, documented extensively in both published and video accounts since their release half a century ago, has only affirmed their historical relevance within the political and generational tensions of the late 1960s and early 1970s.[4] *Let It Bleed* – "Gimme Shelter" in particular (both the song and the film) – has been immortalized as a live broadcast of the abrupt shift from utopian Woodstock ideals of July, 1969 to the crushing dystopian reality – the "Pearl Harbor to the Woodstock Nation"[5] – of the Altamont tragedy only five months later. *Sticky Fingers* is seen as a poetic but dark chronicle of addiction, obsession, dependency, and refuge; and "Sympathy for the Devil," from *Beggars Banquet*, is the ubiquitous point of reference for any discussion of the volatile activism, assassinations, and racial tensions in 1968 America, a country inextricably mired in the Vietnam War and its related protests. Godard's 1968 observational film *One Plus One* [*Sympathy for the Devil*] was remarkably prescient through its resolute focus on the slow evolution of "Sympathy for the Devil" as a metaphor for Marxist anarchy brewing in the streets, a premonition shared even by Jagger: "There's no doubt there's a cyclic change," he says in a May, 1968 interview during the anti-Vietnam protests in Grosvenor Square in London, just prior to the student riots in Paris; "a VAST cyclic change on top of a lot of smaller ones. I can imagine America becoming just ablaze, just being ruined . . ."[6] Finally, *Exile on Main Street*, while breaking no new ground stylistically, frames for posterity the permanent identity of the Stones through the album's themes of both poetic and living geographical exile. It is a summation of the musical diversity introduced by the previous albums in which the deep roots of their style are laid bare in the present: There is no old and there is no new in the musical vocabulary of *Exile*. As Janovitz writes in his study of the album, "[*Exile*] seems to revel in self-imposed limitations. In fact, it sometimes sounds ancient. Other times it sounds completely current and modern. It sounds, at various points, underground and a little experimental, and at others, classic and even nostalgic."[7]

These four releases are not the most popular-selling albums by the Stones, nor do the 57 songs they contain – out of an entire catalog of around 400 – amount to an unusually large concentration of material within any five-year period of their recording history; there is far more music recorded before 1968 and after 1972.[8] But beginning with *Beggars Banquet* of 1968 we see a profound deepening of the vernacular dialects of rock and roll as the group traveled from metropole concerns of urban blues, Mod London, and the middle-class audiences of the Ed Sullivan show on to a new landscape of a vast America and its "distant" traditions of Delta Blues, rural country, and older texts. They infused these genres and their lyrical themes with the raw exilic qualities of distance and authenticity as metaphors for a contemporary culture they saw as revolutionary, disruptive, and teeming with racial and generational strife. Like exiles before them, they were stuck at the crossroads of participation and reflection. While the group recognized deep societal violence and struggle, it remained disengaged from the action at a critical, poetic distance, offering commentary, not combat. As Jon Landau wrote in *Rolling Stone*,

> the most startling songs on the album are the ones that deal with the Stones' environment: "Salt of the Earth," "Street Fighting Man," and "Sympathy for the Devil." Each is characterized lyrically by a schizoid ambiguity. The Stones are cognizant of the explosions of youthful energy that are going on all around them. They recognize the violence inherent in these struggles. They see them as movements for fundamental change and are deeply sympathetic. Yet they are too cynical to really go along themselves.[9]

Symbols of moral and political upheaval abound in the lyrics: a "man of wealth and taste," Lucifer in "Sympathy for the Devil" cavorts among guests at a dinner party but kills both Kennedys; in "Stray Cat Blues" an underage daughter runs away and is raped, but the justification is that it's "no capital crime"; there are marches in the streets; sinners are saints, cops are criminals. At the same time, the Stones' voices are somewhere else: The lyrical and musical Impressionism of "No Expectations" and pentatonic Orientalism of "Moonlight Mile" are reflections, memories, and dreams, not actions; the "Street Fighting Man" is actually uncommitted to the struggle, and the Prodigal Son can't make it on his own, even with his inheritance. So much talk, so little action. In many ways, the only songs offering unequivocal, unambiguous themes are the proletarian tributes "Factory Girl" and "Salt of the Earth." In short, the albums beginning with *Beggars* and ending with *Exile* painted the authentic musical portrait of the Stones that established their most recognizable and durable image, even if it is often contradictory. For fans, every phase of the band since then is a variation on this basic master narrative.

What is this narrative? It might be defined as follows: an exilic and itinerant sense of being – one largely shaped by Keith Richards – derived from the migratory aspects of the blues, and a fearless, ever-deepening search for musical roots of all kinds; a tough, unyielding attitude – again, Richards – that was revolutionary but devoid of overt politics or constituency; a sharp intuition – shaped here mainly by Mick Jagger – about the largely uncharted and fluid sexual and gender boundaries of the day that played out metaphorically and physically in song lyrics, performance, and wardrobe;[10] a deep-seated subversion powered by their reverential identification with African-American and rural idioms; and, importantly, an obsession with the exiled, with Blackness, and culture at the margins, exposing "fantasies of low life and life below the stairs."[11] By the time of *Exile on Main Street*, the Stones, all but Bill Wyman not yet thirty years of age, themselves became the road-tested bluesmen whose deep oral and recorded repertories narrating travel, loss, hopes, lust, and judgement comprised the rich vocabulary of their period in exile.

The period from *Beggars* through *Exile* further coincides with important developments with the band that, in turn, initiated several future directions. 1969 witnessed the first major personnel change as a result of Brian Jones' death in 1968 and the subsequent joining of Mick Taylor, ushering in a period when, musically, the group has never been stronger. Taylor, a young, skilled guitarist whose musical education was formed in the long blues corridors of the John Mayall Band, was a virtuoso bottleneck player, and provided the Stones with their first true "lead" guitarist, resulting in an expansion of their song forms, particularly in live performance, through sections of brilliant solos, distinct tone, and improvisation. 1969 also marks their critical return to touring, following a hiatus from the road of almost two and a half years that was dominated by fighting various drug busts – mainly the well-documented "Redlands Scandal" – and increasing financial distress.[12] The aggregate problems of economic and legal persecution ultimately led to their move in 1971 to the South of France as *vrai* tax exiles. But these years also reveal a new songwriting process in which the system of recording songs for imminent album release is abandoned in favor of longer gestation periods and revision. Much of the material on the *Beggars* through *Exile* albums was, in fact, conceived simultaneously, the composition of many songs begun years before their eventual release – a chronology that is not present prior to *Beggars*. The earliest takes of "You Can't Always Get What You Want" and "Sister Morphine," released in 1969 and 1971, respectively, can already be found in May and November, 1968. Many songs that would appear on *Sticky Fingers* (1971) and *Exile on Main Street* (1972) have their origins already in 1969, including "Brown Sugar," "You Gotta Move," "Wild Horses," "Dead Flowers," "Loving Cup," and "All Down the Line." Similarly, the origins of "Stop Breaking Down," "Sweet Virginia," and "Hip Shake" are found in 1970, prior to the band's move to France and two years before release. This chronology testifies to the musical affinities and common sessions between the four albums that form a distinctive and cohesive creative phase in the history of the Rolling Stones.

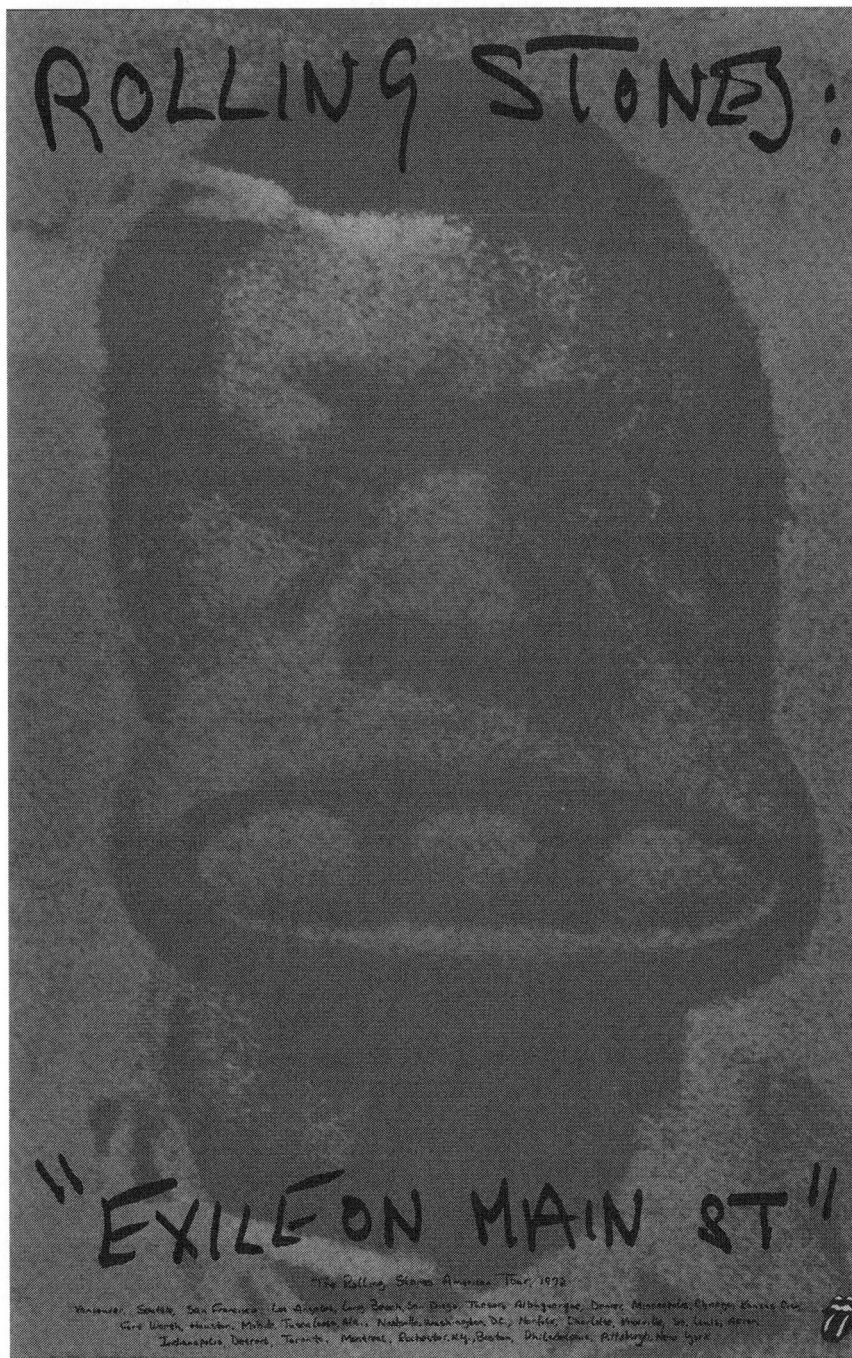

Figure 4.1 Poster for the 1972 "Exile on Main St" American tour. Grybowski Collection, Library and Archives, Rock and Roll Hall of Fame Museum.

Exiles and the Tent Show Queen

No good, can't speak, wound up, no sleep.
Skydiver inside her, slip rope, stunt flyer.
Wounded lover, got no time on hand.
One last cycle.
Thrill freak, Uncle Sam.
All for business, no, you understand?
Judge and jury walk out hand in hand.
Dietrich movies, close-up boogies,
kissing cunt in Cannes.
Protest music, million dollar sad.

"Casino Boogie," from
Exile on Main Street (1972)

The subversive language of "Casino Boogie" is syntactically exclusive to the Stones, and serves to identify and ally the outsider, who is the exile, peering in, and his encounter with others along his journey. Here, it is the characteristic voice of the exile firing cryptic assaults on establishment, convention, and hippie idealism by using the decoys of rich, American gamblers squandering millions in the luxury slum of Monte Carlo's casinos. Indeed, according to Janovitz, the song's lyrics depict "casual disdain for authority, drug-bust martyrdom, and the band's pressure to 'exile' themselves," with the last two lines "captu[ring] the essence of *Exile on Main St:* surreal rock & roll, jet-set sexuality, decadence, and boredom with the tired themes of the 1960s."[13] As a punitive means, exile was imposed on those who could do the most harm, and it recognizes high standing. But exile is also self-imposed, for it is within the "sanctuary" of exile that writers find a powerful voice that is the product of roaming and resistance. It is at once the voice of banishment, homelessness, and encounter with a new world. Linguistically it draws on forms, accents, and syntax that bridge high and low, and finds power and inspiration in dialect and popular forms.

In 1971 the Stones, debt-ridden, literally went into self-exile in the south of France, due to the high taxation laws in the UK that left the group unable to meet their income tax responsibilities. Their exile was also the conclusion to years of systematic arrests by the police on often-fabricated drug and indecency charges that are widely believed to have been part of a particular vendetta against the group. The qualities of exile described above appear throughout *Sticky Fingers*, in which the poetic squalor of practically all of the songs suggests distance and travel. Musically, they call out from elsewhere through an intentional stylistic apartness: the orientalism of "Moonlight Mile"; the long instrumental jam, unique in the Stones' output, at the end of "Can't You Hear Me Knocking"; the Stax-influenced "I've Got the Blues"; and, as noted earlier, the solitary withdrawal of the victim in "Sister Morphine." With *Exile on Main Street*, conceived amidst the rich opulence of the French Riviera, the group moves on to employ a variety of musical styles that take the form of "dialects" that are effectively used to speak in code while simultaneously asserting the Stones' personalities as Others and transients. Within this multi-vocal setting, the Stones employ gospel as a way to mask sex songs ("Let It Loose," "Loving Cup"), country influences to tap into the deep American roots songbook that became more authentic – in tone and technique – through the influence of Gram Parsons, Calypso for a protest song about Black militant Angela Davis ("Sweet Black Angel,", sung in "Caribbean" dialect), and blues for traditional attacks on high-class pastimes.

Exiles and the Circus

Satan was the first exile (Revelation 12.7), followed across the ages by Odysseus, the Holy Family, Dante, Solzhenitsyn, the Dalai Lama, Marvin Gaye, and . . . the Rolling Stones. Historically, the condition of exile is associated with banishment – both real and imagined – the *exiler* becoming a verbal target for reprisal, cryptic assault, and condemnation by the *exiled*. Whether the result of intense political opposition (Dante) or tax evasion (Gaye, the Stones), the sentence of exile amplifies displacement and protest through the use of vernacular dialects, subversive themes, and ancient texts. Nostalgia, mobility, alienation, linguistic variation, encounters with Others, religious themes, and recourse to Scripture are recurring exilic themes. With the Stones, references to the outsider, the use of different voices, vocal delivery, genre, choice of lyrics, stylistic diversity, and sound contribute to this autobiographical notion of exile. Even their recording conditions, in the form of a mobile studio (see Figure 4.2) beginning with the *Exile* sessions, are critical to the decentralized, "exilic" sound and songwriting strategies of the Stones during this period, as they create their own rural musical space in the image of the legendary studios of the American south like Muscle Shoals and Stax.

Reflecting on the end of the group's first American tour in 1964, Keith Richards wrote that he thought the group had "blown it": "We'd been consigned to the status of medicine shows and circus freaks with long hair."[14] Ironically, the image of the circus act is a recurring image in the group's music and overall self-perception between 1968 and 1972. Although the Stones' period of exile is a physical reality in 1971 with their move from England to France, the roots of their displacement can be found at the beginning of this period of creativity, most visibly in the *Rock and Roll Circus* of 1968, a fully realized project intended as a BBC television special that was eventually shelved until its official release on videocassette in 1996.[15] Using the backdrop of a "big top" circus tent (with Mod accents, to be sure), the project features

Figure 4.2 Author in front of the 24-track Helios console inside the Rolling Stones Mobile studio, 2016. National Music Centre, Calgary, Alberta (photo by Tom Knowles).

performances by many of the most popular and emerging British rock and pop acts of the day – the Who, Jethro Tull, the "Dirty Mac" supergroup with John Lennon, Eric Clapton, Keith Richards, and Mitch Mitchell, along with appearances by Marianne Faithfull and Yoko Ono – interspersed with conventional acrobatic routines by authentic circus acts (funambulists, fire breathers, lion tamers, etc.). Intentionally or not, the Stones project here the idea of the rock concert as a circus, its performers likened to trained acts to play before audiences seeking their own vicarious thrills, living perilously on the edge of success and failure, and marginalized – as Richards recounts from the 1964 tour – as a circus act.

Indeed, the circus performer is a classic "exile," especially if in the sideshow. Classified as "misfits," humans with physical deformities, unusual physical abilities, biological difference, and birth defects were leveraged as circus acts alongside other sideshow performers of specious authenticity. The connection between these circus performers and the Stones comes full circle with Robert Frank's cover for the *Exile on Main Street* album, which, taken from photographs he had shot for his legendary book *The Americans*, and in close collaboration with Jagger about the design, featured black and white photos of various circus performers exhibiting their unusual abilities, with some images used individually to promote the 1972 tour (see Figure 4.1).[16] As Richards remembers, "Exile was a double album. And because it's a double album you're going to be hitting different areas, including D for Down, and the Stones really felt like exiles."[17]

Sacred Exiles

Sacred references are frequent in the Stones' music from these years, as they are in Delta blues, not only through allusion or quotes from Scripture, but in the use of sacred *sound* and style. In the song "Far Away Eyes" from *Some Girls* of 1978, the media-driven tele-evangelical movement in America is cleverly (and acutely) parodied through Jagger's drawl, the mimicry of the radio preacher seeking $10 tithes, and the signature pedal steel parts played by Ronnie Wood, but there is nothing really *sacred* about the song.[18] Earlier, however, the allusions were more sober, probing, and authentic. The Stones incorporate sacred idioms from sources as diverse as the English choral tradition, American gospel, and the small-town Salvation Army funeral procession, that, drawing on the emotional arc of the gospel service, provide climactic and conclusive moments within the songs.

"Prodigal Son" (text drawn from Luke 15:11–32), on *Beggars Banquet*, is a moralizing story, a version – calling it a "cover" does not do the song justice – of Rev. Robert Tim Wilkins' "That's No Way to Get Along" that he originally recorded in Memphis in 1929 but later (and after having renounced the life of a bluesman and joined the church) rerecorded as "The Prodigal Son" in 1964.[19] It is this latter version that draws specifically on the story given in Luke and is the immediate influence, both in the guitar work and the lyrics, for the version by the Stones. Appearing on an album whose opening track recounts the destructive history of Satan ("Sympathy for the Devil" [*BB*]) and his contemporaneous killing of the Kennedys, "Prodigal Son" reaches back to the rural style of its author, Jagger mimicking the old bluesman's voice and Richards patterning his strumming in E-tuning after Wilkins, against a duo of harmonicas and a clutter of makeshift-sounding percussion. The effect is that of a street-corner performance somewhere in the Delta for a retelling of the best known of Jesus' three parables, this one foregrounding the themes of greed, reconciliation, family, and ultimately forgiveness. In the end, the song is unlike any other original blues arranged anew by the Stones due to its raw, rural sound, as if one were suddenly listening to one of Alan Lomax's important field recordings of southern Blues.

It is the American gospel tradition, though, that is the most pervasive influence on the Stones in this period. Gospel techniques create call-and-response textures (heard, for example, on "Tumbling Dice" [*EMS*]), they reference gospel's musical progeny, R&B, and they further create climactic moments that recall the rapturous conclusion of gospel church services, heard at the ends of "Salt of the Earth" (*BB*), "You Can't Always Get What You Want" (*LB*), and "Shine a Light" (*EMS*). But the exhilarating crescendos of heavenly gospel textures are also used to celebrate sex ("Loving Cup" [*EMS*]) and, more darkly, sexual surrender ("Let It Loose" [*EMS*]). At a formal level, the fact that "Salt of the Earth" and "You Can't Always Get What You Want" – the final songs of *Beggars Banquet* and *Let It Bleed*, respectively – both conclude with high-energy gospel choruses, suggests that the organization of the albums themselves draws on the plan and rhythm of the gospel service in which confession and community are ultimate themes. Thematically, both albums begin by a stark acknowledgment of evil and tragedy, but they eventually conclude with the same choral exhilaration that accompanies the arrival in the gospel church of the Holy Ghost. In "Sympathy for the Devil" (*BB*) Satan introduces himself by immediately speaking over the macabre, samba-like rhythm of a *Totentanz*, while in "Gimme Shelter" (*LB*) the distant howling (vocalized by Merry Clayton) in the foreboding introduction and relentless three-chord descending progression underlie the premonition of storms, rape, and murder. Halfway through *Beggars* we hear a "sermon" about the Prodigal Son and the lesson of forgiveness; in the case of the much darker *Let It Bleed*, it is rather the grisly fulfillment of the foretold rape and murder by the appearance, halfway through the album, of the Midnight Rambler. In the end, however, both albums banish their evils musically and textually by uplifting gospel choruses.

"Salt of the Earth" (*BB*) – a song that was powerfully revived by Jagger and Richards at the Concert for New York City following the 9/11 attack – begins, as its title suggests, like a boozy, closing-time song in a worker's pub, in which everyone, arms around each other, eventually joins in. It continues the proletarian theme, already introduced by "Factory Girl," to raise a glass to the working class and "lowly of birth" – socialist folk sentiments persuasive enough for Joan Baez to decide to record her own version of this song a few years later. It is often said that those looking for actionable messages in *Beggars Banquet* will not find them. "Street Fighting Man," which would seem to be the most incendiary of the songs on this album, with its megaphone, front-of-the-pack vocal charge, and the driving march of the IV–I chords, recedes into apathy: "But what can a poor boy do/but sing in a rock and roll band?" "Salt of the Earth," too, seems to give a pass to those watching on the sideline: "Spare a thought for the stay-at-home voter/His empty eyes gaze at strange beauty shows/And a parade of gray suited grafters/A choice of cancer or polio." After verses sung individually and together by Jagger and Richards, the song builds to a climax through short, pungent bursts of slide guitar (similar to what takes place in "Jigsaw Puzzle" [*BB*]), until the Watts Street Gospel Choir of Los Angeles enters at the end of the second refrain. Taking over the chorus sung by Jagger and Richards, the choir suddenly (and *characteristically* gospel) kicks the tempo into double time for a foot-stomping, sway-in-the-aisle conclusion. "Salt of the Earth" is an exile commentary about honoring "workers" over the owners, and it could just as easily be a rant against the record industry, the "workers" being the artists under contract.

The Theater of Exile

Richards has cleverly described the song "Midnight Rambler" (*LB*) as an unintentional "blues opera," with its Boston Strangler libretto – many lyrics were taken literally from the confession of the actual Boston Strangler, Albert DeSalvo[20] – and the horrifying, still, recitative section in the middle of the song where the killer, in a whisper punctuated by thrusts of the knife, torments his victim. This kind of dramatic presentation pervades other pieces of the period, as the Stones become more adept at "staging" their songs almost as small one-acts. In "You Can't Always Get What You Want" (*LB*), they employ gospel and sacred sound to force multiple contrasts: the present against the past, England vs. America, black vs. white *rhythm*, and the black vs. the white *church*, all theatrically mounted on a sonic "stage" for this seven-minute-plus finale to *Let It Bleed*. The nostalgic opening of the song is one of the most beautifully written moments the Stones ever produced. The curtain is raised with an Anglican-style "hymn" sung by the London Bach Choir, that, despite some rather awkward text setting (the two-note descending figures given to the one-syllable words "hand" and "man," for example), opens up a spacious and sonorous dimension of time, distance, and memory. As sung by the choir, the scored hymn section provides the day's lesson in an authoritative, didactic fashion. Emerging out of the final note of this first choral refrain is the I–IV strummed riff of Richards' E-tuned capo'd acoustic that appears from yet another seemingly distant part of the space, coupled with Al Kooper's French horn solo sounding, too, *as if* from the distance, like the off-stage horns we hear in Mahler. Thomas Peattie has written about "distant sound" in Mahler's works as being part of a theatrical moment in which instrumental music becomes linked with opera.[21] When the conclusive words ("You get what you need!") of the refrain return after Jagger's first verse (2:01), the transformation is complete: The Anglican choir now gives way to the gospel singers for a joyous community celebration. The refrain, first sung *ex cathedra*, is now familiarized stylistically for the *vox populi*. But, more importantly, it signifies a deepening, a celebration, even the *primacy* of African-American idioms in the Stones' music – an influence that was present at the beginning (the name of the band, of course, comes from the title of a Muddy Waters song), but is now dramatized with a narrative that invites commentary about the Stones and race. Returning to the song, for the next two verses the Bach Choir is silent, but following the bridge section (4:17) the exciting coda unites both the Bach *and* gospel choirs in an ecstatic gospel ending that is propelled – as we heard in "Salt of the Earth" – into the fadeout by shifting into a quick two-beat double-time rhythm.

The spiritual "You Gotta Move" (*SF*), a group arrangement of bluesman Mississippi Fred McDowell's song of the same name (an earlier version he may have known is the Original Blind Boys of Alabama's recording of 1953), is another excellent example of the theatrical imagination of the Stones and how they brilliantly conceive a dramatic and historical narrative out of an acoustic blues. McDowell's riveting performance, recorded in 1965 at the end of the folk/blues revival, features him doubling his vocal line on slide guitar and adding instrumental breaks between the vocal verses, suggesting many adaptable options for the Stones, now with Mick Taylor comfortably integrated into the group. The exilic, dialect vernacular of spirituals is made for the Stones. Spirituals contain irresistible hooks, and many popular R&B songs like Sam Cooke's "A Change is Gonna Come" and Curtis Mayfield's "People Get Ready" were written in the mold of spirituals and freedom songs, as was much of the work of Aretha Franklin and others. That this music became the soundtrack of the civil rights movement was understood by the Stones well before 1971, and other selections on *Sticky Fingers*, like the Otis Redding-inspired "I've Got the Blues," with its signature Stax 6/8 meter, crisp rhythmic shots, "sad" doppler-effect horns, shift to the minor subdominant key for Billy Preston's organ solo, and "pleading" outro, are homages to the classic R&B tradition.[22] Jagger is no Otis Redding, to be sure. But this is no longer a mere cover, as on the early Stones albums, but a new song executed with the authenticity, techniques, and above all performance of the classic R&B tradition.

Equally attractive to the Stones in "You Gotta Move" is the Lord's egalitarian judgement: "You may be high/You may be low/You may be rich, child/You may be poor/But when the Lord gets ready/You gotta move." It is God who decides when your time is up, and you can't pay for your seat in heaven as did the corrupt "kings and queens" during the Great Schism who "fought for decades/for the Gods they made" referenced in "Sympathy for the Devil." But the most interesting part of the song is the theatrical setting they construct for it. Where McDowell's version is rendered in the venerable Delta manner of a solo guitarist singing the blues, the Stones make the song into a Salvation Army funeral procession marching down Main Street of Small Town, USA. With McDowell's original riffs in tow, played here on a twelve-string, improvised harmonies are added on the spot, as are other, spontaneous vocalizations. As the song – and the procession – progresses, more and more instruments are added: A bass drum and clapped hi-hat provide the slow beat of the funeral march as it makes its way, along with the wail of Mick Taylor's electric slide parts (on a vintage 1954 Telecaster, no less) that bring to mind the lacrimose emotions of witnesses to the funeral.

Another excellent example of a staged song drawing on historical references is "Can't You Hear Me Knocking" (*SF*), a loud retelling of the troubadour *alba* in which the exiled poet arrives at the foot of the castle tower for his rendezvous at dawn with his lover. Here, however, he is outside the house trying to smash his way in, weaponized by one of the highest-caliber riffs in Richards' arsenal coupled with Jagger's six-beat window- and door-pounding refrain: "Can't you hear me KNOCK-ing?" With the song's long, suggestive instrumental coda of solos by Mick Taylor and saxophonist Bobby Keys – at times rhythmic and funky, elsewhere bluesy and dreamy – it becomes clear that our troubadour succeeded in entering through the window . . . and stayed awhile.

The final, and most creative example of the dramatic, historical settings the Stones can mount of a Delta acoustic blues is with their staging of Robert Johnson's "Love in Vain Blues," a song recorded twice by Johnson in his only recording session in 1937. Johnson's original, like all of his surviving recorded works, features only him singing and playing. After a short introduction and characteristic chromatic turnaround, Johnson sings three verses without an instrumental break (which he rarely takes on these recordings anyway), followed by a final verse that is vocalized. His guitar accompaniment draws heavily from country blues traditions, with the chord shapes and fingerpicking style, as well as the accented "walking" tempo, emphasizing a light shuffle beat along with a percussive accompaniment achieved through his right-hand strumming and muting technique. The harmonies do not stray from a conventional I–IV–I–V blues scheme, and overall it is one of the most restrained songs, technically and vocally, of Johnson's recorded output. His vocal delivery, perhaps because of the sorrow implicit in the lyrics, is not, like many of his other works, prone to extremes of pitch, shouting, or the use of different "voices." In all, it is a beautiful though sedate song by Johnson, showing off his more lyrical rather than demonic side.

The Rolling Stones make the song into something much different, enhancing it dramatically on many levels. While retaining essential features of Johnson's original, they incorporate country, R&B, and even classical influences, creating a small staged piece of musical theater to evoke the images of travel, loss, and sorrow embedded in the lyrics. Johnson's words are some of the most beautiful in his output, and there is reason to believe that they are autobiographical. In John Hammond Jr.'s 1991 documentary *The Search for Robert Johnson* (UK, Iambic Productions), among several informants who had been in supposed contact with Robert Johnson, Hammond interviews an elderly woman named Willie Mae Powell, who stated that she was Johnson's girlfriend in the 1930s. She must be the "Willie Mae" whose name one can hear Johnson sing off-mic in the final vocalization verse of the recording.

The song opens in the first person with Johnson, carrying a suitcase, following his girlfriend to the train station. Is it her bag that she will take with her when she boards the train, or is it his suitcase because he intends to follow her? We don't know. The second verse opens with the train arriving into the station, and Johnson, sensing that this may be his last chance to patch things up, "looks her [straight] in the eye." Concluding the verse with this line, but offering no resolution, Johnson brings us to the emotional climax of the song within an imagined clamor of steel and brakes as the train stops. In the final texted verse, it is Johnson who stands alone on the platform watching the train depart from the station, taking account of the two lights of the caboose, one blue, the other red, fading into the distance. The verse ends with Johnson musing that the blue light was "my blues" but the "red light was my mind." The final, untexted, verse featuring Johnson vocalizing (and moaning the name "Willie Mae") thus achieves significance as the narrator weeping, shouting, or otherwise emotionally distraught and unable to speak. The whole story, all told in only six individual lines, exemplifies the power of the blues lyric and its well-known themes of travel and loss.

For the Stones, the sentimentality of the verse, its ambiguity, and the rural imagery all inspired a country approach to the piece. Like Johnson, they begin with an introduction on guitar, but instead of the 2/4 shuffle rhythm of Johnson's original, Richards shifts the tempo to a 6/8 rhythm, like a classic R&B ballad, though in this case tilting more towards country music. In addition, his introduction moves beyond the three chords of Johnson's conventional twelve-bar blues setting by adding a minor vi chord before the turnaround (the Stones' version is up a minor third). The addition of the vi chord is a stroke of genius (the progression actually relates to a standard country two-beat scheme of I–vi–IV–V–I), that opens a window "outside" the standard twelve-bar I–IV–V–I progression, similar to the way "Wild Horses" (*SF*) begins on an "unexpected" B-minor chord in the key of G. As verse one begins, using just guitars and voice, we begin to hear the distant train whistles as played on a slide guitar by Keith Richards. The train's arrival into the station in verse two is captured musically by the entrance of the rhythm section, while the train whistles (slide guitar) get louder and more frequent. The Stones' penchant for theatricality is no more apparent than in what happens next: Interrupting the second and third verses, they add an instrumental verse featuring a mandolin solo, played by Ry Cooder, with Jagger singing verse snippets in the background. Although this section is basically instrumental, it provides a crucial explanation to the story. The mandolin is traditionally related to serenades and balcony scenes in Italian opera and usually played by the male lover or seducer: In the seduction aria, "Deh vieni alla finestra" in Mozart's *Don Giovanni*, for example, the Don accompanies himself on mandolin (though modern productions usually have someone in the orchestra to play it). Its use here, in the train station, at the point where Johnson's lover is about to board the train, is a clever adoption of an historical tradition, and it further carves out dramatic action in the absence of words. In the third verse, the full band, including mandolin, accompanies Jagger, who alters a few words ("blues" to "baby"), and the final vocalized verse concludes with a departing train whistle in the distance.

***

By 1973 the group had reached the end of their exile, their narrative of travel, distance, and plurality of voices singularized into language of the city. Their next album, *Goats Head Soup*, recorded back at Olympic Studios in London, revealed fissures that became increasingly visible over the next decade. "There was just this feeling through *Goats Head Soup* that the whole thing was falling to pieces," recounted producer and drummer Jimmy Miller; "It was no longer Mick and Keith's song – it was Mick's song or Keith's song."[23] The 1972 tour barreled across America – Jagger in a jumpsuit and on the cover of *Life* (see Figure 4.3), doing anything and having everything – the basement sessions and their exilic voices that were made far away in Nellcôte now being sung to thousands of fans. The tour exhausted the conceptual period of exile for the Stones; the coarseness around the edges of the tour, as documented in *Cocksucker Blues*, now giving a preview of the group's next phase, in which the landscape of New York City emerges in both theme and sound. The new album initiated a distinct urban period, as the Stones moved from the stories of exile and the redemption of gospel to an often vulgar and more immediate commentary of urban America and its decadence. Wah-wah pedals, increased guitar distortion, the sounds of Leslies, phase shifters, electric clavinet, and blasphemous takes on the innocence of '50s rock ("Star Star") are the

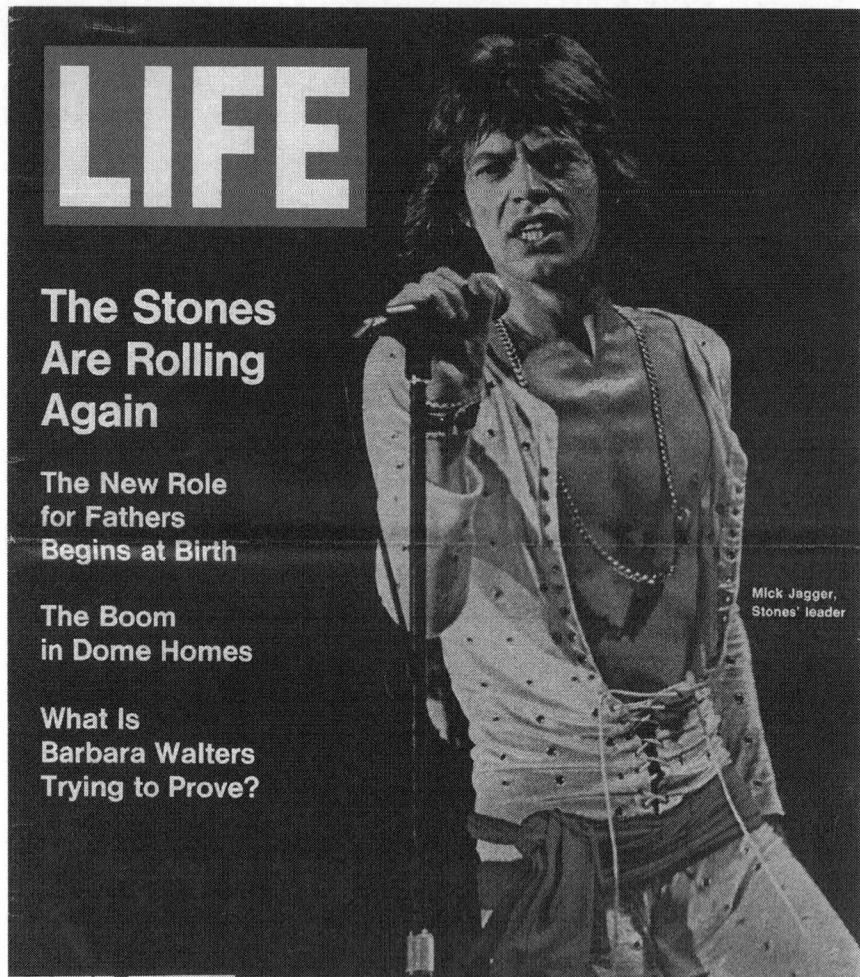

Figure 4.3 Cover of *Life* magazine (July 14, 1972) published during the 1972 tour. Grybowski Collection, Library and Archives, Rock and Roll Hall of Fame Museum.

new sonic expressions for songs about street shootings, overdoses, and groupies "givin' head to Steve McQueen."[24] The New York of *Some Girls* was coming into focus, while the memories of California – the metaphor for paradise in Mick Taylor's elegiac song, "Winter," that closes *Goats Head Soup* – receded into the distance.

Notes

1 Other album releases during these years include the compilations *Through the Past, Darkly (Big Hits Vol. 2)* (1969), *Hot Rocks 1964–1971* (1972) (the latter released through Decca/ABKCO, cashing in on their ownership of the Stones' valuable back catalog after the group left ABKCO in 1971), and the excellent live album *Get Yer Ya-Ya's Out!* (1970), featuring tracks "supposedly"

all recorded at the Madison Square Garden shows during the 1969 tour; see Karnbach & Bernson, 242, 282 (Elliott in *RSCRS*, 123–5, attributes all of the *Ya-Ya's* tracks to the Garden shows as does the booklet contained with the CD/bonus DVD box set *Get Yer Ya-Ya's Out!: The Rolling Stones in Concert* [ABKCO, 2009]). During these years several compilations beyond *Hot Rocks* were rushed out by Decca after the Stones left the label that essentially derive from or duplicate the anthologies mentioned above. For a summary of releases during these years, see Karnbach & Bernson, 279–87.

2 Jack Hamilton, "How Rock and Roll Became White," *Slate Magazine* (October 6, 2016): www.slate.com/articles/arts/music_box/2016/10/race_rock_and_the_rolling_stones_how_the_ rock_and_roll_became_white.html (accessed February 15, 2019). See also his related chapter "Just Around Midnight: The Rolling Stones and the End of the Sixties," in Jack Hamilton, *Just Around Midnight: Rock and Roll and the Racial Imagination* (Cambridge, MA, 2016), 246–76.

3 Letter from Jann Wenner to Mo Ostin, January 13, 1970. Rock Hall, Mo Ostin Collection, Box 17.

4 In addition to the detailed autobiographical accounts of this period in *Life*, 235–323, Wyman*SA*, 485–539 (the coverage of which, however, extends only up to the group's Hyde Park concert in July, 1969), Wyman*RWTS*, 306–405, and the related sessionography in Elliott, *RSCRS*, the Stones have received much respectable, well-researched coverage from journalists, historians, and Stones specialists. Among the best accounts of this period are, for 1968 and *Beggars Banquet*, Jon Landau's review in *RSt* (December 6, 1968), reprinted in Dalton*RS*, 328–31; for the 1969 tour and *Let It Bleed*, Dalton*RS*, 332–4, and Michael Lydon, "At Play in the Apocalypse," *Ramparts Magazine* (March, 1970), 28–54, reprinted as "The Rolling Stones Discover America," in Michael Lydon, *Flashbacks: Eyewitness Accounts of the Rock Revolution* (New York, 2003), 123–86; for a first-hand account of the 1969 tour and Altamont, the central, Stones-authorized source is Stanley Booth, *The True Adventures of the Rolling Stones* (New York, 1984). On *Sticky Fingers*, see the review by Greil Marcus in *Creem* (August, 1971) reprinted in Dalton*RS*, 342–7. For *Exile*, see Lenny Kaye's tepid review in *RSt* (July 6, 1972), the detailed analytical and historical treatment of the entire double album in Janovitz*EMS*, and the famous first-hand account of the subsequent 1972 tour by Robert Greenfield, *S.T.P.* [Stones Touring Party]: *A Journey through America with the Rolling Stones* (New York, 1974), along with its visual auxiliary, Robert Frank's audacious film *Cocksucker Blues* (1972).

5 Quoted from an article by the radical writer Sol Stern, cited in Hamilton, *Just Around Midnight*, 269.

6 From an interview for London underground newspaper *International Times*, reprinted in Dalton*FTY*, 107.

7 Janovitz*EMS*, 8.

8 Just using internal accounts of unit sales of ABKCO album releases through June 30, 1983 (prior to CDs), for example, *Beggars Banquet* totaled 1,065,249, *Let It Bleed* 1,677,647, and *Get Yer Ya-Ya's Out!* 1,252,869, while *Hot Rocks* – the group's largest selling album ever – compiled 3,627,292 units sold, with *More Hot Rocks* selling another half million. Even when considering the early Rolling Stones records releases on Atlantic from 1971 through 1979, *Some Girls* outperformed *Exile* in sales almost fivefold and more than doubled the sales of *Sticky Fingers* (data taken from Rock Hall, Jeff Gold Collection: *Art Collins – Rolling Stones Records/Marketing 1978–1981, 1985*). The most popular non-greatest hits album by the Stones remains *Some Girls*.

9 Landau, review of *Beggars Banquet*, 329.

10 For an excellent, recent study confronting these issues from the perspectives of queerness, gender, and sexuality, see Judith Peraino, "Mick Jagger as Mother," *Social Text* 124 (2015), 75–113.

11 David Dalton, review of *Let It Bleed*, in Dalton*RS*, 333.

12 The Redlands bust is one of the most documented of all the life chapters of the Stones. For a first-hand summary and related band difficulties during this period, see Wyman*RWTS*, 253–73.

13 Janovitz*EMS*, 82–3. Since there is no official edition of Rolling Stones lyrics (as, for example, exists for Dylan), there are many variants to the lyrics of "Casino Boogie" depending on the transcription. The version used here is taken from Janovitz*EMS*, 82.

14 *Life*, 163.

15 Many reasons have been given for the group's decision to shelve the project, for example that their exhaustion from constant filming is evident in their performance; that the Who's own dynamic performance would make them the stars of the program; and that the death of Brian Jones during the editing stages effectively put an end to the planned release. For a faithful account of the project, see Wyman*RWTS*, 316–17.

16 For a discussion of the making of the album cover, see Janovitz*EMS*, 12–27.

17 Keith Richards, in *According*, 159.

18 For a full discussion about this song, see Cyrus R. K. Patell, *Some Girls* (New York and London, 2011), 91–8.

19 In the ensuing discussion of particular songs, references to the four albums under consideration will use initials, as follows: *BB* (*Beggars Banquet*), *LB* (*Let It Bleed*), *SF* (*Sticky Fingers*), and *EMS* (*Exile on Main Street*).

20 *RSG*, 310.

21 See Thomas Peattie, *Gustav Mahler's Symphonic Landscapes* (Cambridge, 2015), 47–8.

22 For an excellent study of the relationship between soul, R&B, and the civil rights movement, with an emphasis on the important role of the recording industry, see Peter Guralnick's *Sweet Soul Music: Rhythm and Blues and the Southern Dream of Freedom* (New York, 1986).

23 Quoted in *RSG*, 399.

24 On the gear used for the *Goats Head Soup* sessions, see *ibid.*, 398–400.

5 Post *Exile*: The Rolling Stones in a Disco-Punk World, 1975–1983

PAUL HARRIS

How, in the 1970s, did a generation whose motto was "never trust anyone over thirty" come to grips with an iconic 1960s rock band whose members were entering their mid-thirties? On the whole, not very well. Mick Jagger, in an unguarded moment, wistfully observed: "I'm afraid rock and roll has no future ... It's only recycled past."[1] The mid-1970s was a time of considerable turmoil and transition for the Stones, and for rock music in general.[2] The music industry was still sorting itself out after the breakup of the Beatles at the very beginning of the 1970s. Historically, the spread of the bucolic culture envisioned by Woodstock already seemed in rot. The 1970s were riven with crises – Vietnam, Watergate, labor strife in Britain, the Troubles in Northern Ireland, global concerns about pollution and overpopulation, the energy crisis, planned obsolescence, the Munich Olympic massacre, the Biafran War, the India-Pakistan War, and the Yom Kippur War, are only a few of the most important calamities that mark the decade. Amidst this turbulence – often simplistically chronicled in rock history by contrasting the Stones' dystopian concert at Altamont with the utopian ideals of Woodstock – the Rolling Stones faced a novel predicament: how to remain at the forefront of rock while entering a stage of life more traditionally associated with conventional adulthood.

By the mid-1970s, the individual Stones were approaching their early to mid-thirties (see Figure 5.1), with the exception of Bill Wyman who would reach the age of forty in 1976. No other iconic refugees of sixties rock had survived more or less intact to this point, and it was not at all clear where the band should be headed musically, or whether they remained relevant, given the "now conventional charges of geriatric redundancy."[3] The Beatles had very messily gone their separate ways, and had already become (literally) figures in the wax museum of Madame Tussaud.[4] The "King of Rock and Roll," Elvis Presley – much further down the road to rock decrepitude, having turned forty in 1975 – was midway through his Las Vegas period, offering increasingly gaudy, louche shows for audiences not much younger than he. Most fans of sixties rock already considered him outdated, and his untimely, undignified death at age forty-two in August 1977 – the apogee of British punk – cemented his status as a tabloid staple and figure of mixed veneration and

Figure 5.1 Atlantic Records promotional photo of the Rolling Stones (1978). Jeff Gold Collection, Library and Archives, Rock and Roll Hall of Fame Museum.

ridicule.[5] Today, rock artists in their fifties, sixties, and beyond have become commonplace, many living comfortably on their back catalog with a large and appreciative classic-rock fan base in tow. But they were at risk of becoming self-satirists in the seventies – it was utterly uncharted territory. In David Bowie's "All the Young Dudes," written for Mott the Hoople in 1972, the generational divide is laid bare: "And my brother's back at home/with his Beatles and his Stones/We never got it off on that revolution stuff/What a drag/too many snags." The Stones were acutely aware that remaining relevant might be their greatest challenge.

How a given music fan experienced, categorized, and evaluated rock music in the early 1970s varied enormously depending on the individual's demographic and geographic situation. Neither Paul McCartney and Wings, nor John Lennon as a solo artist were likely to be considered potential heirs to the predominance of the Beatles in the 1960s; critic Lester Bangs was emphatic about that from his own perspective, describing McCartney's latest works as "Muzak's finest hour" and Lennon as an "infantile" bandwagoner.[6] On a local AM rock station, one could easily hear Tony Orlando and Dawn, Billy Preston, Roberta Flack, Wings, Helen Reddy, Three Dog Night, War, Chicago, the Carpenters, and Sly and the Family Stone cheek to jowl. And, at least for a few months in 1975, the Bay

City Rollers were touted as the "Next Big Thing" in a popular press that remained focused on anointing an heir to the Beatles. Against this background, the Rolling Stones were involuntarily saddled with the principal responsibility for extending the legacy of the Golden Age of Rock into the 1970s. In his review of *Goats Head Soup* for *Creem*, Allen Crowley began: "Sure, I was as full of nervous anticipation as you were. Every new Stones album has to plow through such expectations that the Second Coming would flop first hearing . . . the album isn't ABOUT much. The Stones are still consummate entertainers, but somewhere along the line we began to expect something more than entertainment from them."[7] Faced with such an obligation, the Beatles were fortunate to have disbanded.

The Stones in the Mid-1970s

Their early albums from the 1970s, *Sticky Fingers* and *Exile on Main Street*, are often cited as their finest works, concluding the "core" quartet of albums that began with *Beggars Banquet* and *Let It Bleed*. The albums immediately following are held in much lower esteem. *Rolling Stone* founder and Stones confidant Jann Wenner, in a lengthy interview with Jagger in 1995, pointed to a string of weak albums, namely *Goats Head Soup* (1973), the generally uneven *It's Only Rock 'n Roll* (1974), the compilation package *Made in the Shade* (1975) released to coincide with their 1975 tour, and *Black and Blue* (1976). Asked about the state of the band in this period, Jagger observed:

> General malaise. I think we got a bit carried away with our own popularity and so on. It was a bit of a holiday period [laughs] . . . we cared, but we didn't care as much as we had. Not really concentrating on the creative process, and we had such money problems. We had been so messed around by Allen Klein and the British Revenue. We were really in a very bad way.[8]

While recording *Goats Head Soup*, Richards recalls being generally upbeat but becoming "exhausted. You get busted. For a long stretch, I was either on trial or had a case pending, or we were going through visa problems. That was always the backdrop. It was sheer pleasure to get in the studio and lose yourself."[9]

Music critics in the 1970s were preoccupied with the aging of the Stones and their ability to remain relevant, frequently lamenting that they once "meant" something (although often failing to explain what it meant to "mean" something). Lester Bangs, after musing on whether *Goats Head Soup* would be received as "their latest triumph or the epitaph of old men," posed the following question for Stones fans: "Q: What if the Stones *no longer pay off?* A#1: You desert 'em. After all, they're justa buncha old men. A#2: What kind of friend are you? You grew up with these cats! Christ, are there no values left in this lousy culchuh?"[10] He continues, "There is a sadness about the Stones now, because they amount to such an enormous *So what?*," taking several shots at other emerging rock royalty and declaring his disillusionment with mid-seventies rock in general: "Bowie is a style collector with almost no ideas of his own, Reed's basically just reworking his old Velvets ideas, people like Elton John are reaching back into nostalgia but that's a blind alley, and everybody else is playing the blues. So unless we get the Rolling Stones off their asses IT'S THE END OF ROCK 'N' ROLL."[11] Again there is the notion of the Stones as survivors charged with the burden of continuing the rock legacy of the 1960s. He was similarly dismissive of 1974's *It's Only Rock 'n Roll*: "The Stones have become oblique in their old age ... This album is false. Numb."[12] Bangs' hyperbolic reference to "old age" pointedly illuminates how rock culture was struggling to contextualize rockers over thirty as anything other than nostalgia acts.

The next album, *Black and Blue*, was recorded piecemeal for more than a year between late 1974 and late 1975, and released in April, 1976. Between financial and other business complications, the unexpected departure of guitarist Mick Taylor, the band members living in diverse locales, and Richards' heroin addiction, the group was in disarray. Former Faces guitarist Ronnie Wood, who the Stones all knew well from various side projects, joined the band full time, signaling a new era for the Stones. Critical reception was mixed, but, not unexpectedly, Lester Bangs was disappointed, citing two things to be said: "one is that they are still perfectly in tune with the times (a.k.a., sometimes, trendies) and the other is that the heat's off, because it's all over, they really don't matter anymore or stand for anything, which is certainly lucky for both them and us. I mean, it was a heavy weight to carry for all concerned. This is the first *meaningless* Rolling Stones album."[13] Again, the rhetoric emphasizes the Stones' apparent obligation to somehow encapsulate the times as they were perceived to have done in the 1960s, indicating, perhaps, that the problem was not so much the Rolling Stones as it was the "times," insofar as Bangs acknowledges that they remain perfectly in tune with the era.

Albums were not the only concern. Stones concerts after the 1972 (*Exile*) tour were often rambling affairs, usually starting very late, plagued by bad sound and desultory stage presence, but compensating with stage props and lighting. *Melody Maker* describes one concert from the tour accompanying *Black and Blue*, which saw the band reach into their repertoire of older songs and blues covers, as utterly lacking energy or commitment: "[they were] unable to produce a version of 'Route 66' with half as much vitality as the bands then playing the pub circuit."[14] To top things off, Richards' heroin use landed him on *New Musical Express'* top-ten list of rock stars most likely to die, a position he proudly held for ten years.[15]

Some Girls

By October 1977, the Stones were more than ready to get back to the studio. Richards describes the sessions for *Some Girls* as having a "following wind" from the beginning, a "rejuvenation, surprisingly for such a dark moment, when it was possible that I would go to jail and the Stones would dissolve."[16] Wood describes the album as "a celebration of getting Keith back," as Richards was taking steps to manage his heroin addiction.[17] They moved into the Pathé Marconi studios in Paris with nothing prepared. No other musicians were on hand either; that would all be added later. "It had an echo of *Beggars Banquet* about it – a long period of silence and then coming back with a bang and a new sound."[18]

This was their first album produced by Chris Kimsey, though Kimsey had prior experience with the Stones as assistant engineer to Andy Johns for most of the *Sticky Fingers* sessions of 1969 and 1970.[19] Richards recalls that "We had to pull something out – not make another Stones-in-the-doldrums album. He wanted to get a live sound back and move away from the clean and clinical-sounding recordings we'd slipped into."[20] They recorded in the smaller, less sophisticated rehearsal studio with a 1960s-style, 16-track console (the same board EMI had designed for Abbey Road).

That *Some Girls* is an urban, "New York" album is widely acknowledged. The city was on the verge of bankruptcy in the mid-1970s, with crime, poverty, and political dysfunction at their peak. Jagger observed twenty years later:

> I'd moved to New York at that point. The inspiration for the record was really based in New York and the ways of the town. I think that gave it an extra spur and hardness. And then, of course, there was the punk thing that had started in 1976. Punk and disco were going on at the same time, so it was quite an interesting period. New York and London, too. Paris – there was punk there. Lots of dance music. Paris and New York had all this Latin dance music, which was really quite wonderful. Much more interesting than the stuff that came afterward.[21]

Richards has said that he believed that Jagger was interested in recording a disco album, a claim Jagger emphatically denies.[22] "I just had one song that had a dance groove: "Miss You." But I didn't want to make a disco album. I wrote all these songs – like "Respectable," "Lies," "When the Whip Comes Down."[23]

Punk and Disco on *Some Girls*

Both the Stones and their critics repeatedly acknowledge *Some Girls'* obvious stylistic affinity with disco and punk, two prominent genres of pop music in the mid-to-late 1970s centered in New York. However, these were emergent and rather mutually exclusive styles and subcultures which were likely not representative of average listening tastes. The Stones unanimously deny adopting these styles strategically, but rather suggest that they were "in the air" and absorbed naturally. Watts reports that he and Jagger frequented discos at the time and constantly encountered the four-on-the-floor groove of the kick drum marking all four beats in a measure.[24] Similarly, Wood recalls that the English punk scene was unavoidable as it was "on the news all the time" (although the quote begins with the words "Those punk songs were our message to those boys," thus somewhat negating the lack of intent).[25] Richards claims he was less interested than Jagger in following contemporary pop styles but concedes that disco and punk created "an intriguing juxtaposition."[26]

"Miss You" is typically cited as the Stones' interpretation of disco. It was entirely a Jagger creation, with an early rendition played with Billy Preston in Toronto's El Mocambo ballroom during the period of Richards' drug problems in Canada.[27] According to Jagger, "'Miss You' really caught the moment, because that was the deal at the time. And that's what made that record take off. It was a really great record."[28] Richards agrees, calling it "one of the best disco records of all time."[29]

Simplicity and repetition might reasonably be offered as watchwords for "Miss You," but its formal irregularity and compelling bass line, first climbing and then descending in octaves, give it the quality of an adaptable jam over an insistent i–iv progression organized symmetrically in phrases of 2 + 2. However, while some song components, particularly verses, unfold in classic eight-measure phrases, others are organized into twelve-measure phrases, making this an easy song to mess up – or modify – in live performance unless everyone is paying attention. Richards' opening seven-note riff, duplicated by Jagger's first sung line, is a decorated tonic pitch (indicated with bold text), beginning on an upbeat ("I've **been**") with melodic interest provided by a sus-4 pitch (all caps) on the downbeat (HOLD-ing **out** so **long**). This is the hook for the entire song (except the eight-measure bridge), including the ghostly falsetto gang-vocal sections that almost function as choruses (0:44), as they become the signature sound for the song (similar to the "doo-doo"s comprising the hook to

"Hang Fire" from 1981's *Tattoo You*, although first demoed during the *Some Girls* sessions). Jagger's lead vocal alternates between verses that are sung and others that are recited.

The only disruption of the tonic-subdominant oscillation is the textbook "middle eight" bridge shifting to VI (F major, 1:55) and passing stepwise through E minor to two measures of D minor, but the last measure of the second phrase is the dominant, E major, setting up a strong, traditional harmonic return to tonic A minor. However, this middle eight concludes at almost exactly the midpoint of the song, making its appearance feel, perhaps, a bit premature, especially given that it is followed by a four-measure reduced-texture interlude that basically treads water before a twelve-measure whispered verse that sounds improvisatory and mysterious, as Jagger takes us "off the street" into the shadows of Central Park.

The bass line came from a jam recorded about a year earlier with Billy Preston playing bass after Wyman had already gone home from a recording session. However, when they returned to the song many months later, Wyman took inspiration from the demo, crediting Preston with the basic idea, most likely the octave figuration.[30] The interplay between Wyman and Watts on "Miss You" and the "crisp" production of the drums are noted by numerous critics, not only on *Some Girls*, but on all Stones albums from this point forward. The groove on the record is impeccable. Wyman's bass is prominent, as is essential in disco, and features the disco style of octave leaps on the offbeat, particularly over the D minor chord where he often walks up or down the pitches D–E–F–E over the iv chord (such as at 1:41).

At the other end of the disco-punk spectrum, "Respectable" is routinely cited as the Stones' nod to punk. Even Jagger confirms its "edgy punk ethos."[31] Charlie Watts, while describing Jagger as a great "flavor-of-the-month person," recalls the broader stylistic challenges of playing a disco groove and then "trying to be Johnny Rotten, who was trying to be us, in a way. That's fine with me, because it's really all the same thing."[32] This casual observation problematizes the popular understanding of punk: How can punk reasonably be considered an aesthetic negation of mainstream rock and roll when it so closely resembles it? For example, Tony James, a former bandmate of the Clash's Mick Jones, confirms the debt to early sixties rock during their stint together in the proto-punk London SS, relying heavily on typical medium-tempo covers of the early Stones and early Who until they heard the manic speed of the Ramones' début album in 1976, after which all the British punks "doubled speed overnight."[33]

"Respectable" is a fast, gritty, guitar-driven song, but it is also a traditional modified twelve-bar blues chock full of the Chuck Berry riffs so venerated by Richards. The introduction chugs on a basic two-string boogie pattern on the tonic A major for two measures before two measures of the IV chord (D major), brought in with a massive fill by Watts. The progression returns to I, and then two measures of V (E major) return in full verse texture to the tonic. Jagger starts the verse after only two measures of tonic, making the intro a somewhat irregular ten measures. From this point on, the song unfolds in four-measure phrases following the basic progression of a twelve-bar blues. However, as was the case for "Miss You," some of the song's appeal may stem from its formal irregularity in that the verses and choruses are four measures longer than the standard twelve-bar blues because the concluding phrase ("Get out of my life . . .") is repeated. Jagger sings the lead vocal against Richards' upper harmony which mostly alternates between two pitches creating a variety of intervals with Jagger, but tending to highlight a perfect fifth, for example on the text "we're re-*spect*-able." Basically, this is rockabilly. The next year, the Clash would release *London Calling*, featuring an album cover paying obvious homage to that of Elvis Presley's rockabilly-heavy début album; yet "Respectable" is much closer to rockabilly than anything from *London Calling*. The Clash actually have a twelve-bar blues song, "Brand New Cadillac," on *London Calling*, but it sounds nothing like "Respectable," mostly because of Joe Strummer's shouted, Cockney vocals. The difference between the two is, obviously, not structural, nor is there any real difference in musical materials, but the timbres are completely different. Similarly, the Sex Pistols are not even remotely rockabilly, but guitarist Steve Jones often employs a subtonic figure on power chords reminiscent of Eddie Cochrane's "Summertime Blues" riff. The waters are further muddied when one considers a rather crude-sounding band like the Damned, whose first single (and, arguably, the first punk single ever) "New Rose" is as far from rockabilly as possible – but the record was produced by British rockabilly revivalist Nick Lowe, whose fingerprints are all over early punk and post-punk, particularly with Elvis Costello. So, while punk and rockabilly share very little in terms of sound or "performance style," there is arguably a link at the level of stripped-down aesthetics.

Marxist rock historian Peter Wicke suggests that the widely held view of punks as rebels against the Establishment is pure romanticism, and, extending the work of pop sociologist Simon Frith, argues that the punks were not expressing their disaffection through music, but were merely reflecting the hopelessness and boredom that defined their existence – they weren't trying to *change* anything. The punk subculture provided a sense of community and (pre)occupation.[34] Sociologist Ruth Adams, on the other hand, negates the conventional definition of punks as nihilist and anti-British by focusing on how they reflected traditional English working-class values of satirical dissent against their social "betters." Rotten himself said that he considered *Never Mind the Bollocks* to be "hilarious, from start to finish – pointed, but hilarious, and therefore useful."[35] Adams claims that the punks are, in fact, quintessentially British, discussing them in terms of characters as diverse as the Shakespearean version of Richard III (Rotten rolls his "r's" as he proclaims "Rrrright, now" in "Anarchy in the UK"), through to Dickens' Artful Dodger, a resourceful lower-class pick-pocket (the Pistols' manager Malcolm McLaren's comparison). She further links the Pistols' music to the tradition of English Music Hall, a version of vaudeville originating in London, where the lower classes could safely poke fun at their situation through song and skits.[36] In this respect, Wicke and Adams perhaps find some common ground given the inherent ambiguity of precisely when mere "reflection" of one's situation crosses over to "expression" of that situation for the purpose of effecting change. While the punks never stormed Parliament with pointed sticks, Rotten claimed that he sang about situations that affected him and people he cared about, which is undeniably an act of expression. Other scholarship, acknowledging the diversity of punk musical styles and subcultural variants, suggests that the unifying philosophy of punk rock is not defiance, but merely deviance.[37]

Thus, from a perspective of deviance, "Respectable" succeeds with its imagery of "talking heroin with the President," and the unnamed "queen of porn" who is the "easiest lay on the White House lawn," but it evokes deviance at an élite social level quite foreign to the English punks. Similarly, mirroring Rotten's take on *Never Mind the Bollocks* as pointed satire, Jagger has said that "Respectable" and "Some Girls," both of which generated negative reactions over the misogynistic and racist lyrics, were intended to be funny and not any kind of profound commentary.[38] Arguably, the Stones are reflecting the insouciant culture of the late 1970s, rooting their social protest in satire rather than in the more obvious urgency of "Gimme Shelter" (1969), "Sweet Black Angel" (1972), "Doo Doo Doo Doo Doo (Heartbreaker)" (1973), and serious songs of longing, such as the hit "Angie" (1973).

If "Respectable" is a punk song, then so are "When the Whip Comes Down" and "Shattered." "Whip" is a compound simple verse form comprised almost exclusively of alternating measures of I and IV in regular eight-measure phrases, at least at first. Like many songs on *Some Girls*, the casual listener might recall several iterations of verse-chorus complexes broken by a contrasting bridge in classic AABA form, but it is not that simple. Like "Miss You," this would be an easy song to mess up in concert. Two symmetrical verse-chorus complexes separated by a well-behaved four-measure interlude – a spacer section where the band plays the instrumental track without vocal – make up the first two A sections. However, a third verse seems to begin (1:21), but after only two measures the chorus hook "when the whip comes down" is sung over the next two measures, followed by another four-measure interlude. This equals eight measures, like any verse, but it contains elements of verse, chorus, and interlude. Following this is a normal eight-measure verse (1:36), but the next chorus (1:51) is truncated at only four measures – and then it gets really strange: Another verse seems to begin, but is again cut off by the chorus after only two measures, although this time the chorus section continues for four measures. Finally, rather late in the song, after four (or four and a half?) A sections, a contrasting bridge begins (3:09) alternating between single measures each of VII (G) and IV (D), which, if one considers this to be a modulation to D major, is yet another I–IV progression. However, this bridge, featuring twangy country guitar licks, is not a traditional middle eight, lasting only six measures before a full chorus returns. A guitar solo over verse-chorus music begins at this point (2:34), sounding for all the world like a coda – which it essentially is – but there are two false verses, two distinct changes of texture, and irregular iterations of the chorus still in store. In essence, shortly after the one-minute mark, the song becomes very unpredictable, which is one way the Stones are able to maintain interest over musically static material.

The (Very) Mixed Reception of *Some Girls*

The rock scene around the time that *Some Girls* neared completion in summer 1978 was focused on several stylistically diverse artists, reflecting the multiplicity of popular genres toward the end of the decade. *Melody Maker*, the UK's premier weekly rock music newspaper in the late 1970s, was scarcely able to release an issue that year that didn't have a short teaser or announcement related to Bob Dylan or Bruce Springsteen.[39] With *Some Girls* representing the Stones' first major product in over a year and a half, they ramped up the publicity in the trade magazines. *Melody Maker* of June 3, 1978 featured consecutive full-page ads for the group's pre-album-release single, "Miss You," and its B side, "Far Away Eyes."[40] The other full-page ads went to Springsteen's just-released and bound-for-glory *Darkness on the Edge of Town*, the Alan Parsons Project's *Pyramid*, and Hall and Oates' *Livetime* – a rather eclectic mix of genres, likely more reflective of the advertising budgets of their respective labels than any true barometer of scattered public taste. However, the next week's issue was dominated by the Stones to coordinate with the album's June 9th release. In addition to Chris Brazier's guardedly optimistic feature review of the record, there was a small teaser that the Stones might do a few intimate "surprise" concerts at the Rainbow Theatre in London (where Hendrix had first set a Stratocaster alight ten years earlier), and other surprise gigs in the UK between American concerts scheduled to begin June 17th. *Melody Maker*'s weekly charts listed "Miss You" at number seventeen, behind Boney M's number one "Rivers of Babylon," Olivia Newton-John and John Travolta's number two "You're the One that I Want," Darts' number three cover of Leiber and Stoller's "Boy from New York City," and the Bee Gees' number five "Night Fever." The disco groove of "Miss You" was therefore in good company amongst these dance-pop numbers, even if its lurking malevolence comes from somewhere else. Toward the end of the issue, the "What's New" singles column featured "Miss You" as the first of its list of twenty releases, ahead of new work by Springsteen, the Boomtown Rats, Dusty Springfield, Maria Muldaur, Jackson Browne, and Dolly Parton. Similarly, the adjacent "What's New" albums list had *Some Girls* in second position behind the post-punk stylings of Magazine's *Real Life* – even if the post-punk label itself was still some years in the future. In short, there was considerable rock-industry buzz surrounding the highly anticipated appearance of a new Stones album at the apogee of disco, and the brief flourishing of punk.

Nonetheless, *Melody Maker*'s review was lukewarm. "When the Whip Comes Down," "Lies," and "Respectable" were described as typical Stones "brag and strut," with some interesting guitar-play between Wood and Richards, but the album as a whole was burdened by excessive repetition, absence of melody, and Jagger so low in the mix that his lyrics were inaudible. "The only track which brings Jagger and his lyrics upfront is the title-track, which is of musical interest only for the spit 'n' spite of the first guitar solo and for the hint of blossom in the chorus."[41] However, Brazier calls out Jagger for his "increasingly ridiculous preoccupation" with his jet-set persona, and for the overt racism – which led to public protests of the album (see Figure 5.2) – of stereotypically sexualizing African-Americans. On a more positive note, the review singled out "Miss You," "Shattered," and "Far Away Eyes" as tracks signaling that it was too early to "write off the Stones," thus making *Some Girls* "worthy of investigation."[42] Ironically, these are the three songs that stray furthest from the governing "policy change" of *Some Girls*, namely returning to a classic Stones style.

Some of the repetitiveness that Brazier and other critics sensed on *Some Girls* may come from structural characteristics influenced by the rawness of contemporary punk. Several songs are comprised of verses that alternate between symmetrical iterations of I and IV, which tends to blanch harmonic interest. Jeff Beck alludes to this when, unbeknownst to him, he was auditioning to be Mick Taylor's replacement – without anyone else from the band present – by laying down some demo tracks, allegedly stating

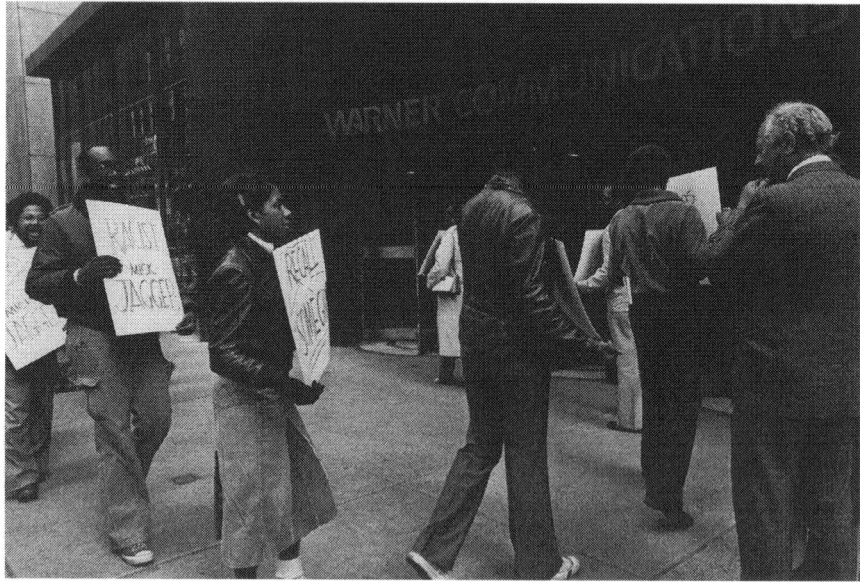

Figure 5.2 African-American protestors of *Some Girls* outside Warner Communications, New York City, 1978. Jeff Gold Collection, Library and Archives, Rock and Roll Hall of Fame and Museum.

that, "in two hours I got to play three chords – I need a little more energy than that."[43] The first four songs, "Miss You," "When the Whip Comes Down," a cover of the Temptations' "Just My Imagination," and "Some Girls," are almost exclusively alternations between the tonic and the sub-dominant, two very closely related sonorities which, depending on one's music-theoretical inclinations, might amount to an essentially static tonic harmony decorated with two upper neighbor tones. A well-known example of this is the opening riff to "Start Me Up" from *Tattoo You*, which began as a reggae number during the 1975 *Black and Blue* sessions in Munich.[44] The Stones could not make it work despite "forty or fifty takes. We would be nagging at it again two years later [*Some Girls*], then four years after that – the slow birth of a song whose perfect non-reggae nature we had discovered in one passing take without realizing it, even forgetting we'd done it."[45] However, this is absolutely standard R&B and lends itself to explorations of groove, an element that text-oriented critics often undervalue.

Paul Nelson's feature review in *Rolling Stone* was also tepid. It opens with the usual litany of the Stones' advancing age, rock music's creeping state of decline, and the suggestion that the Stones bear an ill-defined obligation to do something to reverse this:

> With Bob Dylan no longer bringing it all back home, Elvis Presley dead and the Beatles already harmlessly cloned in the wax-museum nostalgia of a Broadway musical, it's no wonder the Rolling Stones decided to make a

serious record. Not particularly ambitious, mind you, but serious. These guys aren't dumb, and when the handwriting on the wall starts to smell like formaldehyde and that age-old claim, "the greatest rock & roll band in the world," suddenly sounds less laudatory than laughable – well, if you want to survive the Seventies and enter the Eighties with something more than your bankbook and dignity intact, you'd better dredge up your leftover pride, bite the bullet and try like hell to sweat out some good music. Which is exactly what the Stones have done. Though time may not exactly be on their side, with *Some Girls* they've at least managed to stop the clock for a while.[46]

He later suggests that *Some Girls* is to *Exile* what a made-for-TV version of *Rebel Without a Cause* without James Dean would be to the original. The mixed metaphor of handwriting on the wall smelling like formaldehyde (used to preserve corpses), the references to wax museums and leftover pride, as well as a hackneyed reference to the Stones' 1964 cover of "Time Is on My Side," are typical of Nelson's reviews in that they are literary, evocative, and provocative, but often do not make much literal sense. Nonetheless, it is clear that these established critics expect the Stones to *do something* about the state of rock. He continues, acknowledging that there was widespread agreement that this was a return of sorts to classic Stones style, but that it lacked the "passion, power and near-awesome *completeness*" of *Exile*: "Gone is the black and white murk, and the vocals are way up in a nicely messy but pastel mix . . . *Some Girls* is like a marriage of convenience: when it works – which is often – it can be meaningful, memorable and quite moving, but it rarely sends the arrow straight through the heart."[47]

Nelson's penchant for metaphor begs the question of how to reconcile his perception of the vocals "way up" with that of Brazier in *Melody Maker*, who found the vocals too buried, save for "Some Girls." Despite the stripped-down instrumental forces, it seems that seasoned Stones listeners were a bit baffled by the soundscape of *Some Girls*. Elsewhere, Jagger addressed the vocal mix, observing, "With a song like 'Shattered,' however, I thought we had to hear the words a bit, so . . . it's not really just a question of loudness, it has to do with clarity of diction – whether I enunciate properly. And if I don't, you have to have it louder, and even then people don't understand what you're saying."[48] The vocals on "When the Whip Comes Down," however, are clearly difficult to discern, and they are indeed buried in the mix. Ultimately, one wonders how much time various critics spent actually listening to the album.

Jagger was so incensed by Nelson's review that the Stones revoked the press credential for *Rolling Stone*'s tour reporter.[49] To smooth things over, Jann Wenner penned a glowing review of the album and associated concerts in pointed rebuttal to his fellow *Rolling Stone* journalist Paul

Nelson (and likewise Dave Marsh regarding Bob Dylan). He proclaims *Some Girls* "a masterpiece," and much of the review suggests that the senior critics are subconsciously blaming sixties icons for the loss of the sixties themselves.

> Ironically, one of the reasons why Greil Marcus, Dave Marsh and Paul Nelson panned Bob Dylan and the Rolling Stones with such invective is because these critics care so much – not only about Dylan and the Stones but about the entire spectrum of rock & roll. They grew up with it in the Sixties, so maybe it's now necessary for them to slay their figurative fathers and look for new heroes.[50]

Wenner further criticizes them for calling punk the music of the seventies, presciently predicting that the genre will not make it to the eighties, which it arguably does not, at least in the musical mainstream, being superseded by New Wave and post-punk. Having nurtured a very close, but ultimately complicated relationship with Jagger, Wenner defends the group, concluding that "Critical discussions – historical, social, moral – that ultimately revolve around the point of things not being what they used to be are useless. To argue otherwise is to deny the aging of the observer and the observed and to ignore the fact of change."[51]

The 1978 Tour

The American tour supporting *Some Girls* began on June 10, 1978, comprising twenty-five shows in forty-six days in venues as small as 2,000-seat theatres, to hockey arenas and outdoor football stadiums. They rehearsed rather haphazardly – mostly jamming – in Newark for thirteen days before launching the tour in Orlando, billed as "The Great Southeast Stoned-Out Wrestling Champs," with tickets priced at $10.00. Wyman remembers the set as being "not great," but that they gained momentum throughout the summer.[52] They played a mostly post-*Exile* selection including eight consecutive songs from *Some Girls* in the middle of the seventy-five-minute set.

Some of the large stadium shows were problematic. On June 17, 1978, the Stones played the fifth show of the tour, and the first in a large venue, in the cavernous JFK Stadium in Philadelphia to an estimated 100,000 people. Unfortunately, the sound was poor, and the band were reduced to specks for many in attendance.[53] Furthermore, because Jagger was ailing with 'flu, the group played a shorter set than usual, and disgruntled fans, who had sat through many hours of drizzle, began throwing objects on the stage after the Stones disappeared without an encore, a policy strictly followed for the entire tour. It was revealed later that Jagger had performed against doctor's orders with a temperature of 101.[54]

Two nights later, veteran rock journalist Chris Welch reviewed a "surprise" performance at New York's 3,386-seat Palladium Theatre; attendees received tickets via a lottery from WNEW-FM, knowing neither the date nor location. Welch asserts that the eighty-minute show silenced critics, and "reaffirmed faith in the Rolling Stones' ability to rise above the snobbery, the social gossip and the heavy weight of the past ..." He mentions an unnamed *Rolling Stone* journalist seated next to him who complained, "They're just tired old men," echoing the sentiments that Welch reports were made to him the night before by up-and-coming British rocker Tom Robinson, who believed the Stones "should break up and were no longer valid."[55] Welch, however, describes the show in superlative terms, claiming that Jagger, who reportedly had very little stage presence in Philadelphia two nights earlier, "lolled, sidled, wriggled, slumped, rolled over, spun around, leapt through the air and twitched with such violence as to shed teeth, hair and fingernails."[56] Outstanding new songs were "Respectable" and – "the first natural successor" to "Satisfaction" – "When the Whip Comes Down." Welch lauds the move away from the "somewhat ramshackle sound" of the "Honky Tonk Women" days, and describes the rhythm section as "perked up and modernized." Again, we see the divide between critics who bemoan the Stones' loss of relevance and urgency, and those who perceive overall musical growth and adaptation. He claims that his colleague from *Rolling Stone* remained quiet after the show, perhaps unwilling to admit "the old group hadn't been so bad after all," while the rest of the crowd spilled out into the sweltering evening, many singing the falsetto hook from "Miss You." John Rockwell of the *New York Times* agreed that the concert "triumphantly reaffirmed the greatness of rock's most exciting performing band." He echoes Welch, claiming that the new material really ignited the set, particularly a "fierce and desperate account" of "Miss You," and that Jagger performed with a "sense of personal involvement that was always compelling and sometimes almost frightening in its intensity."[57]

Indeed, Jagger's increasing role as a rhythm guitarist changed both the Stones' live sound and their stage show (although he had played guitar on a song or two in concerts starting in 1975). According to Jagger, this gave Richards and Wood more opportunity to solo simultaneously while still supported by Jagger's rhythm guitar, and it permitted any combination of the three guitars to set up counter-rhythms thus more accurately reproducing the textures that Richards had constructed on the records.[58] Jagger claimed that donning a guitar did not inhibit his stage antics as they were now using wireless transmitters.

Postlude: *Emotional Rescue, Tattoo You* and *Undercover*

After releasing *Some Girls* in June, 1978, the Stones were in the studio off and on throughout autumn 1978 to early 1980. In that period, they recorded approximately forty songs, actually finishing twenty-five – more than enough for a new album – and ultimately selecting ten for *Emotional Rescue*.[59] By 1980, Jagger's take on New Wave and punk was that they were no longer new. Referring to the Police and the Clash, respectively, he said: "The music isn't new. It sounds very old . . . I quite like the Clash . . . but they really sound old fashioned . . . *London Calling*'s a great album. But I prefer Elvis Costello's songwriting."[60] Jagger describes his and Richards' songwriting as following no set pattern in terms of who contributes what. In some cases, the songs are written quite separately, whereas in others they are collaborations in highly variable proportions, but all are credited equally. The older tendency for Richards to arrange and Jagger to write lyrics had largely broken down as well. In cases where other members made a significant contribution, such as Wood to "Dance," a co-writing credit was added.[61] When asked by Jann Wenner whether *Emotional Rescue* has "a lot of resonance," Jagger responds that it does not, and that many of the songs were leftovers from *Some Girls*.[62]

The (Less) Mixed Reception of *Emotional Rescue*

Upon its release, the album received generally lukewarm reviews. However, as with *Some Girls*, critical reception has softened over the years, suggesting that both albums might be "growers." On the other hand, the reviews of these releases might simply betray critics' desire for successive albums to be simultaneously groundbreaking yet familiar. Ariel Swartley's *Rolling Stone* review of *Emotional Rescue* was less than effusive.[63] "As far as the music goes, *familiar* is an understatement. There's hardly a melody here you haven't heard from the Stones before. But then that's nothing new. Me, I'd rather be reminded of *Between the Buttons* by the venal, high-speed whine of 'She's So Cold' than revisit 'Miss You' outtakes by way of the interminable 'Dance (Pt. 1),' but there are plenty of rooms available at the current memory motel."[64] Swartley rightly implies that *Emotional Rescue* is heavily informed by cast-offs from *Some Girls*, although it is unclear how aware of this anyone outside the Stones milieu might have been. Swartley makes cunning reference to the ballad "Memory Motel" from *Black and Blue*, which Lester Bangs called the best song on the album, but one that he believed essentially transformed the Stones into an updated Barry Manilow.[65] With prose purple enough to please even Bangs, Swartley waxes poetic, or perhaps metaphysically – if somewhat vaguely – over the role played by the Stones, and rock and roll in general, in their glory years: "With each new album, you had the sense that they were looking over your shoulder, pointing an ironic finger at your most private fantasies. This was what made that devil pose so convincing, even to non-hallucinating brains. The Stones really did seem to have foreknowledge of our causes and concerns. And the mystique of their precognition made rock & roll seem – for a while – to be the intellectual and emotional collectivism that would rule the world."[66] Interestingly, Swartley finds several instances where *Emotional Rescue* fails to live up to *Some Girls*, thus admitting *the latter* into the rock canon: "One thing's for sure: *Emotional Rescue* isn't the newsbreak that 1978's *Some Girls* was."[67]

Michael Watts' review in *Melody Maker* echoed some of Swartley's sentiments, but he found a little more to like. Nonetheless, the review begins with yet another consideration of whether the Stones, now averaging about age thirty-seven (with Wyman already a grizzled forty-three), might be planning to pack it in soon, while pointing out (without evidence) that this is a question rarely asked of Paul McCartney, Roger Daltrey, or even forty-eight-year-old Chuck Berry. He continues: "The public's *idée fixe* of the Stones as ageing *enfants terrible* [sic] is a problem Jagger seems to slyly acknowledge in 'Dance,' the first track of *Emotional Rescue* when he sings 'I think the time's come to get up, get out – out into something new.' The joke – implicit in the sheer bounce of the music – is that the Stones patently have no intention of doing any such thing."[68] Like many seasoned critics, Watts prefaces the review with a discussion of his own diminished expectations – "Like, I suspect, many other long-time Stones fans, I no longer have great expectations" – and points out that there were a few good songs on the post-*Exile* albums, and even half a dozen on *Some Girls*, but that the Stones were now "hostages to their own celebrity, lacking genuine rapport (and, therefore, social context) with a younger audience ... [so that] the Stones now make music whose overall mood is playful and ironic where once its effect was urgent and cutting."[69]

Michael Watts roots the Stones' malaise in Jagger, namely his penchant for the fashionable (which explains the disco of "Miss You" and "Emotional Rescue") plus his campy, "dumb," throwaway humor (to which Watts alludes for Jagger's switching from falsetto to detached spoken passages in "Emotional Rescue" – "the dumbest Stones number since 'Fool to Cry'" – and the "spoof reggae" of "Send it to Me"). He particularly dislikes "She's So Cold," where Jagger "sings and acts as if he were hugging himself whilst locked inside a refrigerating room" (clearly referring to the icy, white-tiled setting for the music video). Jack Nitzsche's horn arrangement for "Indian Girl" comes under fire ("or should it be Kitsche?"), and Jagger's "fake peon voice of revolution in Nicaragua" is mocked as well – "Along this way lies parody, not merely pastiche."[70]

Watts suggests that the rootsy interplay between Richards and the rhythm section typically provides the tension for the Stones, making it ironic that Richards' vulnerability is highlighted on his solo, "All About You." However, Watts' five best tracks from the album, including "She's So Cold," despite his reservations about Jagger, all feature this classic Stones rhythmic dynamic: "Dance," with its Zeppelinesque riff (recalling "Trampled Underfoot" from *Physical Graffiti*) and Latin elements; the rockabilly "Let Me Go"; the "likeably banal" "Summer Romance," which recalls Eddie Cochrane's "Summertime Blues"; and "Down in the Hole," enlivened by Sugar Blue's harp. While acknowledging that five good tracks out of ten is not a bad average, "it's inescapable that they rarely approach the drive and brio of the best newer bands like Graham Parker's or Costello's. Like Chuck Berry, their early mentor, they've become an institution which one may either rail against or draw comfort from. Keeping the ghosts and critics at bay may yet occupy them for years to come."[71] The reference to Graham Parker and the Rumour is interesting, as most North American listeners will never have heard of this solid roots-New Wave hybrid, but the reference does underscore much British criticism in the early eighties that was understandably heavily focused on up-and-coming acts, possibly betraying *Melody Maker*'s desire to court a more youthful audience which tended to favor the *New Musical Express*.

A contrary opinion was provided by the respected reviewer for the *New York Times*, Robert Palmer, who blended interview with review when invited to Stones HQ in New York City to hear the soon-to-be-released album. Palmer, at thirty-five, was only a year or two junior to Jagger and Richards, and reviews the album as much from their perspective as his own. He notes that the album relies less on outside contributions than any album in the last decade, and that it reflects the meticulousness of Richards' post-production efforts and mixing – a process Jagger claims to have almost completely avoided. When asked by Palmer about the "minutiae of instrumental balance and other mixing details," Jagger admits that he "gets bored. That's Keith"; to which Richards answered, "He would say that wouldn't he? Well, I would say that at the moment it feels real natural to be producing the records again."[72] Jagger admits that the entire album is about women, to the point that even a quasi-political song like "Indian Girl," about Central American rebellions, is mostly about the girl. However, he pins this on being a musician in the early 1960s when it seemed that a pop song pretty much had to be about a girl: "But it's very limiting. Basically, it's adolescent fantasizing. I've got to reach for some other things. At my age, I do have experiences to draw on other than picking up waitresses in diners."[73] Palmer acknowledges that the lyrical content has been amply explored in the past, but observes that the "power and originality of the music" more than compensate, and that the detailed work of Richards, both in playing multiple guitar parts on most tracks and in mixing the album, signals his full return to the band. He also praises Jagger's expansion of his timbral variety and voice effects, from the guttural vocal of "Down in the Hole" to the full range displayed on "Emotional Rescue," which includes falsetto and the "playful voodoo hokum of Screamin' Jay Hawkins."[74] However, he believes that the "most effectively sustained emotional resonance" is Richards' lead vocal on the final track, "All About You," described by Jagger as a love-hate song, "plaintively asking 'so why am I still in love with you?'"[75]

The Stones in the Early 1980s

By the early 1980s, the Rolling Stones were all turning at least forty, and the dread surrounding plus-thirty hippies was already moot. The problem, of course, was that the first wave of Stones fans and critics were aging at an identical pace and, perhaps, were coming to see the aging process in a more forgiving light. Anthony DeCurtis shrewdly points out that the Stones albums of the late sixties and early seventies reflected the waning of the Utopian vision of hippie culture. New York, popularly perceived to be in its debt-driven death throes, provided a salient background to the mid-seventies when New Yorkers responded to their plight with a flourishing of urban culture, namely disco and punk.[76] Similarly, Robert Palmer suggests that the Stones in the sixties were more than a rock band – they were news, and they reflected the concerns and aspirations of their generation. But by the late seventies, rock music fans were no longer such an indivisible taste or age cohort, and the Stones were finally able to shed the responsibility foisted upon them by critics of the 1960s and early 1970s.

Critical reception began to turn a corner at the same time. *Tattoo You* (1981) was described by several critics as a triumphant return to form, but with a perspective more suitable to grown men. Writing for *Rolling Stone*, Debra Rae Cohen opined that the Stones of the 1970s dealt with the responsibility of their longevity by adopting a cynical distance to their subjects, and characterizes the punk and disco styles as "grafting unwarranted *au courant* attitudes onto the dependable drive of the rhythm section."[77] While acknowledging that many of the songs from *Tattoo You* had their roots in the 1970s, she perceives greater maturity and vulnerability in songs like "Waiting on a Friend" and the opening track "Start Me Up," where Jagger proclaims "You make a grown man cry" – although she fails to mention the slightly less mature "You make a dead man cum" near the end of the song. Specifically addressing their age, she concludes: "the Stones have settled magnificently into middle age, and . . .

such an adjustment has given them back a power they long ago relin-quished."[78] Similarly, Robert Palmer praises their return to basic rock and roll – eschewing the fashion of disco and the affectations of reggae – and the foregrounding of guitar and vocal, enlivened by crisper, brighter production by Richards and Jagger, engineered by Bob Clearmountain and Chris Kimsey. Echoing Cohen, he concludes: "On earlier albums, the Stones played the role of aging adolescents; they boasted, they swaggered, they portrayed themselves as down-and-out rebels even when they were living in luxury. On 'Tattoo You' they are playing themselves; they have grown up."[79]

The *Rolling Stone* review for 1983's *Undercover* began: "By now, the Rolling Stones have assumed something of the status of the blues in popular music – a vital force beyond time and fashion. *Undercover* . . . reassembles, in the manner of mature masters of every art, familiar elements into exciting new forms."[80] For once, the aged Stones were turning the corner as figures of veneration rather than ridicule. This canonization was doubtless contextualized by processes as diverse as the martyrdom of John Lennon in 1980, the passage of many seventies acts, such as the Eagles, Fleetwood Mac, and the Sex Pistols, well into their thirties, and the radio- and video-driven smoothing out of punk into New Wave and post-punk. Some of the earlier punk artists, such as Joe Strummer (1952–2002) and Chrissie Hynde (b. 1951), were older than most of the first-wave punks – not to mention Patti Smith, Elvis Costello, and the Police, who weren't really punk – and were already past thirty.

Over the ensuing decades the Stones, and innumerable contemporaries, younger and older (but mostly younger), continued as recording and touring acts. Older artists were gradually acquiring guru status to the point that country icon Johnny Cash lends a peculiar gravitas to U2's 1993 *Zooropa* album as vocalist on the concluding track, while Neil Young tutors grunge gods Pearl Jam in joint gigs in the early nineties, ultimately inducting them into the Rock and Roll Hall of Fame in 2017, like a proud parent (or grandparent). Meanwhile, the seventy-year-old Stones and Paul McCartney, and fifty-somethings U2 and Madonna, had some of the largest-grossing world tours in the second decade of the twenty-first century. "Rock music," however one might define it, is increasingly associated with "old" artists, as younger people now display musical allegiance to genres that strain under the label "rock." The tragic deaths of David Bowie (69), Prince (57), and Tom Petty (66) within twenty months in 2016–17 provoked widespread grief, as they were still active, and considered "too young to die." Elvis, on the other hand, was only 42 in 1977, but considered moribund and obsolete. If he had held on for another decade it might have been different.

The Rolling Stones, however, are very much alive and remain active. Richards says: "I'll still be playing rock and roll when I'm in a wheelchair."[81]

Notes

1   Chet Flippo, "Nothing Lasts Forever: Who Will Rescue the Rolling Stones?," *RSt* (August 21, 1980), 38. Flippo describes these remarks as casual conversation with Jagger before a more formal interview.

2   The period saw the second line-up change of guitarists and a major shift in sound as a result of the departure of Mick Taylor and the hiring of Ronnie Wood. The move of rock music towards a transformational business model, which became the catalyst for style change, is discussed in John Covach, *What's That Sound: An Introduction to Rock and its History*, 2nd edn. (New York, 2009), 404–8.

3   Chris Brazier, "More Meat from the Stones," review of *Some Girls*, *MM* (June 10, 1978), 18.

4   The wax figures of the Beatles were already installed in the museum by 1964.

5   See Michael Bertrand, *Race, Rock, and Elvis* (Urbana, 2000), particularly chapter 1, "Race and Class in Southern Juxtaposition: The Forgotten Roots of a (Rock) Revolution," 15–40.

6   Lester Bangs, "Dandelions in Still Air: The Withering Away of the Beatles," *Real Paper* (April 23, 1975), reprinted in *Creem* (June, 1975), and in John Morthland, ed., *Mainlines, Blood Feasts, and Bad Taste: A Lester Bangs Reader* (New York, 2003), 39–46.

7   Allen Crowley, "Mellow Stones: Contradiction in Terms?" *Creem* (December, 1973); see www.timeisonourside.com/lpGoats.html (accessed February 19, 2019).

8   Wenner*MJR*, 66.

9   *Life*, 241, 365–7.

10 Lester Bangs, "1973 Nervous Breakdown: The Ol' Fey Outlaws Ain't What They Used to Be – Are You?," *Creem* (December, 1973), reprinted in *Mainlines*, ed. Morthland, 143.

11 Lester Bangs, review of *Goats Head Soup* in *Creem* (December, 1973), reprinted *ibid.*, 152 (emphasis in the original).

12 Lester Bangs, "It's Only the Rolling Stones" [review of *It's Only Rock 'n Roll*], *Village Voice* (October 31, 1974).

13 Lester Bangs, "State of the Art: Bland on Bland" [review of *Black and Blue*], *Creem* (July, 1976), 63.

14 Brazier, "More Meat."

15 *Life*, 363.

16 *Ibid.*, 398.

17 *According*, 212.

18 *Life*, 398.

19 *RSG*, 190.

20 *Life*, 398.

21 Wenner*MJR*, 66.

22 *Ibid.*

23 *Ibid.*

24 *According*, 213.

25 *Ibid*, 214.

26 *Ibid*, 213.

27 Wenner*MJR*, 66.

28 *Ibid.*

29 *Life*, 456.

30 Wyman*RWTS*, 446.

31 Wenner*MJR*, 66.

32 *According*, 214.

33 Quoted in Clinton Heylin, *Babylon's Burning: From Punk to Grunge* (New York, 2007), 124.

34 Peter Wicke, *Rock Music: Culture, Aesthetics, and Sociology*, trans. Rachel Fogg (Cambridge, 1990), 147.

35 John Lydon [Johnny Rotten] in the Matthew Longfellow documentary *Sex Pistols: Never Mind the Bollocks* (2002).

36 Ruth Adams, "The Englishness of English Punk: Sex Pistols, Subcultures, and Nostalgia," *Popular Music and Society* 31 (2008), 469–88.

37 Lars J. Kristiansen, Joseph R. Blaney, Philip J. Chidester, and Brent K. Simonds, *Screaming for Change: Articulating a Unifying Philosophy of Punk Rock* (Lanham, MD, 2010).

38 Jonathan Cott, "Mick Jagger: The Rolling Stone Interview," *RSt* (June 29, 1978): www.rollingstone.com/music/music-features/mick-jagger-the-rolling-stone-interview-52609/ (accessed February 20, 2019).

39 Others might assign this premier status to the *New Musical Express*, but *Melody Maker* tended to reassert itself in the early 1980s with the rise of New Wave and post-punk.

40 *MM* (June 3, 1978), 15–16.

41 Brazier, "More Meat."

42 *Ibid.*

43 Quoted without attribution in the Wikipedia article on *Black and Blue*, en.wikipedia.org/wiki/Black_and_Blue, accessed February 20, 2019. This was when Beck was moving more towards jazz-fusion (*Blow by Blow* (1975), and *Wired* (1976)), so he may have been less interested in groove-oriented styles that he had mined so thoroughly in the early 1970s.

44 *RSCRS*, 177.

45 *Life*, 379.

46 Paul Nelson, "The Guys Can't Help It," review of *Some Girls*, *RSt* (August 10, 1978), 52.

47 *Ibid.*

48 Cott, "Mick Jagger."

49 Cyrus R. K. Patell, *Some Girls* (New York, 2011), 129.

50 Jann Wenner, "Love in Vain: Dylan and the Stones in the 70s," *RSt* (September 21, 1978), 60.

51 *Ibid.* On the complicated relationship between Wenner and Jagger, see Joe Hagan's *Sticky Fingers: The Life and Times of Jann Wenner and Rolling Stone Magazine* (New York, 2017).

52 Wyman*RWTS*, 447.

53 Chris Welch, "Miss You," *MM* (July 1, 1978).

54 *Ibid.*, 8.

55 *Ibid.*

56 *Ibid.*

57 John Rockwell, "The Stones at Palladium," *New York Times* (June 21, 1978).

58 Welch, "Miss You," 44.

59 Ray Bonici, "Mick Jagger Starts It Up! Hanging Fire Where the Boys All Go," *Creem* (January, 1982), 20.

60 *Ibid.*

61 *Ibid.*

62 Wenner*MJR*, 66.

63 Ariel Swartley, "The Rolling Stones: What Kind of a 'Rescue' is This?," *RSt* (August 21, 1980).

64 The US release of *Between the Buttons* (February, 1967) included "Let's Spend the Night Together" and "Ruby Tuesday," while the UK version did not.

65 See Bangs' review of *Black and Blue* in *Creem* (July, 1976).

66 Swartley, "The Rolling Stones," 46.

67 *Ibid.*

68 Michael Watts, "An Institution Strikes Back," review of *Emotional Rescue*, *MM* (June 28, 1980), 13.

69 *Ibid.*

70 *Ibid.*

71 *Ibid.*

72 Quoted in Robert Palmer, "The Stones Gather Strength," *New York Times* (June 29, 1980): timesmachine.nytimes.com/timesmachine/1980/06/29/111791803.html?pageNumber=95 (accessed February 20, 2019).

73 *Ibid.*

74 *Ibid.*

75 *Ibid.*

76 Anthony DeCurtis, "Love and Hope and Sex and Dreams: Punk Rock, Disco, New York City & the Triumph of the Rolling Stones' *Some Girls*," liner notes to the 2011 reissue of *Some Girls* (Universal), reprinted in Jonathan Lethem and Kevin Dettmar, eds., *Shake it Up: Great American Writing on Rock and Roll and Pop from Elvis to Jay Z*" (New York, 2017), 530.

77 Debra Rae Cohen, "The Politics of Sin," review of *Tattoo You*, *RSt* (October 15, 1981).

78 *Ibid.*
79 Robert Palmer, "The Rolling Stones: Once Adolescent, They've Grown Up [review of *Tattoo You*], *New York Times* (August 26, 1981): www.nytimes.com/1981/08/26/arts/the-pop-life-the-rolling-stones-once-adolescent-they-ve-grown-up.html (accessed February 20, 2019).
80 Kurt Loder, "The Stones: Rock and Roll Without Apologies," review of *Undercover*, *RSt* (December 8, 1983).
81 Quoted in Palmer, "The Rolling Stones."

PART II

Sound, Roots, and Brian Jones

6 The Rolling Stones' Sound: At the Crossroads of Roots and Technology

RALPH MAIER

When we started in England, engineers had no concept of how to record something like this, so
you were fighting almost everything: the technology for what it was (really low believe me) . . .
But there's always been a certain fascination, especially for Mick and myself, about recording.
How do you get what sounds great in the front room or in the bathroom or in the bedroom,
how to make it sound like that in the studio and how do you capture it? I mean, recording is a tricky
business . . .[1]

Traditional analyses of music often overlook sonic elements that are difficult to notate. This is especially true of the way many fundamental aspects of sound, such as timbre, resonance, ambience, stereo placement, and countless other sonic qualities are manipulated during the recording process, but largely ignored in popular music criticism. Yet these elements, so central to recordings of popular music, are as important in conveying expression and meaning as melody, harmony, rhythm, and lyrics. They are an integral part of the music – primary colors in the recording artist's sonic palette.[2]

The extremely close attention paid to the *sound* of their musical production, both live and in the studio, is a primary reason for the enormous longevity of the Rolling Stones, now spanning well over half a century. Listening to them is like peering through the looking glass, observing how they balanced concurrent musical trends with their own fundamental roots in American blues, country, folk music, and rock and roll. As studio artists, the Stones have witnessed monumental changes in recording technology, with their own contributions in particular regarded as innovative and path breaking: One need look no further than the Stones mobile unit and its enormous legacy, the use of cassette tape recorders as "instruments" in songs like "Street Fighting Man" and "Parachute Woman," and the melding of digital technologies with vintage recording methods on *Blue and Lonesome* (2016). If one constant could be found, it would be the sonic embodiment of an attitude that is immediately recognizable and undeniably *Stones*.

Blue Through and Through

We went for a Chicago blues sound, as close as we could get it – two guitars, bass and drums
and a piano – and sat around and listened to every Chess record ever made. Chicago blues hit us

between the eyes. We'd all grown up with everything else that everybody had grown up with, rock and roll, but we focused on that. And as long as we were all together, we could pretend to be black men. We soaked up the music, but it didn't change the color of our skin.[3]

The British blues revival is often regarded as one of the most pivotal events in the history of popular music, and rightly so: it offered escape from the BBC's tightly regimented program of lightweight pop; it served as a training school for eager young players and songwriters at a time when any kind of formal training outside of classical music didn't exist; and it positioned its members as heirs apparent to a venerated lineage that was distant in both geography, race, and culture. As such, American blues was embraced as quintessentially authentic, an "early" music that existed outside of mainstream society and overtly capitalist interests in the same way that American blues musicians, their cultural heritage, and attitudes railed against conservative white society. Admittedly, the relationship between British blues bands and their African-American heroes has had more than its share of problems, its rich history often overshadowed by accusations of cultural appropriation and riddled by legal battles over copyright infringement, with many cases continuing today. In post-WWII London, however, a growing contingent of youth raised on rationing and the clearly defined social strata of an antiquated British class system could easily identify with the plight of African Americans. In retrospect, their unsettled love affair seemed predestined.

On September 2, 1964 the Rolling Stones, along with Andrew Loog Oldham, gathered at Regent Sound Studio to record "Off the Hook," an early Jagger/Richards original, the Drifters' "Under the Boardwalk," and "Little Red Rooster," which was inspired by Willie Dixon's version of a traditional blues tune recorded by Howlin' Wolf just three years earlier.[4] A modest studio with humble facilities on Denmark Street (London's equivalent of Tin Pan Alley), Regent typically catered to the production of demos and jingles. According to Richards, "it was just a little room full of egg boxes, and it had a Grundig tape recorder, and to make it look like a studio, the recorder was hung on the wall instead of put on a table . . . it made it easy for me to learn the bare bones of recording . . . One of the reasons we picked it was because it was mono, and what you hear is what you get."[5] Oldham recalled that it was "no larger than an average good-sized hotel room," with the control room the size of the hotel's bathroom, "but for us it was magic."[6] While the Stones had garnered considerable success over the past year with numerous performances at home and abroad, along with television appearances as well as recording sessions at legendary Chess Studios during their first US tour, they had yet to produce an LP or release any original music.[7] Their insistent focus on blues and R&B covers (many of them B sides) is significant. Years later, Richards remembers the decision to cut "Little Red Rooster" as:

> a daring move at the time, November 1964. We were getting no-no's from the record company, management, everyone else. But we felt we were on the crest of a wave and we could push it. It was almost in defiance of pop. In our arrogance at the time, we wanted to make a statement. "I am the little red rooster/Too lazy to crow for day." See if you can get that to the top of the charts, motherfucker.[8]

"Little Red Rooster" begins with a standard blues riff performed by Brian Jones on slide guitar with Bill Wyman delivering a more than credible simulation of Willie Dixon's upright bass on his Framus Star electric. Richards doubles the riff on his single cutaway Framus Jumbo acoustic, replacing the piano and second electric guitar of Wolf's recording while hearkening back to the Delta blues of Bukka White, Lead Belly, and the band's recent discovery of the recordings of Robert Johnson.[9] Watts, sitting far enough forward in the mix to suggest a club performance, gently applies brushes to his Ludwig kit, avoiding full snare in favor of rimshots, the bounce of his kick drum seemingly casual but tight. When Jagger enters at the first chord change of this subtly altered twelve-bar blues progression, the mild distortion that colors the edges of his voice conjures shades of the natural grit of Howlin' Wolf's earthy timbre. The vocal delivery and its spare accompaniment are restrained, punctuated by the occasional barnyard outburst of Jones' slide guitar; the sparse texture, exaggerated by studio reverb, offers a perfect analog to the austerity of post-World War II Britain.

Despite the monaural mix, the performance is remarkably spacious, strangely resonant, atmospheric, and bleak, the generous use of reverb particularly arresting. As a sonic resource, reverberation is an especially powerful tool: it enhances and enlarges the signal it is applied to; it transports the listener into an imaginary performance space; and it can suggest boundaries – both physical and temporal – between performer and listener. Its presence is at least as old as rock and roll, and indispensable in communicating the power of its possessor. When describing the innovative use of slap-back echo and heavy reverb in 1950s recordings of Elvis at Sun Records and RCA Studios, Richard Middleton points out: "Elvis Presley's early records, with their novel use of echo, may have represented a watershed in the abandoning of attempts to reproduce live performance in favor of a specifically studio sound; but the effect is used largely to intensify an *old* pop characteristic – 'star presence': Elvis becomes 'larger than life'."[10]

Mimed television performances of "Little Red Rooster" become particularly interesting in this context, where the auditory cues provided by Jagger's reverb-soaked voice are completely at odds with the visuals of the performance: The singer and his band appear unaffected by the physical laws of reality.[11] Sexually charged, mysterious, and detached from the mundane, the Stones are cast in an image of power in the same way that their idols used the blues as an expression of personal and cultural empowerment.

Black and White

[JAGGER:]   Andrew wanted to make the Rolling Stones the anti-Beatles, so if you've got heroes you've got an anti-hero, like in a movie, you've got good guys and bad guys. Andrew decided that the Rolling Stones were the bad guys ... It helps to have people that go along with it or fit the bill; it's good to have an actor who will play the part ...

[RICHARDS:]   The Beatles got the white hat, you know. What's left? The black hat.[12]

By 1966, popular music's sonic landscape was rapidly changing, a transformation expedited by technological advances in the production, mediation, and reception of recorded music and encouraged by the ever-expanding psychedelic movement born of the London underground scene and its American counterpart, San Francisco's Haight-Ashbury district. The increasing popularity of hi-fi stereo systems, the relatively new phenomenon of immersive personal listening enabled by John Koss' invention of the stereo headphone a scant eight years earlier, and cutting-edge trends in the stereo transmission of popular music via FM radio in the United States dramatically altered the ways in which listeners engaged with recordings.[13] Their significance notwithstanding, none of these industrial advances matched the cultural impact of *The Psychedelic Experience*, Timothy Leary's hallucinogenic-assisted tour of the *Tibetan Book of the Dead* that became the manifesto of the counterculture. For pop musicians in the latter part of the sixties, it provided an impetus for unprecedented experimentation.

Recorded at RCA Studios in Los Angeles in early December of 1965 and early March of 1966, *Aftermath* marked a critical turning point for the Stones.[14] Jagger described *Aftermath* as a landmark album, noting its eclecticism, sound quality, originality, and deliberate departure from blues covers:

> It's the first time we wrote the whole record and finally laid to rest the ghost of having to do these very nice and interesting, no doubt, but still cover versions of old R&B songs – which we didn't really feel we were doing justice, to be perfectly honest, particularly because we didn't have the maturity. Plus, everyone was doing it. [*Aftermath*] has a very wide spectrum of music styles: "Paint It, Black" was this kind of Turkish song; and there were also very bluesy things like "Goin' Home"; and I remember some sort of ballads on there. It had a lot of good songs, it had a lot of different styles, and it was very well recorded. So it was, to my mind, a real marker.[15]

Brian Jones had become increasingly interested in instruments other than the guitar and blues harp, performing dulcimer on "Lady Jane," marimba on "Under My Thumb," and sitar on "Paint It, Black," the latter released in the UK as a mono single in May, 1966 and as the opening track for the US release of *Aftermath* later that year in stereo. The acquisition of his first sitar likely occurred within a few days of the release on December 3, 1965 of the Beatles' *Rubber Soul*, which contained George Harrison's ground-breaking sitar-playing on "Norwegian Wood." After initial experiments, Jones took lessons with a half-Welsh, half-Indian friend named Hari who had studied with Ravi Shankar for twelve years and was called in to coach Jones for the recording of "Paint It, Black."[16]

The intentional shift away from the blues towards an eclectic style clearly illustrates the more cultural and historical inclusivity of pop music during the latter 1960s. The Stones' songs now evoked images as diverse as Victorian England in "Lady Jane" to eastern pilgrimages along the hippie highway in "Paint It, Black," at once demonstrating the band's musical authority and versatility, while announcing their willingness to push forward and take stylistic risks rather than play it safe. The group's predilection towards eclecticism takes on even greater significance when considering composer Luciano Berio's observation that, "when instruments like the trumpet, the harpsichord, the string quartet, the recorder are used with electric guitars (or in place of them) . . . they seem to assume the estranged character of quotations of themselves . . . [and] develop into a sort of sound drama . . . in the form of a *collage*."[17] The end result of this interplay of styles and influences is the creation of a complex network of associations contained within the fabric of these songs. Building on Berio's notion of "sound drama," the song becomes the stage upon which a multiplicity of diverse musical characters interact, each one clothed in an immediately recognizable social/cultural/historical costume.

"Paint It, Black" certainly opens in dramatic fashion, the first iteration of its exotic minor melody heavily reverberant and in stark isolation, rhythmically unencumbered and panned far right in the stereo field. The calm, meditative pretense of its brief introduction is immediately shattered by Watts' bellicose entrance on his four-piece Ludwig drum kit, the tom-toms cast as stand-in tablas panned far left. The full complement of players enters quickly, gathered around opposite sides of the soundstage: The sitar, overdubbed Gibson Hummingbird acoustic guitars played by Richards and Jones, as well as Richards' performance on his Guild Freshman M 65 electric guitar, inhabit the right side of the stage; Wyman's performance on his Vox Wyman bass along with doubling on the organ pedals of a Hammond B-3, added for weight, join Jack Nitzsche's piano and Watts' drums on the left;[18] Jagger is the last to enter, the anti-hero in what quickly reveals itself to be an angry, menacing narrative, center stage amidst the propulsive syncopation of the instruments.

The timbre and ambience of the voice are essential elements of the ensuing drama, and clear indicators of the protagonist's inner conflict; the abrupt changes between Jagger's relaxed, sombre lower register and his choked, aggressive upper range that demarcate each half of the first four verses highlight his turmoil. The use of reverb, applied globally over the mix, adds an additional layer of meaning and invites several potential readings. Serge Lacasse points to the use of reverb in early French radio broadcasts and later, in the films of Alfred Hitchcock, as aural indicators of a perspective taken from within the character's mind. Drawing on the observations of French cinema and radio theorist Étienne Fuzellier, he states, "the advent of electrical vocal staging [via reverb] . . . allowed [for the representation of] a psychological action directly from the interior, literally eavesdropping on a character's mind, or to create parallel worlds . . ."[19] Here, the presence of reverb, heavy in the first half and light in the second half of each verse, highlights Jagger's torn emotional state and implies a continually shifting discourse. This effect is amplified by the width of the voice in the mix. For example, during the opening "I see a red door and I want it painted black," the spectrum of Jagger's voice is incredibly wide, covering the area roughly between 40 degrees (left) and 140 degrees (right) of the 180-degree stereo field. Conversely, during the second half of the verse beginning "I see the girls walk by dressed in their summer clothes," the sitar disappears and the stereo width of the voice suddenly collapses, suggesting the juxtaposition of internal monologue and external declamation.

Lacasse also explores pre-electronic vocal staging in past cultures and non-Western traditions, noting its universal association with ritual and spectacle, and that the diffuse quality of such resonant sounds creates the illusion of sound coming simultaneously from everywhere and nowhere, suggesting power and mystery.[20] If such is the case, then any aspirations toward transcendence evoked by the ambient quality of the mix and the allusion to non-Western music/spirituality are especially ironic. Superficially, many of the song's musical attributes might parallel the music of the Beatles and their contemporaries; but for a counterculture that looked eastward for spiritual enlightenment and an alternative to their normative Judeo-Christian upbringing, the stark juxtaposition of "Paint It, Black"'s bleak narrative with sonic links to hippie idealism borders on satire.

As "anti-Beatles," the Stones actively cultivated their image as outsiders, a contrarianism that was particularly glaring at the height of 1960s bohemianism. The nihilistic tone of "Paint It, Black," or later works like "Midnight Rambler," "Stray Cat Blues," and "Sympathy for the Devil," embraces themes far removed from the majority of their contemporaries while remaining central to those of the satirist: madness, violence, and apocalyptic chaos. As true satirists, the Stones enacted and performed madness through their recordings and live shows. Their representations of excess – violence, obsession, addiction, and sexual glut – shone a spotlight upon the ills of society.[21]

After *Their Satanic Majesties Request* (1967), their first album without Andrew Loog Oldham, the Stones – at the recommendation of engineer Glyn Johns – began their enormously successful (and as it turned out, regrettably short) partnership with Jimmy Miller, the American producer brought to England by Chris Blackwell to work with the Spencer Davis Group. Miller's five-year tenure with the Stones, beginning with *Beggars Banquet* (1968), marked what is often regarded as their finest work.[22] The album's opening song, "Sympathy for the Devil," left no doubt – if there ever was any – as to the color of hat the Stones wore.

Recorded at Olympic Studios' relatively new home on Church Road in Barnes, the two-day evolution of "Sympathy for the Devil" from its folky, Dylanesque beginning as brought into the session by Jagger into its densely textured, frenetic samba, serves as the musical centrepiece to Jean-Luc Godard's film *One Plus One*. Later retitled *Sympathy for the Devil*, against the director's wishes, the film documents the song's gradual transformation interspersed with scenes depicting contemporaneous revolutionary ideology (see Figure 6.1). Although band members remain grateful for its existence, their responses to the film as a whole are at best ambivalent: "Nobody, I think, has ever quite honestly been able to figure out what the hell he was aiming at . . . I'm glad he filmed that but Godard! . . . The film was a total load of crap . . ."[23] Issues of intelligibility aside, *One Plus One* offers valuable insights into the band's characteristically free approach to recording in which seminal ideas are allowed to develop in an organic and largely spontaneous process.

Olympic Studios is synonymous with British pop, its roster of employees and list of clients representing the most famous names in the industry.

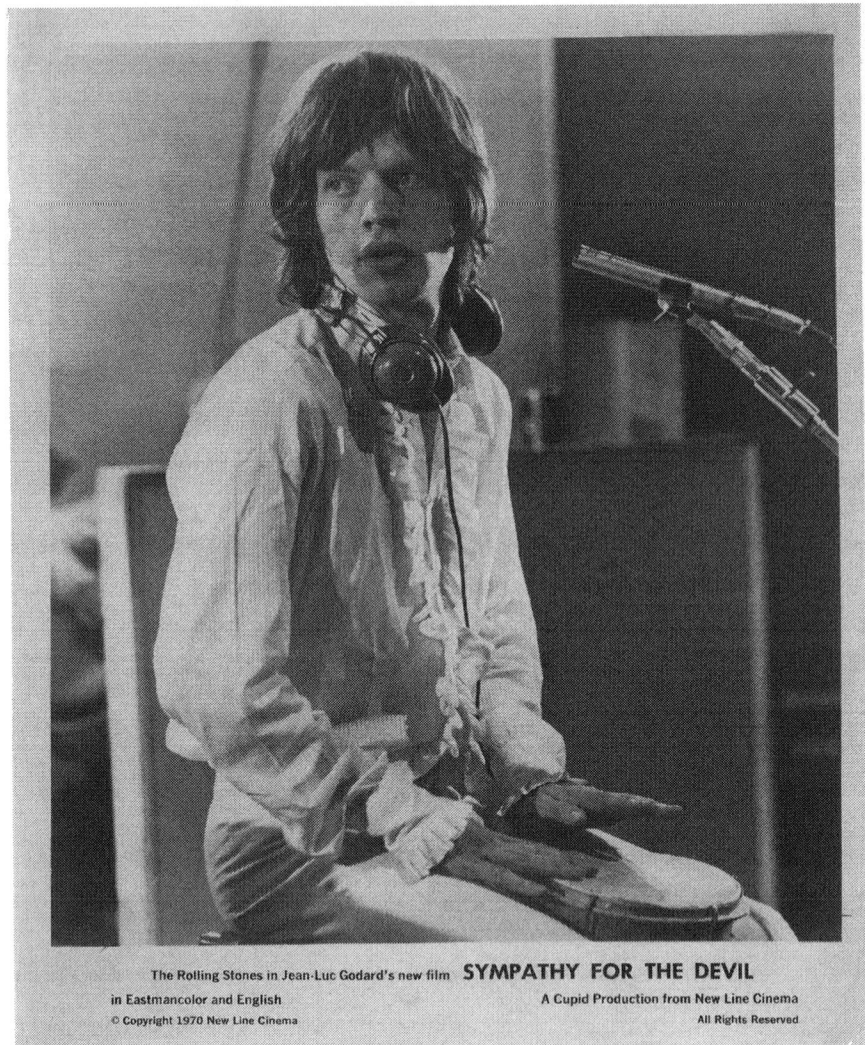

The Rolling Stones in Jean-Luc Godard's new film **SYMPATHY FOR THE DEVIL**

in Eastmancolor and English   A Cupid Production from New Line Cinema

© Copyright 1970 New Line Cinema   All Rights Reserved

Figure 6.1 Publicity shot with Mick Jagger for Godard's *Sympathy for the Devil* [*One Plus One*], 1970. Jeff Gold Collection, Library and Archives, Rock and Roll Hall of Fame and Museum.

Originally located on Carlton Street near Piccadilly, it served as the location of the Stones' first hit recording in 1963 of Chuck Berry's "Come On."[24] In 1966 an expiring lease forced Olympic to move, settling eventually on a former television studio in the Barnes area of Richmond. A once derelict building, massive renovations for the studio included the construction of walls with no parallel surfaces in Studio One, and the design of Studio Two as a completely floating box, suspended by rubber pads on seventeen tons of steel framework.[25] Revolutionary, ergonomic wrap-around mixing consoles for both rooms were conceived by studio manager and chief engineer Keith Grant, and were hand built by chief technician Dick Swettenham.[26] They featured Lustraphone transformers and germanium transistors, the resulting third-order harmonic distortion a vital component to the Olympic sound. Clearly, the Stones found the venue more than acceptable: From 1966 to 1972 they recorded the better part of six albums there. In 1969, Jagger was even recruited as interior designer and decorator for Studio Two.[27]

"Sympathy for the Devil" is an absorbing passage through an evolving soundscape, where the music's gradual thickening texture, its slowly increasing volume and pitch, and its increasingly harsh timbre coincide with the narrative's path from prehistory to modernity. According to Jagger, the main character in "Sympathy for the Devil" is:

> a very long historical figure – the figures of evil and figures of good – so it is a tremendously long trail he's made as personified in this piece . . . It has a very hypnotic groove, a samba, which has tremendous hypnotic power . . . it's also got some other suggestions in it, an undercurrent of being primitive – because it is a primitive African, South American, Afro-whatever-you-call-that rhythm. So to white people, it has a very sinister thing about it. But forgetting the cultural colors, it is a very good vehicle for producing a powerful piece.[28]

The introduction of "Sympathy for the Devil" opens on a primeval scene with Watts performing tablas on the far left of the stereo field, then joined by percussionist Rocky "Dijon" Dzidzomu playing congas on the far right. Jagger's voice enters, a distant animalistic yowl panned slightly left that echoes into the far right. The setting is expansive, mysterious, even frightening. The successive layering of maracas, soft laughter, and grunts and groans positioned at various points across the soundscape quickly surround the listener, setting the stage for the following encounter and effectively foreshadowing the piece's overall shape in miniature. The entrance of the anti-hero is startlingly abrupt, his voice dead center at the front of the mix, the complete lack of ambience suggesting an uncomfortable closeness: The devil is crooning in your ear, with carefully elongated sibilants of his prefatory, "Please allow me to introduce myself, I'm a man of wealth and taste," unsettlingly serpentine. Flanked by Richards on bass guitar panned near-left and Nicky Hopkins on piano near-right, his importance is reinforced by their long, held chords in an ironic evocation of gospel music.[29]

In the ensuing discourse, various musical elements accompany the character's relentless passage through human history. At references to the Crucifixion during verse one, the bass (played by Richards) adopts the dance rhythms of the percussion ensemble. Far right, the brief chatter of the backing singers that frames the first statement of the song's chorus signals their growing restlessness. In verse two the story moves forward through the bloodshed of the last Russian czar and the stench of mechanized Blitzkrieg, where the piano also becomes rhythmically infected by the samba's irresistible allure, intensified by Watts' cymbal splashes on the downbeat. In the following verse, we are drawn into the present by the carnivalesque "oo-oohs" of the now unconfined backing singers, co-celebrants in humanity's shared guilt at the demise of the Kennedys. Appropriately, the next musical figure to enter the soundstage is Richards' overdubbed electric guitar just past the midway point of the song, the first incontrovertibly modern sound to appear. Playing on his Les Paul through a highly overdriven Vox AC-30 tube amplifier, his center-panned guitar is distorted and abrasive, perfectly matching Jagger's timbre and momentarily becoming the Devil's voice as Jagger reverts to sporadic grunts and vocalizations further back in the mix. Not surprisingly, the riffs are unmistakeably blues based.

Jagger's vocal trajectory matches that of the instrumental texture, gradually moving from low to high and from clear to rough. In verse one, the melody occupies a fairly narrow range situated closely around b. During the first chorus, the rising melodic line is centered around d♯′, at times reaching e′. In the first half of the second verse, Jagger's vocal grows increasingly forced, insistent, and agitated; at "I rode a tank at the general's rank" the vocal suddenly jumps to e′, becoming mildly distorted and growly, and in the following chorus the range is higher yet, circling around f♯′ and getting as high as g♯′ before returning to e′. The melody of verse four begins where it was left on e′, but now with many blue notes reaching g′, and during the third chorus Jagger's vocal is distorted further with even more time spent around g♯′. Here the guitar solo begins, its first two licks ending on the same note where the vocals left off, then gradually climbing to settle a full octave higher. The following, final chorus is punctuated by Jagger's frequent deployment of g′ blue notes, conspicuously placed on strong beats or at the beginning of phrases, his ever-growing excitement signalled by an increasingly strained vocal timbre. The closing jam session over the final 1:46 of the song sees Jagger's falsetto extend a full octave higher, sometimes screaming, bordering on caricature in a blues-like call and response with Richards' guitar. As the music gradually fades, the vocal returns to its primal state, echoing from near-left to far-right, apparently unaffected by the passage of time and leaving the listener to wonder if the dance will ever end.

Streets Running Red

I don't think they understand what we're trying to do . . . or what Mick's talking about, like on "Street Fighting Man." We're not saying we want to be in the streets, but we're a rock and roll band, just the reverse. Those kids at the press conferences want us to do their thing, not ours. Politics is what we were trying to get away from in the first place.[30]

Although some may disagree, until their inevitable transition from angry young men of the 1960s into respected post-1980s rock royalty, the Rolling Stones epitomized rock's subversive, rebellious image – and in many ways, they still do. While it's true they rarely engaged in overt political activities as visibly as John Lennon and Yoko Ono's Montreal "bed-in," one can't overlook Jagger's arrest for participating in the 1968 anti-Vietnam protest march on the US embassy in Grosvenor Square, whose violent culmination helped inspire "Street Fighting Man."[31] Jagger later sent the song's hand-written lyrics to New Left leader Tariq Ali, who published them in the November 1968 issue of the radical *Black Dwarf* newspaper. Ali and many of his brothers-in-arms felt the song's message was perfectly clear: "Well, I thought they [the lyrics] were very ultra-left actually, when we heard the song and tried to sing it we thought, 'God, it's a bit far out even for us.' But it reflected the mood. This is a sleepy town, why aren't we doing anything!"[32] Later, Jagger attributed "Street Fighting Man" to the political turmoil at home and the violent upheavals in France that resulted in the near collapse of DeGaulle's government.[33]

"Street Fighting Man" opens the second side of *Beggars Banquet* and balances side one's opening "Sympathy for the Devil," the exposed positioning of both songs made all the more conspicuous on an album composed almost entirely of rural Americana. In March of 1968 the Stones, together with producer Jimmy Miller and engineer Eddie Kramer, began pre-production for the album at RG Studios in Morden where several demos were produced, including "Primo Grande," which became "Did Everybody Pay Their Dues" and ultimately evolved into "Street Fighting Man."[34] Sessions at Olympic Studios commenced in March and lasted until June 10.[35]

By now, Richards was in a process of reinventing his playing style, adopting an open D-tuning (a standard open E-tuning lowered to D) following the example of blues players from the 1920s and 1930s. In addition to playing a Fender Precision bass for the song, Richards layered as many as eight acoustic guitar parts, a Gibson Hummingbird tuned variably in open D, in standard tuning, and in open five-string G-tuning using a capo in various positions. "There's lots of guitars you don't even hear. They're just shadowing."[36] Other instrumental overdubs included

Watts' Ludwig kit, Jones on sitar and tambura, Nicky Hopkins on piano, and Dave Mason on shenhai, an Indian double-reed instrument brought in by Jones.

The main instrumental bed was recorded with the group huddled around a Phillips EL3302 portable recorder and its stock dynamic microphone owned by Richards, an early model cassette recorder that had no built-in limiter to prevent distortion. The idea came from Richards, who used the machine to record rough drafts of the band in his home and thought it was a shame they couldn't get the same sound for the finished song. Jimmy Miller suggested transferring the cassette to 4-track. The session saw Richards and Jones playing acoustic guitars, positioned behind Watts playing a portable, suitcase practice kit with Jagger on maracas. This was then piped through studio monitors to an Ampex 4-track tape machine and then transferred to 8-track tape.[37]

It's no wonder that "Street Fighting Man" caught the interest of Tariq Ali's New Left. If visions of charging feet, fighting, and revolution set to a driving, hard-rock march weren't enough to capture listeners' attention, then the song's powerful, rebellious sound surely would have. Aural representations of power abound, starting with Richards' introductory cassette-recorded guitar riff, the heavy distortion of saturated tape completely subverting conventional hi-fi aesthetics and rendering its otherwise acoustic earthiness harsh, technological, and urban. Panned far-right, it begins in solitary isolation but is joined after two bars by Watts' heavy tom-tom shots on the left. The two are soon augmented by hi-hats and a second, clean acoustic guitar on the left, Watts playing his cassette-recorded suitcase kit along with Jagger's maracas panned right, followed by the driving ostinato of Richards' overdubbed bass in the middle.

Jagger's voice joins the fray, its heavily syncopated rhythm avoiding resolution until the final word of the line, "boy," in a melodic setting clearly evoking the sound of a police siren. His track is doubled and the twin Jaggers are panned on opposite sides of the stereo field, lending additional weight to the text and suggesting strength in numbers. Upon reaching the chorus, the ranks swell further with more acoustic guitar "shadowing," additional percussion, and the drone of Jones' sitar highlighting the song's hook and reinforcing its countercultural ties. This is further strengthened during the outro with the appearance of Dave Mason's droning shenhai, surprisingly placed within the structure in a spot conventionally accorded to the guitar solo. As the principal musical forces begin to fade, Nicky Hopkins' piano moves slowly forward in the mix performing a triplet pattern set in rhythmic opposition to the main beat and contradicting the harmonic stasis of the music. Has the fighting just begun?

Rock music has provided auditory symbols of rebellion, subversion, and empowerment for its participants since the beginning; this is nowhere more evident than in songs like "Street Fighting Man" and "Gimme Shelter," the opening track to *Beggars Banquet*'s follow-up album, *Let It Bleed*. Of the many elements used to convey these symbols, distortion is one of the most essential. In his seminal book *Running with the Devil*, Robert Walser discussed its importance at length, noting its tendency to enlarge and empower the audio signal to which it is applied. Further, its subversion of hi-fi norms is an overt act of transgression and helps reinforce the music's rebellious attitude. Finally, the sound of overdriven electronics is analogous to the sound of the overdriven, distorted cries of vocal screams and assists in communicating extreme agitation or uncontained, irrepressible emotion.[38]

In February of 1969, the Stones reconvened at Olympic for a series of sessions that would ultimately produce the bulk of *Let It Bleed*. Brian Jones' continual deterioration and eventual dismissal from the band meant that Richards carried the bulk of the guitar duties for the majority of the songs on the album (in truth, this had already been the case for some time) until Mick Taylor was brought in as Jones' replacement late in May. Jagger also played guitar on several tracks.[39]

Jagger remembered the period around the recording of *Beggars Banquet* and *Let It Bleed* as a tumultuous one:

> Well, it's a very rough, very violent era. The Vietnam War. Violence on the screens, pillage and burning. And Vietnam was not war we knew in the conventional sense . . . It was a real nasty war, and people didn't like it. People objected, and people didn't want to fight it. The people that were there weren't doing well. There were these things that were always used before, but no one knew about them – like napalm . . . That's [i.e. "Gimme Shelter"] a kind of end-of-the-world song, really. It's apocalypse; the whole record's like that.[40]

The bed tracks for "Gimme Shelter" were among the last completed for the album. Richards played an Australian-made slimline hollow-body electric Maton SE777 through a Triumph Silicon 100 amplifier whose built-in tremolo forms an integral part of the track's sound. The guitar literally fell apart just as the last chords of the final take were struck, coming to its own apocalyptic end. Additional musicians included Nicky Hopkins on keyboards and Jimmy Miller on tambourine.[41] Singer Merry Clayton was called in as a replacement for Bonnie Bramlett, originally slated for the job. According to engineer Glyn Johns, Clayton was late-term pregnant, unimpressed at being summoned from bed by a group she had never heard of, and only acquiesced to come to the late-night session to satisfy the pleas of her husband. Johns recounted, "none of us had ever heard anything quite like what she produced that night. I practically had to stand her in another room, her voice was so powerful. She did three amazing takes, standing there with her hair still in curlers, and went home."[42]

The sense of rising frustration and apocalyptic dread reflected in Jagger's previous comment are apparent within the first few iterations of the song's opening chord progression, initially performed on Richards' solitary Maton electric and quickly joined by backing vocals, percussion, and Watts' light accompaniment on kick, snare, and cymbals. Several additional guitars augment the gradually thickening texture, set against a single-note ostinato played on the bass immediately imitated on the lower keys of the piano. The general direction is one of descent, both in terms of the succession of instrumental registers and the downward C#–B–A of the chord progression. At around 0:40, two bullet shots on Watts' snare shock the instrumental collective into a single, unified statement of the riff before settling in to a monochordal groove that serves as the verse's bed. All of the instruments are placed unusually close to the center of the soundscape, with Richards' pulsating guitar, fat and crunchy, occupying both sides of the stereo field simultaneously.[43] A final blues lick on a center-panned electric guitar, prominently forward in the mix, marks the end of the introduction and announces the arrival of Jagger's vocal.

Jagger enters nearly overwhelmed by the crowded instrumental texture; his melody occupies the same range as the proceeding guitar and his voice sounds similarly effected and compressed. Indeed, their sonic resemblance and ongoing exchange throughout the song identify them as co-narrators. The chorus is marked by Merry Clayton's dramatic, emotionally charged entrance, soaring above Jagger's warning: "Oh, children, it's just a shot away, it's just a shot away!" She is joined at around 2:00 by her own co-narrator, a blues harp whose severely distorted sound closely matches her intense vocal quality and emotional distress. During the song's climax, Clayton reaches the threshold of her range and the limit of self-control: Her voice breaks repeatedly with her cries of, "Rape, murder, it's just a shot away, it's just a shot away!" to the relentless accompaniment of the riff.

The release of *Let It Bleed* on December 5, 1969 just a day before the tragedy of Altamont was sadly prophetic: The deteriorating events culminating in the death of Meredith Hunter are often seen as a turning point away from the optimism of the late 1960s to the pessimism of the following decade. The gradual hardening of the Stones' sound over the course of their first decade runs parallel with the growing frustration of the counter-culture. Despite wishes to remain politically ambivalent (or at least aloof) the Stones found themselves front and center of politics. As generational spokesmen, the Stones challenged existing institutions and helped forge a new identity for youth without the need to be overtly political, bringing leftist ideology squarely into the center of mainstream consciousness.[44]

Earth Tones

I firmly believe that if you want to be a guitar player, you better start on acoustic and then graduate to electric. Don't think you're going to be Townshend or Hendrix just because you can go *wee wee wah wah*.[45]

As hard-rocking as their sound and image often is, even the most casual listener could likely name a song or two by the Stones featuring acoustic instruments; it is an aspect of their sound as fundamental as their grounding in American folk, country, and Delta blues. For a counterculture emerging from the turmoil of the late 1960s and looking to the unfolding decade with growing mistrust, acoustic music hearkened nostalgically to the innocence of the movement's early optimism and Dylan's assertion that the times were a-changin'. A similar situation existed for British audiences still within earshot of the skiffle craze of the late 1950s and the Marxist leanings associated with their own folk revival in the 1960s.

By the early 1970s, however, the landscape of popular music was often dominated by technological sounds: overdriven electric guitars and basses, keyboards such as the Hammond B-3, the mellotron with its "canned" orchestral sounds, and the futuristic resonances of the synthesizer and studio processing that completely transformed the natural qualities of instruments and voices. For contemporaneous listeners, recourse to acoustic instruments and "natural" vocal performances signified a shedding of the trappings of technology in a romantic return to a simpler, more authentic experience.

The use of acoustic instruments and connotations of authenticity are completely embedded in music of the period. One need only look to Bob Dylan's controversial performance on electric guitar at the 1965 Newport Jazz Festival, where the show was repeatedly interrupted by booing. The strong link between perceived authenticity and acoustic performances also extends to the British blues revival as experienced first-hand by Richards during a performance by Muddy Waters on electric guitar around 1961: "Muddy and the band were playing great. It was a knockout band . . . But for this audience, blues was only blues if somebody got up there in a pair of old blue dungarees and sang about how his old lady left him . . . What did electric have to do with it? . . . They wanted a frozen frame . . ."[46]

As unfortunate as some of these perceptions were, the integration of acoustic elements by the Stones and their contemporaries fulfilled several important functions: Like their connection with the blues, it linked the Stones with earlier musical traditions, positing them as informed scholars of popular music's greater history; it also allowed them to demonstrate their versatility and true skill as players without the benefit of modern technology (Richards' "wee wee wah wah"); finally, it offered enormous potential for experimentation and dramatic tension, especially when acoustic and electric instruments were deliberately set against each other on an album or within a song.

In "Sister Morphine," the Stones used the acoustic/electric dialectic to great effect. An early version of the song was released as a 1969 single sung by Marianne Faithfull with Mick Jagger on acoustic guitar, Ry Cooder on electric guitar, Charlie Watts on drums, and Jack Nitzsche on piano. Work on a Stones version began early in 1969 during the Olympic sessions for *Let It Bleed* and was completed for release on *Sticky Fingers* (1971).[47] The song begins in stark isolation, with Richards' melancholic acoustic guitar accompanying Jagger's soft vocal, "Here I lie in my hospital bed. Tell me, Sister Morphine, when are you coming 'round again?" The lack of ambience is disquieting, especially on an album where vocal enhancement via reverb, echo effects, console saturation, and augmentation by backing vocals is more evident. Here, the thin timbre and barren soundscape convey a sense of fragility and isolation unlike any other moment on the album.

As early as 1936, film theorist and perceptual psychologist Rudolph Arnheim described the impact of sounds recorded in deadened vs. resonant spaces, noting that sounds devoid of ambience imply that the recorded sound comes from the same space that the listener occupies, since it bears the same sonic footprint. Ambient sounds, on the other hand, create the sense of listening in on a foreign space.[48] In "Sister Morphine," the protagonist is located squarely within the listener's ambient space, narrow and focused in the center of the stereo field. Devoid of studio enhancement, accompanied by a solitary acoustic guitar, he is organic, natural, and vulnerable.

The unfolding narrative reveals an accident victim's return to consciousness, accompanied by fleeting images of his ordeal, his growing understanding of his predicament, and the unavoidability of his approaching death.[49] Although Jagger has stated that the story is meant to be taken at face value, associations with drug addiction are surely viable, especially in light of the song's auditory cues. The first figure to disturb Jagger's space is Ry Cooder's slide guitar on the far right; the generous use of reverb marks it as an outsider and its thick electric timbre throws the acoustic guitar's woody naturalness in sharp relief while Jagger confides, "The scream of the ambulance is sounding in my ears." As his voice rises in pitch and intensity, it also becomes lightly impacted by reverb, joined now by Wyman's fretless bass encroaching on the left during the line, "What am I doing in this place?" The final word in the closing line of verse two is heavily soaked in reverb: "Can't you see, Sister Morphine, I'm trying to *score*." In the following verse, the instrumental texture is further thickened by the palpitating heartbeat of Watts' bass drum, dry like Jagger's vocal and sharing his placement in the center of the stereo field. This is suddenly followed by Nicky Hopkins' angular piano flourishes: Significantly, the sound of the keyboard is so heavily treated with reverb as to render it almost unrecognizable and place it effectively *behind* the vocal. Watts' pulse quickens as he engages more of his kit, his once dry, natural sound tainted by reverb and echo. The protagonist is caged in on all sides of the soundscape, his once natural acoustic presence slowly enclosed in sounds twisted by machinery. During the song's long fade, his final shouts of "hey" become part of the ambient wash: Has the story teller shed his mortal coil or succumbed to his addiction?[50]

Blues at the Crossroads

The silence is your canvas, that's your frame, that's what you work on; don't try and deafen it out.[51]

From their inception as green but passionate artists of a nascent 1960s British blues revival through to their most recent album *Blue and Lonesome* (2016), the Rolling Stones have been working on their canvas for well over half a century and show no signs of stopping. Convening at Mark Knopfler's British Grove Studios in London, sessions for *Blue and Lonesome* marked the first time in over a decade that the band would begin work on a new album. According to Knopfler, the studio "is probably analog's last great shout ... But it also incorporates the best of the latest digital technology ..."[52] Knopfler's long-time co-producer Chuck Ainlay described the facility as "a monument to past and future technology. The studio has an API Legacy in one of the rooms and a new 96-frame Neve 88R in the other room with a bunch of older Neve-style modules. There are also two old EMI consoles ..."[53] After several days in British Grove with little new material to show for it, Richards suggested a new tack:

> I called Ronnie up a few weeks before the session, I say, "Get this blues track down, just because we might need it to get the sound in the room together ..." After two days, it proved to be true that this room is fighting us, so I said, "Ronnie, 'Blue and Lonesome'." And after that, it all fell into place ... This record just sort-of happened ... it imposed itself.[54]

Over the course of five days, twelve tracks were recorded, and to their own surprise the Stones produced the first album comprised entirely of blues covers in their long history.

"Just Your Fool," the raucous Buddy Johnson/Little Walter opener on *Blue and Lonesome*, perfectly encapsulates the Stones' longstanding alignment with the blues. Within the first twelve bars, before Jagger has uttered a word, the band has told us everything we need to know about their roots: the harmonica, Jagger's surrogate voice, moans and wails front and center amidst a soundscape bristling with energy, driven by Watts' steadfast pulse, now as in the past always a calculated hair or two behind Richards' lead. The electric guitar is distorted and crunchy as the bass throbs below, adding to the riff's thickness and weight. Occasionally, distant snatches of honky-tonk piano evoke the ghost of Ian Stewart. Jagger's voice enters with authority and swagger, its timbre as crunchy as the guitar, the distortion and heavy proximity effect signalling his insistence on being heard. The club-like ambience of the track envelopes the full collective of musicians and for a moment, against all we know to be true, we are transported to a small bar in Ealing or Richmond to reconnect with the past and reaffirm long-shared beliefs.

Just how long the Stones will be guiding listeners through the Crossroads remains an open question, but according to Richards there are no immediate plans to retire: "It's what we do man – we enjoy doing it and there's thousands of people out there and they enjoy it too. You can't be a party pooper, right?!"[55]

Notes

1 Beckotube, "Rolling Stones: Keith Richards on *Blue and Lonesome* with Becko from Triple M," Sydney, December 6, 2016: www.youtube.com/watch?v=0aHpFAujp7Y (accessed February 22, 2019), transcription by the author.

2 Serge Lacasse, "'Listen to My Voice': The Evocative Power of Voice in Recorded Rock Music and Other Forms of Vocal Expression" (Ph.D. diss., Liverpool, 2000), 16–18. The most significant study of this type is Albin J. Zak, *The Poetics of Rock: Cutting Tracks, Making Records* (Berkeley and Los Angeles, 2001).

3 *Life*, 103–4.

4 *RSG*, 137–8; for a complete account of the September 1964 Regent sessions, see *RSCRS*, 46–7.

5 *Life*, 128.

6 Quoted in Janovitz*RO*, 29. The Regent Studio still stands but has been repurposed as an instrument retail shop. On display are Stones memorabilia as well as the Studer mastering tape machine used through the 1960s and 1970s.

7 For details of the Chess sessions, see *RSCRS*, 51–2. On early Stones songs recorded by other artists, see the chapter by John Covach in this volume, 10.

8 *Life*, 160–1.

9 A detailed account of the instruments and amplifiers used in the Regent Sound sessions can be found in *RSG*, 104–5. Columbia Records' 1961 release of *King of the Delta Blues Singers* first introduced British audiences to the music of Robert Johnson.

10 Quoted in Lacasse, "Listen to My Voice," 124.

11 The band's November 20, 1964 British TV appearance on *Ready, Steady, Go!* is a good example; see *RSCRS*, 52.

12 From *The Rolling Stones: Crossfire Hurricane*, directed by Brett Morgen (Milkwood Films/ Tremolo Productions, 2013), transcription by the author.

13 Stereo mixes were nevertheless a relatively new phenomenon, and album releases in stereo often followed initial monaural releases, with or without the involvement of the band during mixing. Mono releases of singles, the mix that most listeners would have experienced, continued to be the norm until the end of the 1960s.

14 The Stones worked prodigiously at RCA during this period. See *RSCRS*, 68–75, 77–81.

15 Quoted in Wenner*MJR*, 57.

16 *RSG*, 220–1. Jones vehemently denied accusations of following the Beatles, saying, "What utter rubbish . . . You might as well say that we copy all the other groups by playing guitar." Quoted in Janovitz*RO*, 94.

17 Zak, *The Poetics of Rock*, 62. See also Brita Renée Heimarck's chapter in this volume, 142–61, applying the synchronous term, derived from Deleuze, of *assemblage*.

18 *RSG*, 219–23.

19 Lacasse, "Listen to My Voice," 78. The editorial emendations clarify Lacasse's original: "the advent of electrical vocal staging also allowed to represent a psychological action directly from the interior. . ."

20 *Ibid.*, 70, 39.

21 Michael Powers, "The Rolling Stones: Danceable Mythic Satire," *Popular Music and Society* 10 (2008), 46.

22 *RSG*, 274.

23 *Life*, 252.

24 *RSCRS*, 18.

25 The avoidance of parallel surfaces in acoustic spaces is to minimize undesirable reflections and frequency buildup or "room modes."

26 Swettenham came to Olympic from Abbey Road and later founded Helios Electronics Ltd. Swettenham and Helios were hired for the custom build of the Stones mobile unit's mixing desk.

27 An insider's account of the history of Olympic Studios from the early 1960s to its closing in 2009 is in Matt Frost, "Keith Grant: The Story of Olympic Studios," *Sound On Sound* (August, 2012), 146–53.

28 Wenner*MJR*, 58.

29 Early scenes from Godard's *One Plus One* show Hopkins playing organ, an instrument whose historical association with the church would have created a similar (or greater) sense of irony.

30 From a 1969 interview with Keith Richards, quoted in Patrick Burke, "Rock, Race, and Radicalism in the 1960s: The Rolling Stones, Black Power, and Godard's *One Plus One*," *Journal of Musicological Research* 29 (2010), 275–94, at 287.

31 Joseph Foy, "How Come You're So Wrong, My Sweet Neo-Con?" in *The Rolling Stones and Philosophy: It's Just a Thought Away*, ed. L. Dick and G. Reisch (Chicago, 2011), 203.

32 Leo Burley, "Jagger vs Lennon: London's Riots of 1968 Provided the Backdrop to a Rock 'n' Roll Battle Royale," *The Independent* (March 9, 2008): www.independent.co.uk/arts-entertainment/ music/features/jagger-vs-lennon-londons-riots-of-1968-provided-the-backdrop-to-a-rocknroll- battle-royale-792450.html (accessed February 22, 2019).

33 Wenner*MJR*, 60.

34 *RSG*, 275.

35 Engineer Eddie Kramer was replaced by Glyn Johns for the Olympic sessions; see *RSCRS*, 98–103, 105–6.

36 *RSG*, 274–9.

37 *RSG*, 277–80; see also Robert Greenfield, "Keith Richard: The Rolling Stone Interview" (August 19, 1971): www.rollingstone.com/music/music-news/keith-richard-the-rolling-stone-interview- 238909/ (accessed February 22, 2019). "Jumpin' Jack Flash" and parts of "Gimme Shelter" are recorded in a similar fashion; see *Life*, 240.

38 See Robert Walser, *Running with the Devil: Power, Gender, and Madness in Heavy Metal Music* (Middletown, 1993); on the relationship of amplification and distortion to expressions of race and Blackness, see Steve Waksman, *Instruments of Desire: The Electric Guitar and the Shaping of Musical Experience* (Cambridge, MA, 1999), chapters 4 and 5.

39 *RSG*, 310.

40 Wenner*MJR*, 60–1.

41 Richards had by this point developed his signature open five-string G tuning, influenced in part by Ry Cooder's involvement on some of the sessions; see *RSG*, 313. Unlike Cooder and traditional blues players, Richards dispenses with the slide bar and explores the potential of alternate tunings and the new, fingered chord shapes they necessitate; see Richards, *Life*, 241–6.

42 Glyn Johns, *Sound Man* (New York, 2014), 148. Vocal overdubs were done at Sunset Sound and Elektra Studios in Los Angeles.

43 Richards had discovered a method of overheating his Triumph amplifiers to the point of near failure in order to produce the unique sound captured on "Gimme Shelter." See Janovitz*RO*, 176.

44 Foy, "How Come You're So Wrong," 203.

45 *Life*, 70.

46 *Ibid.*, 83.

47 See Wenner*MJR*, 64, and Greenfield, "Keith Richard"; Marianne Faithfull filed suit and was eventually credited as co-author with Jagger and Richards.

48 See Lacasse, "Listen to My Voice," 101.

49 According to Marianne Faithfull (*Faithfull*, 167–8), who wrote the lyrics, "People tend to assume that 'Sister Morphine' comes from an incident in my life, that it is a parable of a junkie's last hours . . . [but] 'Sister Morphine' is the story of a man who has had a terrible car accident. He's dying and he's in tremendous pain and the lyrics of the song are addressed to the nurse."

50 The use of multiple levels of ambience is discussed in Zak, *The Poetics of Rock*, 82–5.

51 *Life*, 58.

52 Rick Clark, "Mark Knopfler – Best of Old and New," *mixonline.com*, May 1, 2005: https://www.mixonline.com/recording/mark-knopfler-375278 (accessed March 5, 2019).

53 *Ibid.*

54 Beckotube, "Rolling Stones," transcription by the author.

55 Scott Colothon, "LISTEN: Keith Richards Talks UK Tour, New Rolling Stones Album and Retirement," *Planet Rock* (February 27, 2018): www.planetrock.com/news/rock-news/listen-keith-richards-talks-uk-tour-new-rolling-stones-album-and-retirement/ (accessed February 22, 2019).

7 Driving Stones Country in Five Songs

DANIEL BELLER-MCKENNA

Fashioning identity has always been at the heart of the Rolling Stones' music and mystique. From their origins as white English teenagers delving as deeply into black American rhythm and blues as any band in Britain (or the States, for that matter) at the time, to their post-sixties forays into glam rock, reggae, disco, and other diversions, they rode into the twenty-first century as a self-defining "classic," parlaying their status as one of the most accomplished and longest-lasting bands of the rock era into a self-sustaining mega act. Through it all, the initial connection to the blues remains the stylistic marker to which they are most often associated, an influence that has come full circle with their recent Grammy Award-winning album of blues covers, *Blue and Lonesome* of 2016. As they came to public attention, the overtly African-American implications of the blues provided the Stones with an edgy cultural distinction. To be sure, other British invaders built their sound on a foundation of blues artists from the 1930s through the early 1960s, but as the Stones rose to prominence among such acts, they were drawn into a binary relationship with the Beatles, whose style was more obviously eclectic and whose identity was driven by the commercial agenda of their manager Brian Epstein. This proved especially true in the States when each group arrived for tours in 1964. It is no surprise, for example, that when the Beatles had a few days off on their initial visit to the USA in February, 1964, they remained in Miami (where they made their second appearance on the Ed Sullivan Show) to take in nightclub acts at the Deauville Hotel or fishing and riding speed boats around Miami harbor, whereas the Stones took advantage of a five-day gap in their eight-city, cross-country tour to fly to Chicago to record new songs at Chess Studios – to them, a virtual R&B Valhalla. And while they jammed there with heroes like Muddy Waters, Chuck Berry, and Ray Charles, the Beatles' only close contact with a black cultural figure came in a light-hearted photo-op with Muhammad Ali (then Cassius Clay), who was in Miami training for a title fight.

Painting the Stones "black" and the Beatles "not black" is, of course, overly simplistic to the point of being misleading. The Beatles incorporated plenty of R&B (and more still, Tamla Motown) influences into their version of the "Merseybeat" sound. But like many other influences, it is a skillful amalgamation with a wide variety of musical styles, from pre-war

Music Hall tunefulness and Sun Records rockabilly, to the Bakersfield twang of Buck Owens. The Bakersfield-influenced "I Don't Want to Spoil the Party," recorded and released in September of 1964, predates their overt nod to Owens with the cover of "Act Naturally" in 1965. By the same token, the Stones' cultivation of the black roots styles dug up a host of musical idioms that are tangled up in the blues. Once one travels back beyond the post-war style shifts occasioned by the introduction of the electric guitar, it becomes harder to draw distinct lines between the rural blues and white folk styles. That admixture did not surface much in the Stones' early albums, but *Beggars Banquet* in 1968 saw a turn towards acoustic instruments, in the aftermath of ever trippier tracks during the preceding year. Keith Richards remarked:

> There was a lot of country and blues on *Beggars Banquet*: "No Expectations,"
> "Dear Doctor," even "Jigsaw Puzzle." "Parachute Woman," "Prodigal
> Son," "Stray Cat Blues," "Factory Girl," they're all either blues or folk
> music ... We had barely explored the stuff where we'd come from or that
> had turned us on. The "Dear Doctor"s and "Country Honk"s and "Love
> in Vain" were, in a way catch-up, things we had to do. The mixture of black
> and white American music had plenty of space to be explored.[1]

The blues half of this equation was quickly recognized as a reboot for the group, returning to their "roots." But the same impulse also spawned a number of country tracks across *Beggars Banquet* and the succeeding albums through the 1970s, a group of songs that form a distinct subset in the Stones' songbook.

The group's early blues covers and originals grew consistently from the electrified R&B of the 1950s. But when the Stones turned to country, they presented a far more variegated picture of an American style that (rightly or wrongly) can be seen as separate from the black musical influence that was so bound up with their own musical identity up to this point. A number of factors led to the heterogeneity of the Stones' country songs; but, more so than the relatively specific locales – Chicago, the Delta, Texas – that the blues represented to them, the diversity in their country output allows these songs to plot a road map representing the geographic sweep of America that the label "country music" covers. Moreover, while the return to the blues in 1968–72 was marked most strongly by the push back beyond the fifties R&B that had been the Stones' earlier inspiration (covers of Muddy Waters, Jimmy Reed, Chuck Berry, Howlin' Wolf, and others on earlier LPs were replaced by ones of Robert Johnson, Fred McDowell, and Robert Wilkins), their foray into country embraced similarly retro styles but also up-to-date country-rock syntheses, reflecting the wide range of the Stones' country influences.

Country Learnin'

Preceding any outside influences, members of the band each brought their own familiarity with country music to the table. Jagger claimed that he and Keith Richards had listened to, written, and recorded country music long before *Beggars Banquet*:

> As far as country music was concerned, we used to play country songs, but we'd never record them – or we recorded them but never released them. Keith and I had been playing Johnny Cash records and listening to the Everly Brothers – who were *so* country – since we were kids. I used to love country music even before I met Keith. I loved George Jones and really fast, shit-kicking country music, though I didn't really like the maudlin songs too much.[2]

A penchant for country music would not make Jagger or Richards unique among sixties British rockers (the Beatles had been penning Bakersfield-influenced songs since 1964: "I'm a Loser," "I Don't Want to Spoil the Party"), but they had displayed only a little interest before *Beggars Banquet*. At least, not on any released material. On a trio of demo recordings from the summer of 1964, Stones manager Andrew Oldham enlisted a number of outside players (members of the "Oldham Orchestra"), including several guitarists who were already highly respected (Big Jim Sullivan) or destined to become major figures (Jimmy Page and John McLaughlin). Someone among them played pedal steel guitar to lend a country tinge to the songs.[3] These tracks only surfaced a decade later on the UK LP *Metamorphosis* (only "Heart of Stone" appeared on the US release of the LP), but demonstrate an early curiosity about country sounds, at least on the part of Oldham: Mick Jagger may have been the only member of the band participating in one or more of these recordings. Of the songs in question (all Jaggers/Richards compositions), "Some Things Just Stick in Your Mind," "We're Wasting Time," and "Heart of Stone," only the latter was rerecorded and released a few months later as a single in the USA, with the pedal steel replaced by Keith Richards' baritone guitar.

It would take a while for the group to air their country interests. A live cover of Hank Snow's "Movin' On" from late 1965 owes more to Ray Charles' 1959 cover than to the original. Months later, on *Aftermath*, the Jagger/Richards song "High and Dry" does more to validate Jagger's claims. As a country song it is a hodgepodge: Richards' overdubbed acoustic guitars are as much a bow to folk music as country, while the relatively loose ensemble conjures an earlier era in country recordings. As in the more frequently referenced country songs in the Stones' output (discussed below), neither Bill Wyman nor Charlie Watts display much affinity for country rhythms. The latter's ringing hi-hat serves to avoid a rock back-beat, but fails to capture the terse simplicity of 1960s country drumming. "I love Hank Williams and Bob Dylan's *Nashville Skyline*, but the whole Nashville thing I'm not that enamoured of," Watts commented years later. "I can enjoy Buck Owens and Bob Wills's swing band and George Jones, but it's not something I'm particularly good at."[4] At the same time, Wyman's repeated notes in "High and Dry" oversimplify the root-fifth alternation of a typical country bassline. Both members would grow and adapt in the country songs of the coming years, but the rhythm section helped to mark these numbers as Rolling Stones tunes, no matter how deeply Richards delved into the world of "Three Chords and Truth" (a phrase widely attributed to legendary Nashville songwriter Harlan Howard) or how often Jagger affected a Southern drawl.

On *Aftermath*, "High and Dry" is one of several forays into new styles for the group, including the quasi-Elizabethan "Lady Jane," the artsy "I Am Waiting," and a smattering across the album of a variety of instruments from outside the rock band line-up.[5] It shows less an interest in exploring country music than in exploring various styles beyond the band's core blues sound. That impulse to widen their stylistic horizons led to the nearly obligatory diversion into the Summer of Love, culminating in the least Stones-like Rolling Stones album of the decade, *Their Satanic Majesties Request*. Though some elements of psychedelia lingered beyond *Majesties*, 1968 marked the band's decisive turn, as noted above, back to the blues on *Beggars Banquet*. By the time the album was released at the end of that year, two critical outside influences had redirected the Stones' stance toward country music: Gram Parsons and Ry Cooder. Their impact on and interaction with the group could hardly be more different. In May, the group encountered Parsons while he was on tour in the UK during his brief stint with the Byrds (indeed, his initial conversations with Jagger and Richards about the band's upcoming tour of Apartheid South Africa convinced Parsons to drop out of the Byrds).

Although Parsons' influence was more personal and more widely acknowledged, Cooder's contribution must be considered for an understanding of what "country" meant to the Stones in the 1970s. Cooder was brought over from the USA by Jack Nitzsche in June of 1968 to jam with the Stones, in order to percolate ideas for a film project (*The Performers*) back in Los Angeles, for which Cooder was to write the soundtrack. While his most notable impact on the group was turning Richards onto the five-string open-G tuning (with which Richards claims he was already experimenting), Cooder also deserves credit for helping to steer the band towards pre-Chicago blues, an era when white and black "country" music were often indistinguishable, when Lesley Riddle could collaborate with the Carter family and Woody Guthrie could sing alongside Lead Belly.[6]

A number of the Stones' songs, from *Beggars Banquet* onward, tap this earthier, organic vein of country music: "Sweet Virginia" from *Exile on Main Street*, and "No Expectations" from *Beggars Banquet*, for example. Nowadays, we might not think to label those songs country, but the concept of "country rock" was broad enough at the end of the sixties to encompass the loose Americana aura of The Band (touted on the cover of *Time Magazine* as "The New Sound of Country Rock"), the straight-ahead honky-tonk of the Byrds' *Sweetheart of the Rodeo*, and the tight-harmony and steel guitar-laden styles coming out of southern California from Poco, The New Riders of the Purple Sage, and others. By contrast, Cooder was himself a product of the late-sixties LA music culture, and his own albums around this time illustrate his interest in everything that scene had to offer, not just the emerging sound of hippie-twang. Through Nitzsche, a record company insider with his own eclectic tastes, Cooder was in contact with other roots-seekers in LA: Randy Newman, Leon Russell (who had already played on many recordings there as a member of the studio band, the Wrecking Crew), and Lowell George, to name a few.[7] Some of that mix probably was conveyed to the Stones in London. Although they had little (documented) contact with those artists, echoes of all the aforementioned can be heard throughout their string of albums from 1968–72, and Russell actually first recorded the Stones' gospel-influenced song "Shine a Light" a few years before it appeared on *Exile*, for his eponymous album of 1970.

Just how much of those influences were directly communicated through Cooder and how much was a matter of a shared musical language is hard to gauge. The relationship between him and the band soured a year later when he was once again brought in by Nitzsche, at the planning stages for the 1969 album *Let It Bleed*. Although he is credited on "Love in Vain" (mandolin) here, and later on "Sister Morphine" (slide guitar) from *Sticky Fingers* (1971), Cooder vented in a 1970 *Rolling Stone* interview about his presence during the *Let It Bleed* sessions, claiming that his riffs were copied by Richards and formed the core sound of the album:

> The Rolling Stones brought me to England under false pretenses. They weren't playing well and were just messing around the studio ... When there'd be a lull in the so-called rehearsals, I'd start to play my guitar. Keith Richards would leave the room immediately and never return. I thought he didn't like me! But, as I found out later, the tapes would keep rolling ...
>
> In the four or five weeks I was there, I must have played everything I know. They got it all down on these tapes. *Everything*.[8]

For their part, the Rolling Stones have downplayed Cooder's influence, allowing only as how he showed Richards many ways to utilize the open G-tuning that became a hallmark of Richards' playing from that point on.

By contrast, Gram Parsons is often assumed to have given the Stones as much material as Ry Cooder complained that they took from him. Yet unlike Cooder, Parsons never claimed any credit or begrudged the band any bits and pieces they might have borrowed. In part, this speaks to the deep personal connection he felt to the band, and to Richards in particular, who spoke of Parsons as a "long-lost brother."[9] On three stints – the first at Richards' Redlands estate in the summer of 1968 following Parsons' decision to abandon the Byrds in July; the second in the fall of 1969 when the Stones took up residence in southern California to complete *Let It Bleed* and prepare for a US Tour; and the third in the summer of 1971 at Richards' Villa Nellcôte in the south of France, where the Stones were recording what would become *Exile* – Parsons and Richards bonded in lengthy explorations of the country canon, with Parsons bringing Richards' youthful familiarity with honky-tonk up to date. His Southern *bona fides* notwithstanding, Parsons himself had only warmed to country music when he arrived in Cambridge, Massachusetts to attend Harvard in the fall of 1965. During his single (mostly truant) semester there, he fell in with a band that would move to the Bronx within a year and become the International Submarine Band. ISB guitarist John Nuese takes credit for immersing Parsons, along with the rest of the band, in the Bakersfield sounds of Merle Haggard and Buck Owens: "Gram knew nothing about what was going on with country music in the sixties and he quickly became an avid fan ... He took on that music and made it his own."[10] Neuse recounts long nights singing through material that jibe with Parsons' later marathon singing sessions with Richards as the latter recalls them:[11]

> [W]e played music without stopping. Sat around the piano or with guitars and went through the country songbook. Plus some blues and a few ideas on top. Gram taught me country music – how it worked, the difference between the Bakersfield style and the Nashville style. He played it all on piano – Merle Haggard, "Sing Me Back Home," George Jones, Hank Williams ... Some of the seeds he planted in the country music area are still with me, which is why I can record a duet with George Jones with no compunction at all.[12]

By the time Parsons met Richards, he had cajoled the International Submarine Band into moving to Los Angeles, where they disbanded in 1968, shortly before Parsons and Neuse scored a record deal with Lee Hazelwood and produced one album (*Safe at Home*) with a hastily assembled new line-up. Over the next five years of his short life (he died of a drug overdose in 1973 at the age of twenty-six), Parsons established a pattern of gathering other musicians around him, only to lose interest, focus, or both, or to try the patience of his collaborators through his unreliability, which was largely fueled by his substance abuse. His fame and influence (almost entirely posthumous) are wildly disproportionate to the amount of music he wrote and recorded, and speak more to his vision of "Cosmic American Music," in which the various strands of late 1960s popular music – country, R&B, and rock – could be harmoniously blended. Parsons recognized this quality in the Stones as he encountered them in 1968. Prompted by an interviewer's leading comment ("'Wild Horses' is very unlike most of their writing"), Parsons calls the song "a logical combination between our music and their music." As Parsons tried to explain in his ensuing remarks, the Stones had sent the original masters to Parsons' band, the Flying Burrito Brothers, who actually released the first version of the song.[13] This remark touches on a subtle but critical facet of his relationship with the Rolling Stones and on the very nature of the Stones' country songs. For all the hours Parsons and Richards spent drilling down into the country songbook, from Hank Williams to Merle Haggard, the idea of replicating the style of those songs and the sound of those recordings was not Parsons' agenda during the years he was close to the Stones. Rather, he was after a synthesis of various strands of American music, and it is that vision that ultimately influenced Richards and his bandmates. That, however, leaves a more nebulous mark, which makes it hard to pin down Parsons' impact, on the one hand, and easy to imagine it everywhere, on the other. Richards says as much: "That country influence came through in the Stones. You can hear it in 'Dead Flowers,' 'Torn and Frayed,' 'Sweet Virginia,' and 'Wild Horses,' which we gave to Gram to put on the Flying Burrito Brothers record *Burrito Deluxe* before we put it out ourselves."[14]

The fact that those four songs come across as quite different from one another stylistically speaks volumes about the Stones' approach to country stylings in their own music. Whereas their early focus on rock and roll and R&B provided some unity to their sound through 1966, the diversity of their country-influenced numbers reflects the wide range of their country inspirations and the relative novelty of the genre for the group. Moreover, since the country influence of Ry Cooder leaned more towards what we would nowadays label "roots" music, a mix of vernacular styles from which both country and the blues would emerge, and because Gram Parsons – for all of the Nashville and Bakersfield tutorials he shared with Richards – interacted with the group while pursuing his own path of blending country, blues, and rock under the banner of Cosmic American Music, it is not surprising that Stones Country is an itinerary of disparate places that don't connect along one road; there is no country route to replace the Highway 61 of the Stones' blues background.

What follows, then, is a tour of an imaginary musical landscape. Each of the songs discussed below has to be taken on its own merits, considered for its unique representation of country within the Rolling Stones' core style. To help navigate them, however, I have grouped some songs together, leading from those older primordial mixtures of country and blues (The Old Country), through numbers that wear country on their sleeve – maybe a little too overtly (Deep Country), to songs that incorporate country elements in a decidedly modern manner to produce something entirely at home at the turn of the decade (Stones Country). This list hardly exhausts the songs that display country influence – much less the influence of Parsons and Cooder – but represents rather a survey of significant landmarks. Well-known examples ("Wild Horses," "Country Honk," "Torn and Frayed") will be bypassed in order to focus on a handful of songs that raise particular issues of the Rolling Stones' engagement with country music styles.

The Old Country: "No Expectations" and "Sweet Virginia"

One of the obstacles to defining Stones Country is the inherent blending of country and blues once one looks back beyond the honky-tonk era of Hank Williams and Ernest Tubb. Country music was only defined as a type in the wake of the "Big Bang" at Bristol in 1927, when Ralph Peer recorded Jimmie Rodgers and the Carter Family (along with numerous other aspiring regional acts) for the Victor Talking Machine Company in the first week of August. Although many white Appalachian string bands were recorded in the 1920s and early 1930s, their repertoire and playing styles often overlapped considerably with African-American blues artists (their counterparts in the "race" catalogues of Victor and other early recording companies). No one better illustrates the cross-fertilization between hillbilly music and the blues (and Tin Pan Alley, for that matter) than Rodgers himself, whose "Blue Yodel" series of songs all follow the twelve-bar blues form while borrowing vocal inflections and lyrical clichés from the black side of the "race records" divide.

At least two Stones songs from the cluster of albums between 1968 and 1972 dwell in that interstice. "No Expectations" from *Beggars Banquet* (1968) would seem to derive from straight blues material. Commentators frequently point to Reverend Gary Davis' "Meet Me at the Station," and Robert Johnson's "Love in Vain" – which Richards claims the band had only discovered in 1967. "No Expectations" has the distinction of being the last recording to include Brian Jones, whose Hawaiian-style acoustic slide guitar quickly conjures the country blues of the 1930s. But if the lyrics vaguely tap various stock lines from early rural blues recordings (for example, "I followed her to the station," from Johnson's "Love in Vain," becomes "Take me to the station" in the Stones' hands), details in the musical setting decenter the song's blues identity. Most notably, the verses alternate three times between a pair of chords (A major and E major), launching each iteration with a softly altered version of A major as Keith Richards lets a note from the other chord in the pair ring through in his part. Pre-war guitarists certainly may have added notes to these chords, but they would be flatted and would have added a bite, not the melancholy tone struck here. Jones' limpid slide guitar lines do little to sharpen the effect. The result is neither blues, nor the rootsy early country of Jimmie Rodgers, Charlie Poole, and the like, but rather a comfortable blending of the two that pays homage to their interconnectedness, while injecting just enough poetry ("Our love was like the water/That splashes on a stone/Our love is like our music/It's here, and then it's gone") to render the song modern. Like some other songs in Stones Country, the country element in "No Expectations" is mostly latent, as evidenced by the stronger presence of country idioms in covers that range from bluegrass renditions by John Hartford and Bill Keith, to outlaw statements from Johnny Cash and Waylon Jennings, and a retro-roots version by Nancy Griffith and Son Volt.

"Sweet Virginia" (*Exile on Main Street*, 1972) similarly carries more country potential than it realizes (although in this case there is no bank of country covers to plead its case). The opening of the song seems as generically "country"-sounding as a song could get in 1972. Richards' unadorned, jingle-jangle guitar could derive from any era in country music up to that time. But – as a country song – the track quickly loses its moorings. Although we could still hear "Sweet Virginia" as traditional country of one sort or another when Mick Jagger's harmonica enters five bars in, followed in short order by Mick Taylor's lead acoustic guitar, things start to take a right-angle turn when the drums and bass enter (0:47). A country vibe is maintained through the first verse but dissipates as the piano (Ian Stewart) and saxophone (Bobby Keys) enter with the chorus, and the entire ensemble morphs into something more like a Bayou blues jam than an Appalachian string band. In other words, "Sweet Virginia" crosses the same blurry boundary from country to blues that "No Expectations" had traversed, only here it occurs sequentially rather than simultaneously. Lost in the raucous romp into which the song extends from its mid-point on is a perfectly plausible modern country, 2/4 beat. To be sure, Charlie Watts' snare shots are raspier and looser than one would expect from the average Nashville or Bakersfield drummer of the day (compare, for example, the drumming on Merle Haggard's nearly contemporaneous [1971] cover of Roger Miller's "Train of Life"); they might sound more at home in Memphis or New Orleans. Nevertheless, the underlying rhythm to Watts' pattern can be traced back to any number of early country songs – again, Jimmie Rodgers provides a ready example in "Waiting for a Train," in which the boom-chick of Watts' pattern is ably represented by Rodgers' guitar. If the drumming on "Sweet Virginia" leans towards blues or something more soulful than we tend to associate with country, it is merely a reminder of how interconnected country's origins are with other "roots" genres.

Acknowledging the crossover from an ostensibly country opening into something "other" also helps explain the frequent suggestions (beginning with the members of the Rolling Stones themselves) that "Sweet Virginia" reflects the influence of Gram Parsons.[15] On the surface this is a curious claim, as there are no Parsons songs that come close to sounding like this. Only "Do You Know How it Feels," included on both the International Submarine Band's *Safe at Home* and Burrito's *Gilded Palace of Sin*, has any resemblance, sharing the underlying drum pattern (though much closer to Jimmie Rodgers than Charlie Watts). But that lack of a specific match serves as a reminder that Parsons' influence was as much a concept as a sound. In this case, the blending of country and soul leads backwards more than forwards, and thus Parsons' Cosmic American Music is not the best label for what the Stones achieve in "Sweet Virginia": we are still in the Old Country. As much as Parsons' idea was predicated on the common roots from which country, R&B, and rock and roll had sprung, he was aiming towards a newer synthesis. Stones tunes making up a second group from the period in question fall short of that ideal by seizing solely on the country explorations that Parsons and Richards undertook at Redlands and Nellcôte. Perhaps it is no surprise that these songs feel less like Rolling Stones songs, and more like role-playing or parody.

Deep Country: "Dear Doctor" and "Far Away Eyes"

For all of Keith Richards' and Mick Jagger's legitimate interest in and knowledge of country before encountering Ry Cooder and Gram Parsons, they defined themselves first as Rolling Stones – as asserted at the beginning of the chapter – through the passion for R&B and blues that they shared with Brian Jones. With a nod to the Animals, the Stones were the "blackest" of the British Invasion bands. Reflecting on blackness as an attitude and ominous demeanor (rather than race) after Altamont, Robert Christgau posited that whereas the Stones and the Beatles shared an appreciation for the "tough, joyous physicality of their Afro-American music," the Stones "came from a darker angrier place." But Christgau takes issue with the idea that Jagger was trying to be black:

> Early analyses of their music veered between two poles – Jagger was either a great blues singer or a soulless thief – and both were wrong. Like so many extraordinary voices, Jagger's defied description by contradicting itself. It was liquescent and nasal, full-throated and whiny. But it was not what Tom Wolfe once called it, "the voice of a bull Negro," nor did it aspire to be. It was simply the voice of a white boy who loved the way black men sang – Jagger used to name Wilson Pickett as his favorite vocalist – but who had come to terms with not being black himself . . . His style was an audacious revelation. It was not weaker than black singing, just different, and the difference always involved directness of feeling.[16]

Christgau is speaking specifically of Jagger's voice. While the adoption of black musical style might have harnessed the frustration of British youth in the post-war era, Jagger did not need to adopt black vocal mannerisms to get the point across. His verbal articulation may have been just as muddy as that of the Chicago bluesmen he studied as a teenager (Jagger claimed he would put his ear directly up to his record player's speaker in order to decipher the lyrics of his favorite songs), but as Christgau avers, his was a different voice whose blurred diction was founded on "directness of feeling," not verbal blackface.[17] One glaring exception to this rule is Jagger's rendition of Robert Wilkins' "Prodigal Son" (a song that draws its refrain from Wilkins' "That's No Way to Get Along") on *Beggars Banquet*. As the only song on that LP not penned by Jagger and Richards, Jagger could be heard to pay homage to Wilkins through his affected delivery.

Jagger's vocal style in the Rolling Stones' most overtly country songs is starkly different. In contrast with the avoidance of a black voice in the Stones' generic rock style and blues numbers, Jagger falls into a mannered drawl in the two songs I have grouped under Deep Country. In both cases, his voice is only the most overt projection of the Stones' parody of a specific country song type. Rather than absorbing country as a new facet of their identity, as one could argue they had in "Sweet Virginia," these songs find the band holding country at arm's length, something not only beyond their identity, but far enough removed from it to be an object of ridicule. In Jagger's words: "The country songs, like 'Factory Girl' or 'Dear Doctor' on *Beggars Banquet* were really pastiche. There's a sense of humor in country music, anyway, a way of looking at life in a humorous kind of way – and I think we were just acknowledging that element of the music."[18] "Dear Doctor" is nothing if not comedic. However, the humor lies not in the nature of the country music it parodies (per Jagger's assertion), but rather in the exaggerated manner in which the Stones play up the stereotypes and clichés of the genre. At its core, "Dear Doctor" is a country waltz – a type with a rich tradition going back at least to the Carter Family. More often than not, country waltzes are wistful, either retelling a sad tale or recalling a tender moment. This offers a perfect context for the singer's tale of woe, driven to drink "like a sponge" as he is pushed by his mother to marry a "bow-legged sow" – a far cry from the lost loves of Pee Wee King's "Tennessee Waltz," Bill Monroe's "Kentucky Waltz," Webb Pierce's "The Last Waltz," and from a few years later (1974), "As Soon As I Hang Up the Phone," by Loretta Lynn and Conway Twitty. Jagger makes sure to let the listener know they are intentionally missing the emotional mark of their models by tagging the rhyming words "jar," "sour," and "hour" (a little less so on "heart"). Richards' harmony vocal doubles down on the spoof at those moments, slightly overshooting his note every time. The farcical falsetto with which Jagger delivers the lines in the missing bride's letter to her jilted fiancé in the last verse ensures that no one will miss the send-up. At best, the Stones are providing some relief on an otherwise heavy album. More likely though, they are displaying their own discomfort: with the maudlin nature of those legitimate country waltzes, the oh-so-white character of the straight country-waltz beat, and the idea of representing straight country music in one of their own songs. The song was recorded in May of 1968, before Richards embarked on the first of his extended country music deep dives with Parsons, so the aura that country would soon take on for Richards and the group had not yet materialized.

That said, Jagger and Richards knew how a country song works, and they dialed up several stereotypical features of the genre in "Dear Doctor." For example, the reiterative melodic beginning of the chorus ("Oh help me"/"Dear doctor"/"I'm damaged") mimics a similar melodic profile in such country waltzes as Hank Williams' "I'm So Lonesome I Could Cry," and "Tennessee Waltz" (where the pattern breaks with the third iteration, moving the repeated phrase ["I was dancing"/"with my darling"] up an octave ["to the Tennessee Waltz"]). Harmonically, the Stones seize on a tendency for country waltzes to move directly from their opening I chord to firmly establish a higher one on IV (in the case of "Dear Doctor," the move is from the tonic D major harmony to a G major harmony). That is hardly an unusual move, but it is ubiquitous in well-known country waltzes ("Tennessee Waltz," "Alabama Waltz," "I'm So Lonesome I Could Cry," "Blue Moon of Kentucky," "Waltz of the Angels"). Finally, the climbing dissonant harmonies that land in a higher range (from 1:32–1:39) tap a category of country songs that shift key for a portion of the song, following the same interval of a fourth, now at the level of key (not simply harmony). Unlike their genuine models (Willie Nelson's "Family Bible," Buck Owens' "Sweet Rosie Jones," Merle Haggard's "House of Memories," Conway Twitty's "Next in Line"), in which the shift occurs briefly within the verse of the song or as a bridge, "Dear Doctor" never comes back down to its original key, and ends with the chromatic, dissonant climb: another comical gesture, perhaps.

Humor at the expense of country stylings in "Dear Doctor" is not subtle, but neither is it over the top. Partly that is because the basic make-up of the band is present. Bill Wyman strips down his bass line as one would expect of a country player, but he approaches the chord roots at the downbeat of each measure from a minor third above or a second below – sticking to rock conventions and belying any Nashville or Bakersfield authenticity. Accordingly, Richards' acoustic guitar parts are still bluesy enough to remind us that this is not a country band, and Jagger delivers the lyrics with an unaffected British accent for enough of the song (when he isn't exaggerating his "R"s) that we have no trouble making sense of it as part of *Beggars Banquet*.

Through the run of albums from *Beggars Banquet* to *Exile on Main Street*, any further forays into country would be delivered more deftly (and we will consider some of those cuts below). But the country parody returned with a bang on *Some Girls* in 1978. After a few LPs following *Exile* that garnered mixed reviews for their musical content as well as for the Stones' apparent lack of direction, *Some Girls* was generally received as a return to form and, more importantly, relevance.[19] The album proved that the group could still provoke a response, from its cover featuring the band members in drag (replacing the real faces of some celebrities who insisted their faces be removed), to the gendered and racial offenses of the title track.[20] At the same time, *Some Girls* also demonstrated that the Stones could adjust to current pop music trends: disco with "Miss You"; new wave with "Shattered"; and punk with "Lies." The other clear "style" piece on the LP is "Far Away Eyes," which goes far beyond "Dear Doctor" in evoking the sound and flavor of country music. Of course, a lot had changed in country music and with the Rolling Stones during the intervening decade (see Figure 7.1). In 1977, the top of the country charts was in mid stream, represented on the one hand by the classic styles of Conway Twitty, Loretta Lynn, Waylon Jennings, and Charley Pride, and on the other by the forerunners of the soon-to-crest Urban Cowboy movement: a revamped Dolly Parton, Ronnie Millsap, Glen Campbell, and Crystal Gale. (Ironically, much of the changing sound of country music by the late 1970s was a reaction to the blending of country and rock that Gram Parsons had helped initiate in the late 1960s.)

Figure 7.1 Mick Jagger and Dolly Parton following her performance at the Bottom Line, New York, May 14, 1977. Jeff Gold Collection, Library and Archives, Rock and Roll Hall of Fame and Museum.

For their part, the Stones had moved on from founding member Brian Jones, through Mick Taylor, to Ron Wood, their new guitarist. On "Far Away Eyes" and at least three other tracks that were recorded for the LP (two only emerging decades later on rereleases of *Some Girls*) Wood plays pedal steel guitar, the quickest way to mark a track as "country." Although Wood never developed stellar technique on pedal steel (he added steel tracks to several later songs as well), the playing here is decidedly more in tune and passable than on the 1964 demos mentioned earlier. The bright sound of the steel guitar's whine is matched by Richards' brittle Fender Telecaster, a combination that supplied the core of the Bakersfield sound a decade earlier. And unlike the country-influenced tracks at the turn of the 1970s, "Far Away Eyes" features a very passable execution of a laconic country rhythm track from Watts and Wyman. The comparison with the earlier songs from Stones Country is driven home by the strong similarity in musical content and structure with "Sweet Virginia." Where the earlier track ran amok, spiraling into a swampy blues number, this one maintains the initial country flavor throughout, despite the nearly identical harmonic structure (the chord progression is extremely similar, save for the second chord in each song's pattern) and formal similarities.

But the straight country delivery in "Far Away Eyes" is overshadowed by the very specific subcategory to which the lyrics assign the song: the country talking-blues. Examples dot the history of country music, from Hank Williams' preaching songs under the name Luke the Drifter, to numerous examples by Johnny Cash, to the narration songs of Red Sovine, most memorably the ghost-trucker song, "Phantom 309." The most recent hit in the style also had been a trucking song, C. W. McCall's 1975 "Convoy." Jagger uses the built-in hokum of the genre as a license to expand the parody element he had explored in "Dear Doctor." In place of the hillbilly saga there, Jagger invokes Bakersfield and radio preachers to drench "Far Away Eyes" in country *bona fides*. And whereas the earlier Stones country songs let an occasional drawn-out "R" punctuate a line, Jagger laces this track with an exaggerated drawl throughout, where rolled "R"s are no longer necessary to put the effect across. The straight country playing behind the vocal allows the joke to stay front and center throughout, as the protagonist recounts running ten straight red lights with God's blessing ("Thank you Jesus; thank you Lord!"), and the preacher's exhortation to send ten dollars "to the church of the Sacred Bleeding Heart of Jesus located somewhere in Los Angeles [pronounced Ange-*leez*], California."

In a *Rolling Stone* interview several months after the song was released, Jagger cites the origins of "Far Away Eyes" in the real experience of driving through Bakersfield on a Sunday morning, specifying: "all the country-music radio stations start broadcasting live from L.A. black gospel services." When prompted by the interviewer (Jonathan Cott), Jagger initially denies the influence of Gram Parsons, but then immediately circles back to him:

JC: I sense a bit of a Gram Parsons feeling on "Faraway Eyes" – country music as transformed through his style, via Buck Owens.

MJ: I knew Gram quite well, and he was one of the few people who really helped me to sing country music – before that, Keith and I used to just copy it off records. I used to play piano with Gram, and on "Faraway Eyes" I'm playing piano, though Keith is actually playing the top part – we added it on after.

> But I wouldn't say this song was influenced specifically by Gram. That idea
> of country music played slightly tongue in cheek – Gram had that in
> "Drugstore Truck Drivin' Man," and we have that sardonic quality, too.[21]

Since Jagger raises the tongue-in-cheek element, it is hard not to also hear
an echo of the last song on the Flying Burrito Brothers' *Gilded Palace of
Sin*, the Parsons and Chris Hillman original "Hippie Boy," and from there
to trace "Far Away Eyes" back further and more specifically within its
genre. In "Hippie Boy," Parsons' churchy organ chords and wild piano
runs accompany Hillman's spoken tale (partly based on real events) of
intrigue and deception, leading to the death of an innocent hippie at the
calamitous 1968 Democratic National Convention in Chicago, ending with
a screeching choral allusion to "Peace in the Valley."[22] For Parsons and
Hillman, one need look no further than their beloved Louvin Brothers for
a precedent. "Satan is Real" (1959) supplies sonic elements (the church
organ) to the Burritos' song while presaging the religious trappings (a
preacher's reply to the call to warn the congregation about the realities of
Satan) in the Stones' later parody. For the Stones, all of this is fodder for a
send-up of country music and one of its core values, evangelical religion.

Stones Country: "Dead Flowers"

Ironically, in "Far Away Eyes," the Rolling Stones sound the most convin-
cingly country when they are distancing themselves from it most strongly.
Jagger and Richards back up their various claims of having known and
appreciated country music before Cooder and Parsons arrived on the
scene, but they don't want to be tied directly to it. Despite the cachet of
numerous country-rockers, "outlaws" (Willie Nelson, Waylon Jennings,
etc.), and progressive singer-songwriters by 1978, the Stones did not feel
they could treat country music as simply as the newer styles represented
on *Some Girls*. But they could have. A 2011 CD reissue included eleven
previously unreleased tracks, mostly from the original recording sessions
for the album from October 1977 through March 1978. Among those (and
two from slightly later sessions) are two country covers that might have
situated the Stones very differently in relation to country. Their recording
of Hank Williams' classic "You Win Again" uses much the same line-up
and basic core sound (with a touch of slap-back echo added) as "Far Away
Eyes," but there is no trace of parody or distance; it is as sympathetic a
reading as they gave any of the R&B songs they had ever covered. Jagger
injects a heavy dose of blues inflection to the vocals, befitting a serious
Rolling Stones track. Most surprising is how deftly Wood handles the

pedal steel guitar. Whereas his licks on "Far Away Eyes" were limited (the sort of pedal mashing any guitarist might engage in when dabbling), he strings phrases together on this track passably and he shows more feeling for the idiomatic use of the instrument. Wood also deserves kudos for his pedal steel playing on "Shattered," which required more imagination since there is nothing remotely country about the song, and thus no models to fall back on. (Nevertheless, he is probably not the first to use pedal steel on a New Wave or punk track; that distinction likely goes to Walt Andrews of Root Boy Slim and the Sex Change Band, whose eponymous LP débuted in June, 1978, but who had been performing in the Washington, D.C. area for a few years before that.) Another cover, "We Had It All," was captured in the wash of material the Stones recorded in 1978, but included the same line-up heard on *Some Girls*. Written by established country songwriters Troy Seals and Donnie Fritts, the song had been previously recorded by Waylon Jennings and Dobie Gray (among others); Richards – who, according to Jagger, heard it off the Jennings album *Honky Tonk Heroes*[23] – gives a haunting version singing and accompanying himself on piano. By now, Watts and Wyman have assimilated country rhythm playing and can apply it without the audible eye roll (confirmed by the official music video) that seeps through on "Far Away Eyes." Whereas the latter could have been taken as an affront by a generation of alt-country artists who would emerge a decade later, Richards' gripping rendition of "We Had It All," along with the band's gritty but subdued instrumental tracks, could have been held up as a road map for later pioneers like Jay Farrar and Ryan Adams. Reversing roles from earlier country-influenced tracks, Watts and Wyman lay down a country beat, and Richards and Wood move beyond that into a place that is neither country, rock, nor blues.

"Dear Doctor" and "Far Away Eyes" demonstrated that the Rolling Stones could never feel at home in Deep Country. They had to maintain their distance by playing the fool; the Stones' parody of country idioms clearly pegs them as outsiders. However, this is not to say that they couldn't incorporate country music into their sound, which is why "You Win Again" and "We Had It All" are so important for demonstrating that, by 1978, the Stones had figured out what they *could* do with country music. Several songs from the core LPs from 1968–72 chronicle their gradual assimilation of country. The high-water mark among these is "Dead Flowers," recorded in 1969–70 and released in 1971 on *Sticky Fingers*. Perhaps more than any other track discussed here, "Dead Flowers" is widely recognized as the Stones' most direct country song, even though it falls short on many country style points. All of the exaggerations of the earlier "Dear Doctor" are toned down and delivered with more finesse, starting with the lyrics. What had been a redneck romance is replaced by an uptown/downtown relationship gone wrong. And whereas the substance of choice in the earlier song was corn whiskey ("She plied me with bourbon so sour"), "Dead Flowers" makes a veiled (albeit thinly) reference to heroin use in the second verse: "I'll be in my basement room with a needle and a spoon/And another girl to take my pain away." Indeed, the title of the song itself and its addressee, "Little Susie," may even allude to heroin. These codenames may be more urban legend than reality: they are mostly discussed in internet chat rooms rather than in any authoritative sources.[24] Given the group's well-publicized troubles with heroin and any number of other controlled substances by this time, "Dead Flowers" brings the story closer to home. It is not autobiographical, however; Jagger and Richards' lyric locates the protagonists in the South with a reference to "Kentucky Derby Day."

Just as tellingly, they also tie the song to some heavy Southern class symbolism: the pink Cadillac. As an icon, the pink Cadillac goes back to Elvis Presley. In his 1955 recording of Arthur Gunter's "Baby, Let's Play House," Presley alters Gunter's first verse:

> You may go to college/May go to school
> You may get religion, baby, don't you be nobody's fool.

Elvis changes the opening of the second line to "You may drive a pink Cadillac." Shortly after recording the song for Sun Records, Presley bought himself a custom pink 1954 Cadillac sedan – the first of several pink cars he would own. Greil Marcus recognizes the pink Cadillac as central to Elvis' rags-and-resentment-to-riches story, even tying it to some of Jagger's earlier songs:

> The Pink Cadillac was at the heart of the contradiction that powered Elvis's early music ... When he faced his girl in "Baby, Let's Play House" (like Dylan railing at the heroine of "Like a Rolling Stone," or Jagger surveying the upper-class women who star in "19th Nervous Breakdown," "Play with Fire," and "You Can't Always Get What You Want"), Elvis sang with contempt for a world that had always excluded him.[25]

Jagger's protagonist has contempt less for the social class that separates him from his ex than for her hypocrisy: holding forth with her rich friends while supplying his heroin (she is, after all, the "queen of the underground"). Situating her in her pink Cadillac, in contrast to his heroin-tainted basement room, marks her as a social climber – someone who, like the singer, does not belong with her rich friends. Some, all, or none of this may derive from actual relationships the Stones found themselves in through their rise to stardom in the preceding decade, but all of the dynamics at play (drugs, class conflict, bitter break-ups) are plausible and relatable aspects of the band members' lives. Right off the bat, then, before even turning one's attention to the music to which the lyric is set, this is a more legitimate country song than anything the Stones had done before, since it relates a "real" story.

As with the lyrics, the excesses of "Dear Doctor" are tamed in the musical setting of "Dead Flowers." Richards' sprawling acoustic guitar parts are replaced by a more organized trio of Jagger on acoustic and Richards and Taylor with terse, intertwined electric riffs. Charlie Watts' drumming, barely present on "Dear Doctor," now supplies a tight, steady pulse through the verses, and Wyman reins in his bass line to include primarily rhythmic repeated-note interjections. But the song's country flavor derives from a host of details, not its basic instrumental features. Among those details are things that are *not* there. For one, nearly all blue notes and seventh chords have been eliminated from the standard Rolling Stones musical language. Likewise, the chord patterns, while not necessarily "country" harmonic progressions *per se*, are dominated by root position major chords, which are the stuff of standard country music. In fact, only the "Three Chords and Truth" trio of harmonies are employed here: I, IV, and V (or D, G, and A). Significantly, the tell-tale VII chord is completely absent, stripping the harmony of a standard blues and rock marker. (The VII chord is ubiquitous in the Stones' music. Some notable appearances in songs discussed so far include: "High and Dry" ["High and dry, well *I'm up here with no warning*"]; "No Expectations" ["I've got no expectations *to pass* through here again"]; and "Dear Doctor" ["It's sleeping, it's beating, can't you *please tear it* out"]). Finally, the overdriven sound of the electric guitar is missing as well, as both Taylor and Richards maintain a clean signal in their respective channels. While not *de rigueur* for a rock guitar sound, overdrive and distortion were a base-line sound of rock by 1971. Their absence makes it that much easier to assign "Dead Flowers" to another style.

Perhaps the clean guitar sounds only point specifically to country due to Taylor's many pedal-steel-like string bends, one of two country details that were added to the mix. More significant is Jagger's vocal delivery. By now it may seem redundant to raise the issue of an affected Southern accent, after the observation of hard "R"s and other drawled words in "Dear Doctor" and "Far Away Eyes." However, Jagger's Southern persona in "Dead Flowers" is entirely different. Just as the drug-riddled back story accords with the Stones' reality at that time, Jagger pulls punches in the delivery here to remove the comic edge that pervaded the songs of Deep Country. To be sure, final "R"s are hit hard, and some "L"s are drawn out ("You know I could never be a-*Lone*"; "Rose pink cadi-*LL*-ac") so as to highlight the drawl of the ensuing vowel. Yet at no point does the song sound like a parody. In some ways it foreshadows Jagger's much later solo recording, "Evening Gown" (1993), with its even more subtle hint of a Southern accent to fit the song's country styling. In some ways, the more sincere he makes his Southern accent, the more unambiguously Jagger can turn a Rolling Stones song into a "country" song. Perhaps this is why songs like "Torn and Frayed" from *Exile on Main Street* (despite its use of pedal steel guitar) and *Let It Bleed*'s "Country Honk," with its aggressive fiddle, make less of a claim. As anyone who has witnessed the rise of Bro country can attest, sometimes all that connects a song to a country claim is the singer's Southern accent. We might not notice when the singer identifies as an American Southerner and dons a cowboy hat or boots, or a plaid flannel shirt, but it is to some degree the very essence of country. When the scarf-adorned poster boy for British rock puts on the accent, however, we are forced to take notice and contemplate the country identity of his song. Our attention is drawn even more compellingly when that singer and his band are so strongly identified with decidedly African-American musical styles, and, most critically, when that core association is achieved without an overreliance on a parallel affectation of black vocal idioms. The Southern accent is the strongest relic of the Old Country and Deep Country that imprints its sound on Stones Country, precisely because it reminds us how these songs draw a distinction from the Rolling Stones' core sound and identity.

Notes

1 *Life*, 238.
2 *According*, 112–13.
3 Martin Elliott chronicles these sessions in *RSCRS*, 43 and 45. Margotin & Guesdon credit Big Jim Sullivan with the pedal steel part for two of the songs (they do not list the demo of "Heart of Stone"), 442 and 446.
4 *According*, 138.
5 Including sitar, Appalachian dulcimer, marimba, and harpsichord; see *RSG*, 216–23.
6 Richards has commented frequently on Cooder's influence regarding open G-tuning. See, for example, Stephen Davis, *Old Gods Almost Dead: The 40-Year Odyssey of the Rolling Stones* (New York, 2001), 244. See also Brita Renée Heimarck, "A 'Gust of Fresh Air': Brian Jones, *Assemblage*, and World Music," in this volume, 159, n. 20.
7 Barney Hoskyns, *Hotel California: The True-Life Adventures of Crosby, Stills, Nash, Young, Mitchell, Taylor, Browne, Ronstadt, Geffen, the Eagles, and their Many Friends* (Hoboken, 2007), 87–90.
8 Quoted in Davis, *Old Gods Almost Dead*, 283.
9 *Life*, 247.
10 David N. Meyer, *Twenty Thousand Roads: The Ballad of Gram Parsons and his Cosmic American Music* (New York, 2007), 161.
11 *Ibid.*, 157.
12 *Life*, 248.
13 Bud Scoppa, "Gram Parsons Interview: Burrito Deluxe," in Sid Griffin, *Gram Parsons: A Music Biography* (Pasadena, 1985), 101.

14 *Life*, 310.

15 Margotin & Guesdon, 378. Parsons' influence on "Shine a Light" notwithstanding, his actual participation on the record, long of interest to Stones scholars and fans alike, cannot be firmly established. Neither of Janovitz's informants, Mick Taylor and *Exile* session-player Al Perkins, confirms Parsons as singing backing vocals, as some have claimed (Janovitz*EMS*, 102–3). Elliott establishes the first takes of the song as occurring in 1970 at Olympic Studios, with a possible origin earlier in the *Let It Bleed* sessions of 1969. In the version recorded at Nellcôte, Elliott can only conclude that "one of the backing singers may have been Gram Parsons" (*RSCRS*, 134–5). Janovitz cites other possible country inspirations for "Sweet Virginia," including the "reedy" harmonica style of Roy Acuff and Faron Young's references to California wine growers in "Wine Me Up" (Janovitz*EMS*, 96–101).

16 Robert Christgau, *Any Old Way You Choose It: Rock and Other Pop Music, 1967–1973*, Expanded edition (New York, 2000), 223–4. Christgau's quote can be found in Tom Wolfe, *The Kandy-Kolored Tangerine-Flake Streamline Baby* (New York, 1965), 174.

17 Jagger's listening habits are recounted by John M. Hellman, Jr. in "'I'm a Monkey': The Influence of the Black American Blues Argot on the Rolling Stones," *Journal of American Folklore* 86 (1973), 368. The story stems from an October 12, 1968 *Rolling Stone* interview with Mick Jagger, reprinted in Dalton*RS* (New York, 1972), 103.

18 *According*, 120.

19 For critical reviews of the albums immediately preceding *Some Girls*, see Paul Harris' chapter in this volume, "Post *Exile*: The Rolling Stones in a Disco-Punk World, 1975–1983," 75–97.

20 Davis, *Old Gods*, 430; see also Harris, *ibid.*, xxx.

21 Jonathan Cott, "Mick Jagger: The Rolling Stone Interview," *Rolling Stone*, June 29, 1978, reprinted in Peter Herbst, ed., *The* Rolling Stone *Interviews: 1967–1980* (New York, 1981), 331. Jagger returns to this same idea in a *Rolling Stone* interview almost two decades later, when in answering a question from Jann Wenner about "Far Away Eyes," he states that "a lot of country music is sung with the tongue in cheek, so I do it tongue in cheek. The harmonic thing is very different from the blues. It doesn't bend notes in the same way, so I suppose it's very English, really. Even though it's been very Americanized, it feels very close to me, to my roots, so to speak." See Wenner*MJR*, 64.

22 Bob Proehl discusses the background of "Hippie Boy" in *The Gilded Palace of Sin* (New York, 2008), 71–2.

23 *RSCRS*, 221.

24 The song title is referenced, however, by Robert Palmer as "Heroin . . . as in crushed poppies"; see Anthony DeCurtis, ed., *Blues and Chaos: The Music Writing of Robert Palmer* (New York, 2009), 217.

25 Greil Marcus, *Mystery Train: Images of America in Rock 'n' Roll*, 6th edn (New York, 2015), 151. Martin Elliott muses on Blind Willie McTell's "Lay Some Flowers on My Grave" as a possible influence for the song's refrain, "And I won't forget to put roses on your grave" (*RSCRS*, 130). Given the Stones' interest in rural blues during this period, one could also wonder whether Blind Lemon Jefferson's "See That My Grave Is Kept Clean" plays a role.

8 A "Gust of Fresh Air": Brian Jones, Assemblage, and World Music

BRITA RENÉE HEIMARCK

A breath of air is exteriority coming in.[1]

An assemblage of forces organized inside an individual is characterized by a new possibility of life . . . a distribution of affects – a new mode of existence.[2]

The French philosophies of Gilles Deleuze (1925–95), in particular his theory of *assemblage* (introduced in his 1980 book with Félix Guattari, *Mille plateaux*), provide a useful approach towards understanding the musical and overall aesthetic contributions of Brian Jones. In this chapter, I will apply Deleuzean philosophical concepts to the life and world music interests of Jones as a means of highlighting his creative work as a "breath of fresh air" (*un courant d'air*) within the prevailing blues and rock standards and influences that have more consistently represented the Rolling Stones. In particular, I will explore the assemblage of life and musical events that make up the broad stylistic mixture we now associate with Jones, concentrating on his founding role and decade-long connection with the Rolling Stones.

Jones brought a wide range of musical instruments, styles, skills, and cultural associations to the Rolling Stones, enhancing the band's sound with unique qualities of assemblage that would otherwise have been absent and sorely missed. This kind of musical assemblage refers to the musical syncretism Jones introduced. He was not just a talented and instinctual musician drawn to notions of authenticity (or as Wyman put it, "hung up on musical integrity"[3]), but a sound artist who explored the rich sonic techniques of American blues harp and slide guitar, and subsequently dulcimer, sitar, recorder, and marimba on distinct occasions. On the one hand, assemblage may be viewed as a single work of art that combines diverse influences; on the other, it can describe an individual life that develops through distinct events in such a way that diverse influences may be incorporated over time. In the visual arts, assemblage may be defined as "a work of art made by grouping found or unrelated objects." This definition may be transferred to a musical assemblage or syncretic work, which I define here as a merging or combination of diverse musical sounds or influences in a given work or *oeuvre*. At the same time, I utilize Deleuzean philosophy to explore assemblage as a theoretical model for a set of relations that is not static, but rather, "infused with movement and change."[4] The life events that fostered Jones' musical contributions to the Stones can be viewed in Deleuze's philosophical manner as an assemblage of events that have musical and social repercussions; some of them are immortalized in the compositions and recordings of the Stones, whereas others may have triggered the downward spiral towards Jones' early and tragic death.

Assemblage and Deleuzean Philosophy

Deleuze uses the image of a breath or gust of air to refer to the invigorating impact of philosophers he admired, such as Spinoza, Foucault, and Sartre,[5] and this idea is useful to illuminate the musical contributions of Brian Jones to the Rolling Stones. Here we can distinguish three levels of inspiration at work: (1) philosophical influences as a *courant d'air* for Deleuze; (2) Deleuze as a *courant d'air* for my exploration of Brian Jones; and (3) Brian Jones as a *courant d'air* for the Rolling Stones and through their work as an influence on blues, rhythm and blues, and rock and roll in general. In his construction of philosophical concepts, Deleuze was concerned with the fundamental consequence of "events" over time, rather than an accumulation of things, and with the idea that an individual might be characterized "as a flow of events and not as a person."[6] In other words, the individual (in this case, Jones) is characterized by his or her actions, not his or her attributes.[7] In my characterization of Jones within the context of the Rolling Stones I will focus on the flow of events that gradually introduced certain musical instruments and associations to Jones, as a means of constructing a concept of his life.[8] This flow of events becomes the assemblage, indicating the emergent and heterogeneous world music interests of Jones in his ever-shifting incorporation of non-Western, or at least non-standard, sounds into the Stones' music. "The assemblage is productive of difference (non-repetition). It is the ground and primary expression of all qualitative difference."[9] Assemblage enables a combination of diverse components, thus allowing something different to emerge. Deleuze replaces the idea of *content* with an arrangement or "assemblage" (*agencement*) of relations.[10]

Jones as Harbinger and Casualty of the Stones' First Decade

Jones was a harbinger of the musical path the Stones would take in his founding passion for American blues and his vision to incorporate rhythm and blues into the British rock scene. Jones also anticipated the interest among pop musicians in different traditions of world music, an influence already present in George Harrison's use of the sitar in "Norwegian Wood" of 1965 (which predates Jones' use of the instrument in "Paint It, Black" by almost six months), but one that would be more deeply explored by such artists as Paul Simon, Sting, and Peter Gabriel, to give just a few famous or infamous examples. Simon and Sting incorporated not just influences, but world music singers into their own songs – consider the significant role of Joseph Shabalala from Ladysmith Black Mambazo on Simon's *Graceland* album of 1986, or Sting's song "Desert Rose" with Algerian singer Cheb Mami of 1999 – and Gabriel organized world music festivals and concerts, such as his WOMAD festivals (World of Music, Arts and Dance) begun in 1980.[11] Jones' idea to combine his own music not only with American blues and soul, but even distant "Elizabethan" idioms, and more importantly, his fascination with recording the Master Musicians of Joujouka in Morocco (1967–68), were visionary for their time.[12] Jones had an almost ethnomusicological leaning in his desire to make field recordings of the Joujouka musicians' ritual music in its authentic location and to share at least portions of these recordings along with information about the musical rite with audiences beyond its borders. He also reveals an early interest in mastering and ultimately combining diverse instruments, which became perhaps his most original and key contribution to the Stones.

Jones, however, was a casualty in his devastation both by the perverse attempts by some in the band to share each other's women – something that he also participated in over time, but which cost him the opportunity to be a father to his son Julian with Pat Andrews – and by his fraught relationship with Anita Pallenberg.[13] Jones was furthermore a casualty of the Stones' first decade – and to some extent the broader countercultural movement – in his succumbing to the drugs and alcohol that ultimately consumed and claimed his life. Jones' bandmates reflected on his tragic demise and their role in it. Charlie Watts recalled: "He got much nicer just before he died – in the last few years of his life. But I felt even sorrier for him for what we did to him then. We took his one thing away, which was being in a band. That's my opinion."[14]

Jones drowned in his own pool late at night in 1969 after celebrating too heavily the promise of incoming funds to his account, but he was also perhaps bemoaning the loss of his place in the band he was so instrumental in founding.

Overview: Jones' Musical Impulses

Almost all writings about Jones cite his abundant creative impulse to search for broad and meaningful musical influences. From his "hauntingly beautiful" recorder melody – generally reminiscent of early music – in the ballad "Ruby Tuesday" and blues harp and slide guitar playing, to the marimba riff in "Under My Thumb" and his fascination with Indian sitar timbres and technique, Jones combined diverse elements into a cohesive whole.[15] As in the philosophy of Deleuze – who coincidentally began writing just after

WWII, not long after the most dominant Rolling Stones members were all born (Jones, 1942; Jagger and Richards, 1943) – Jones achieves difference through diverse musical influences and a wide range of instruments he played on various songs and albums. In the process, Jones developed an assemblage of style uniquely his own. Despite constant comparisons to the Beatles, whose stylistic breadth and technological innovations pushed other groups to follow suit, the Stones struck a path that veered away from the love and peace message of the Beatles, toward a darker representation of sex and power with a strong American blues influence.

Blues Influences

Jones was unquestionably the most versatile, unconventional, and exploratory musician in the Rolling Stones, and he founded the band with his passion for black R&B in mind; he instigated the core passion that fueled the formation of the Rolling Stones and their ongoing fascination with black American blues artists and culture. Of course, Jagger and Richards shared this fascination, and that is what brought them all together at the Crawdaddy (blues) Club, but Jones had been diligently practicing and imitating the American blues style and performing numerous gigs prior to this meeting. Jones' mastery of the pitch-bending style of American blues harp playing was already evident when the Beatles came to see the Stones playing at the Crawdaddy Club by invitation of the owner, Giorgio Gomelsky; John Lennon's response to Jones is described as "something like hero-worship. 'You really *play* [emphasis mine] that harmonica, don't you,' he said. 'I can't really play – I just blow and suck.'"[16]

The degree to which the Stones introduced vast American television audiences to Howlin' Wolf and Muddy Waters is telling of the influence the band had on bringing great American blues musicians in the twilight of their careers into the limelight of music on television.[17]

> It was on May 20, 1965 that Jones built a bridge over a cultural abyss and connected America with its own black culture. The founder Stone introduced Chester Burnett, aka Howlin' Wolf, on ABC's *Shindig!* . . . This was truly a life-changing moment, both for the American teenagers clustered round the TV in their living rooms, and for a generation of blues performers who had been stuck in a cultural ghetto.[18]

The British rockers' admiration for these longstanding American blues artists became an indelible part of the long-term image of the band.

Jones learned to play cross harp and taught blues-style harmonica to Jagger as well.[19] In addition, concerning the focus on "roots" (blues) music, Trynka is emphatic that

> [i]t was Brian who first searched out the early music of Robert Johnson,
> Charley Patton and Son House, Brian who persuaded his fellow Stones of its
> potency, and Brian who showed Dick Taylor and Keith how to play in Open
> D, Open E and Open G tunings.[20]

In terms of rhythm and blues, however, it was Richards who taught Jones
more about Chuck Berry.[21]

The Stones' early recorded sound became distinctive through the impact
of several renowned American studios: RCA studios (where post-Memphis
Elvis recorded), marking the beginning of Jack Nitzsche's important relationship to the band, and the famous Chess Records studios in Chicago,
whose records of artists Chuck Berry, Muddy Waters, Howlin' Wolf, Jimmy
Reed, Willie Dixon, and Sonny Boy Williamson were at the root of the
formation of the band itself. "Did we hit it off? [recounts Richards concerning his encounter with Jagger on a train] You get in a carriage with a guy
that's got *Rockin' at the Hops* by Chuck Berry on Chess Records and *The
Best of Muddy Waters* also under his arm, you are gonna hit it off."[22]

At Chess Studios, they met Muddy Waters and began work on a soul
song by Bobby Womack, "It's All Over Now," under the expert supervision
of house engineer Ron Malo, famous for his work with Chuck Berry and
Bo Diddley. They also met some of the great legends of the blues
and talked to them at Chess. Richards described recording at Chess and
receiving support from the artists they admired so much as "a shortcut to
heaven."

> Muddy Waters dropped in frequently to talk to the Stones during their
> session. So did two more of their great Chicago blues idols, Willie Dixon and
> Buddy Guy. The bluesmen were naturally full of benevolence towards the
> young Britishers who had given their songs a new lease of life. Later on, even
> the great Chuck Berry came in to inspect them. Rock 'n' roll's poet laureate,
> though not best known for charity towards young musicians, thawed
> considerably in the light of the composer's royalties the Stones were earning
> him. He praised their version of Reelin' and Rockin'.[23]

The Rolling Stones and Race

The Stones acknowledged their rhythm and blues influences and the
African-American artists they revered, but they also could not deny
their own significant impact and charged reception. In an article for
Melody Maker in 1964, quoted by Jack Hamilton, Jagger acknowledged
that

> it's the system that's sometimes wrong. Girl fans, particularly, would rather have a copy by a British group than the original American version – mainly, I suppose, because they like the British blokes' faces,

implying that "the singer recognized that the Stones' skin color had given them an undue advantage among audiences."[24] Despite their varied backgrounds and appearances, the Stones emulated the timbres and vocal style of black American music along with the actual genres and specific compositional styles. Notably, in the BBC's initial rejection of the Stones, one key criticism was that "the singer sounds too coloured."[25] Jagger's vocal and gestural swagger, whoops and growls drew a great deal on the vocal style and dance moves of James Brown and other soul and blues artists. Yet even beyond musical style, there were social associations. Hamilton connects British blues with the "perceived danger and subversive liminality" of the Southern American blues tradition, which was steeped in the violence and racial terror of the American South. "Fantasies of the blues' 'threatening' capacity for social rebellion . . . took on uniquely powerful imaginative dimensions in England, where black American bodies were generally absent."[26]

> The Stones' obsession with black music and black musicians simply became part of the Rolling Stones, the band who'd wanted to be Muddy Waters now surrounded by a world of rock musicians that wanted to be them. This transition – the shift from the Rolling Stones being heard as the authenticated, to the Rolling Stones being heard as the authentic – is among the most significant turns in the racial imagination of rock.[27]

Jones, Jagger, and the Image of the Rolling Stones

Another play with authenticity developed by the Stones was through the cultivation of their image. Brian Jones was one of the first (if not the first) of the group to master a grand, theatrical appearance. Jones was well dressed, well spoken, well educated, and "obsessed with music."[28] His mother recalls that he started piano lessons when he was six or seven, and when he was twelve he joined his school orchestra and learned clarinet.[29] His father notes his penchant for listening to Modern Jazz Quartet records for hours on end. "The reverberations used to drive me crazy," Mr. Jones says, "These records were playing morning, noon, and night."[30]

In addition to diligent musical studies, Jones had a distinctive rock star image.

His clothes were a harlequin of velvet and psychedelic patterns. A long scarf trailed from his neck across the lap of the Alice in Wonderland girl who sat next to him, holding his hand, her eyes wide and bright and her hair the same fine natural blond as Brian's. She wore a tiny dress of tatty lace, and scarves. An antique lace shawl was draped half over them and half in the large woven straw shopping basket they'd brought with them. They were the centerpiece of the party, like an eighteenth-century tableau.[31]

As the sixties progressed, the Stones quickly shifted from suit and tie to more stylish clothing. Numerous photographs show Jones in colorful and dramatic attire. He wears red corduroy pants with a black turtleneck sweater, white blouses, pinstripe suits and polka dot shirts, all kinds of striped or plaid pants and furry or silken vests, fur coats, white hats, velvet jackets, colorful scarves, and occasionally all-white outfits. His hair is carefully coiffed, another obsession of his. Jones exhibited a heightened awareness about his clothing and appearance within the band, but he was not the only one who stood out. On their American tour, Tom Wolfe described the excitement at their appearance:

And, finally, the Stones, now – how can one express it? the Stones come on stage –

"Oh, God, Andy [Warhol], aren't they *divine*!"

– and spread out over the stage, the five Rolling Stones, from England, who are modeled after the Beatles, only more lower-class-deformed. One, Brian Jones, has an enormous blonde Beatle bouffant.

"Oh, Andy, look at Mick! Isn't he *beautiful*! Mick! Mick!"[32]

Jagger was aware of the central importance of his image and his fashion, saying:

The images you project are really important. Musicians always like to talk that it's only about the music. It isn't, of course. It's about what you wear, what you look like, what your attitudes are – all of these things. (*Exhibitionism*, "Style.")

On the Ed Sullivan show, a program that is central in the history of rock and roll for exposing prime-time audiences to rock groups of the 1960s, and in many other videos of the Stones' performances, Jagger's style as evident in his clothing gives off an operatic theatricality. In a 1966 performance of "Paint It, Black" he wears a tangerine silk shirt with a black patterned jacket; and in his famous 1967 performance of "Let's Spend the Night Together" – which Jagger sings (in high camp) as "let's spend *some time* together" to comply with the show's prudish censors – he wears a white frilly shirt underneath a shiny golden jacket. Much later, he simplifies his sex appeal to the more masculine white undershirt with crossed straps in back, flexing his biceps and waving his arms. In these later years, he moves from the bisexual theatricality of silk and stars to jeans and a white undershirt, betraying his father's longstanding influence in teaching him to stay fit, exercise, and lift weights from his childhood days onward. Whatever the outfit, when Andrew Loog Oldham first saw the Stones, he believed their image and marketability could be summed up in one word: sex. Oldham saw the Stones as representing sex, musically and metaphorically, and he quickly arranged to represent them.[33] Over time, the Stones came to stand for the British countercultural movement of the 1960s: long hair, fashionable stylishness, and ultimately drugs, sex, and rock and roll.

In the language of assemblage, these traits are not important for what they are, but for what they *do*.[34] Thus the sexy and fashionable image manifested by the Rolling Stones – combined with their music – creates the powerful effect of the band on stage, and their lingering presence.

Jones as Sound Artist

"I love the SOUNDS. I like to experiment. I think that is the real reason I prefer harmonica to guitar. I can wail on harmonica."[35] Jones taught Gordon Waller (of Peter and Gordon) to play the harmonica, he showed others how to bend the notes to play blues harp, and in general his passion for blues harp was longstanding. In 1965, Jones met folksingers Richard and Mimi Fariña – the latter, Joan Baez's sister – several times during his visits to Los Angeles, and their "explorations of stripped-down Appalachian music" led directly to Jones' purchase of a dulcimer.[36] Subsequently, when recording the song "Lady Jane" during the *Aftermath* sessions at RCA Studios in Hollywood, Jones created a counter-melody on the dulcimer, which, along with Jack Nitzsche's contributions on harpsichord, provides the "Elizabethan" melancholy that is unique to this piece, and, according to Elliott, "confirmed Andrew Oldham's belief that the band's mid-60s musical success was due to [Jones'] instrumental elaboration."[37]

Aftermath

The fourth (in America, the sixth) Rolling Stones album, *Aftermath*, released in April 1966, represents perhaps the artistic high point of Brian Jones within the group. Although all of the songs are credited to the writing partnership of Jagger/Richards, it clearly reveals the pronounced compositional stamp of Jones and his "virtuoso playing . . . on a range of instruments seldom seen before in a pop recording studio" along with a corresponding "lack of interest" in the electric guitar.[38] The origins of Jones' use of the marimba in "Under My Thumb" are found in the 1966 *Aftermath* sessions at RCA Studios in Hollywood. As luck would have it, the Mexican Baja Marimba band

> had left their instruments – including a marimba – in one corner of the huge RCA studio. Jones went over, started experimenting, and after a few minutes came up with what Eddie Kramer, one of the Stones' key engineers at Olympic studios in west London, describes as "genius. A riff that makes sense of what could have been a nonentity. Because he could think out of the box."[39]

Kramer believes Jones was unique in his understanding of tone color. "His sense of tone colour was magnificent, that's how he'd think out of the box, to put a different tone colour on something to make it speak. That's exactly what he did with the marimba part."[40] In the song, Jones plays a fluid, expressive melody on the marimba, which develops and repeats over time. The interplay of an instrumental melody that supports Jagger's vocal line but also adds a counter-melody in between the verses encapsulates a key aspect of Jones' musical contributions to the Stones generally, and to this album specifically, as represented by an array of varied instruments and world music components he introduced in different songs.

Jones acquired his first sitar during the RCA recording sessions from December 8–10, 1965. His response to what the sitar had to offer again demonstrates his desire to experiment with diverse musical sounds. "I love the instrument," he told the *Melody Maker*, "it gives you a new range if you use an instrument like that. It has completely different principals [i.e. harmonics] from the guitar and opens up new fields for a group in harmonics and everything."[41] Jones experimented with the sitar on his own and later found a teacher in a former student of Ravi Shankar named Hari whom he met in New York. Like George Harrison, Jones studied the sitar with serious intent for some time.

Bill Wyman recalls his own messing around on the pedals of an organ in the creation of "Paint It, Black," and the subsequent *collaborative* development of the piece: "Charlie immediately took up the rhythm and Brian played the melody line on sitar ... Funnily enough, it was never credited as a Nanker Phelge composition – I can't think why."[42] Whatever the exact development of this piece, it is clear that Jones' melody and the distinctive sound of the sitar formed an important part of this powerful synthesis.

When the Stones performed "Paint It, Black" on the Ed Sullivan Show in 1966 as well as for *Ready Steady Go* (see Figure 8.1), Jones plays the instrumental equivalent of the Other in his performance on the sitar. For

Figure 8.1 Brian Jones playing sitar on *Ready Steady Go*, 1966. Jan Olofsson/Redferns/Getty Images.

the Ed Sullivan Show Jones is dressed all in white and sits in a circumscribed white circle as if in a world apart from the others (who stand separately in white circles of their own); still, he contributes closely to the song and more broadly represents an important part of the sixties exploration of the East: Indian music, fashion, and yogic philosophies as witnessed in the transformation of the Beatles in this regard.

Figure 8.2 Rolling Stones concert at the Berlin Waldbühne, September 15, 1965. From l–r: Bill Wyman, Brian Jones, Mick Jagger. Photo: Alexander Enger, Preußischer Kulturbesitz; bpk Bildagentur/Art Resource, NY.

The transformation of the Beatles, the Stones, and the sixties decade can be traced in performances by both bands. When the Beatles appeared on *Ready Steady Go* in 1964, their hair was short and tidy, and they all wore matching white-collared shirts, dark ties, and suit jackets, as people danced around their lip-synced performance. When the Stones performed "Under My Thumb" semi-live on the same show a few years later, girls are screaming in the audience, and bouncers are struggling to hold the crowd back, away from the band. Despite the overall trajectory of transformation, one element that was already at a feverish pitch in the mid-sixties was the mania of the fans for both the Beatles and the Stones. There are numerous accounts of Rolling Stones concerts being disturbed by riots and fans trying to grab them on stage or tear apart the hall (see Figure 8.2).

Marianne Faithfull recalled the long creative process of "Ruby Tuesday," a song that underlines the assemblage process in Jones' desire to combine his interests in two genres at opposite ends of the stylistic and historical spectrum, Elizabethan lute music and Delta blues.

> "Ruby Tuesday" took forever to get down. It began, as I recall, with a bluesy Elizabethan fragment that Brian was fiddling with in the studio. Brian was obsessed by his notion of a hybrid of Elizabethan lute music and Delta blues, and would hold forth on the essential similarities between Elizabethan ballads and Robert Johnson to anyone who would listen – a bemused Mike Bloomfield or an incredulous Jimi Hendrix, for instance.[43]

Described as a "cross between Thomas Dowland's 'Air on the Late Lord Essex' and a Skip James blues," "Ruby Tuesday" evolved from Jones' recorder melody spun out of this unlikely stylistic pairing, and is an example of one of the closest collaborations between Richards and Jones, with no musical contribution by Jagger other than the vocals.[44] Faithfull remembers that for several weeks it remained as just an instrumental track: "just this beautiful melody . . . Brian's recorder dominates that song. It's a second vocal, a plaintive gull hovering over the song. It was Brian and Keith's song."[45] Despite Jones' compositional involvement in this song, the Jones/Richards partnership was never acknowledged; instead, all the Stones songs were credited to the Jagger/Richards duo with obvious financial consequences for Jones. According to Trynka, "Stan Blackbourne, the Stones' accountant from 1965, was one of many who thought this completely inequitable. 'I used to say to Jones, "What on earth are you doing? You write some of these songs and you give the name over as if Mick Jagger has done it. Do you understand, you're giving 'em thousands of pounds!"'"[46]

The Rolling Stones *Rock and Roll Circus*, 1968

The Rolling Stones Rock and Roll Circus of 1968 – a TV project, eventually abandoned, featuring the Rolling Stones and other groups along with real circus acts – begins with Jethro Tull, the Who, and John Lennon with Eric Clapton, then features Yoko Ono performing with a classical violinist, and finally the Rolling Stones. Jones, clearly in physical distress, plays guitar on some songs and begins the circus performing on a dark wooden flute. He stands relatively still, almost sedated, in a purple jacket, ivory pants, and his shaggy blonde hair, sincerely adding chords, slide guitar, or a specific maracas rhythm to fill in and enhance the sound, with an effect that is neatly woven together yet propulsively electric. Jones' musical *modus operandi* delineates another key definition for assemblage: the act or an instance of fitting together, or, an object made of pieces fitted together.

Jagger is unquestionably the most charismatic by this time, with his clear blue, big expressive eyes and large singing mouth, dancing lithely all the time and propelling his waist in a Latin pelvic thrust over and over, drawing the audience in to what appears to be *his* circus event. He talks with John Lennon in one scene before introducing the Dirty Mac supergroup, then later Lennon silently introduces the Rolling Stones with sign language. By now, Jagger is the central focus, with the long stories of "Sympathy for the Devil" and "You Can't Always Get What You Want" expressed with a theatrical flair, inviting the audience into his world. His dark auburn hair framing his light sparkling eyes is a memorable sight.

Jones is understated but musically adept, contributing to the overall sound without a need to be the center of attention. He is musically a core member but has been almost entirely removed from the action. One exception in the later sixties period is the "Jumpin' Jack Flash" promotional video, where, "wearing bug-eye alien specs, silver lipstick and an ice-blue Telecaster, Brian dominated the visuals alongside Mick,"[47] yet even in this instance Jones appears alienated and removed, in a world of his own. Concerning Jones' increasing isolation from the core members of the band, Faithfull remembers that the composition of "Ruby Tuesday" had

> taken on an almost desperate significance for Brian. This collaboration [with Richards specifically and the Stones generally] was to be their last, and perhaps Brian could sense that. He knew it was one of the best things he'd ever done. He wanted everyone to say "That's great, Brian, wonderful! Good work!" But, of course, nobody did.[48]

After Jethro Tull – Ian Anderson with his long frizzy hair, an unhinged stare directly into the camera, and his frequent placing of his left foot on his right knee like a yogic posture or court jester – and the perhaps founding primal-scream sound artist in Yoko Ono who wails into the microphone on and off key for minutes, the Rolling Stones seem positively cool and collected, like a well-seasoned rock band. For all the previous acts the audience listened and stood up to clap enthusiastically at the end, but for the Rolling Stones, audience members, now garbed in variously colored cloaks, immediately started to dance. The percussive groove the Stones create, using Latin rhythms combined with drum kit, invites the collective bodies to move, illustrated first and foremost by Jagger's ever-fluctuating arms, legs, feet, and body gesturing for all to join in. When they conclude with "Salt of the Earth" ("Let's drink to the lowly of birth"), Marianne Faithfull conceals her face under her light brown suede hat, possibly because she is the daughter of a baroness from Austria, not of "common birth" at all.

Morocco and an Ethnomusicologist's Bent

In Morocco (March, 1967) Jones was introduced to the sounds of the Master Musicians of Joujouka by Brion Gysin and the owner of the 1001 Nights restaurant, Mohamed Hamri, whose uncle was leader of the musical group. Gysin described a ceremony intended to contact Pan, the goat God, considered to represent "sexuality itself," wherein the protagonist had to wear a goat skin newly removed from a sacrificed animal. Trynka describes the importance of this iconic image of Pan for Jones both musically and sexually: "Pan had brought syncopated, dangerous sounds into our world, was the ultimate progenitor of what some righteous people called the Devil's music, and was the god of fertility." Studio engineer George Chkiantz went to Morocco with Jones in August of 1968 to record *Pipes of Pan of Joujouka*. The week-long festival was not taking place at that time but they did go and record for a long evening until dawn.

> It was the first time any serious recording had been done up there, apart from my little Uher [a portable German open-reel tape recorder], and there was some uncertainty among the musicians. It was the first time some of them had ever "heard" themselves. In general, there was quite a commotion because they thought that Brian Jones was very funny and not really of this world, with his long blond hair and furry hippie togs. Remember, they'd never seen anyone like this before. It was very new to them.[49]

The recording did not appear until October 1971, several years after Jones' death, on the Rolling Stones' own label. Bob Palmer wrote in *Rolling Stone* (October 14, 1971):

> Whatever vibrations Brian Jones may have felt his one night in Jajouka, we know that he spent the next few weeks in Tangier, listening and relistening to his tapes, finding his way in the music. He heard it running forward, he heard it running backward, he heard it overlaid upon itself, and he recreated his multi-directional hearing with considerable expertise in a London studio.[50]

Jones added some electronic effects, "a backward drum track here, a backward melody there," and drew on the unusual stereo effects of the recording, since the recording engineer "stood with his Uher 4400 in the center of the musicians, crossing his two microphones in one hand while they marched around him in a revolving figure 8."[51]

The CD liner notes end with Jones' description of the project:

> What exists here is a specially chosen representation of the type of music which is played and chanted during the festival. The pieces and therefore the climaxes are necessarily shortened and when one considers that many of these chants continue for hours and hours, one will realize this necessity. We apologize for the virtual inaudibility of the lead singer during the chanting of the women but they are chanting an incantation to those of another plane, and while we were recording her, she hid her beautiful voice behind the drum she was playing. It was not for our ears. Anyway we hope to have captured the spirit and magic of Jajouka.[52]

A memo from Andy Wickham to Mo Ostin of Warner Bros delineates their concerns that the release of this album not be seen as "exploitation of a dead man's myth and so on." Ultimately, they believed the audience could be convinced that "Brian would have wanted it this way." Wickham concludes: "No matter what anyone says, it is a finished recording, Jones would probably have released it had he lived and in no way can we fairly be accused of extortion. An official Rolling Stones endorsement would, of course, be advantageous in all this." (See Figure 8.3.)

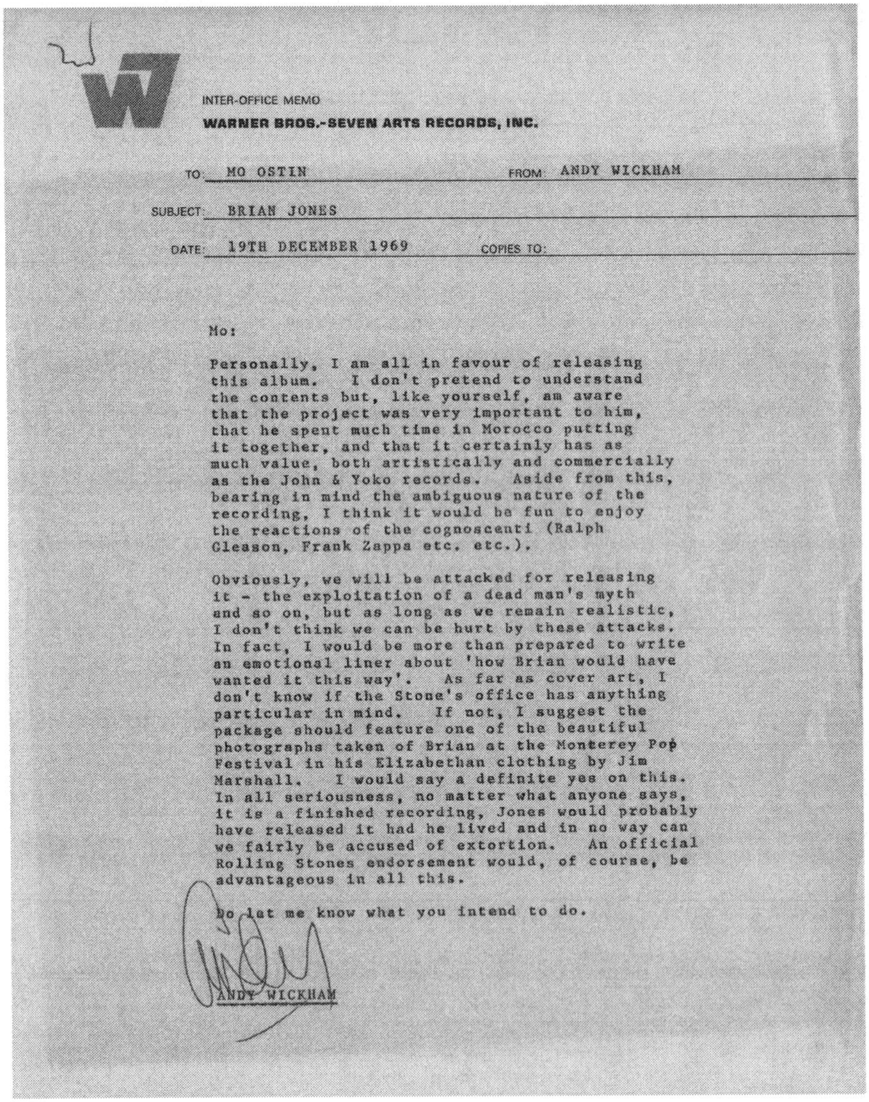

Figure 8.3 Inter-Office Memo from Andy Wickham to Mo Ostin, December 19, 1969. Mo Ostin Collection, Library and Archives, Rock and Roll Hall of Fame and Museum.

Devil Imagery and the Dark Side

The Stones highlight devil imagery in the title for *Their Satanic Majesties Request* (1967) and in the 1968 recording of "Sympathy for the Devil." [53] In the 1968 film of *The Rolling Stones Rock and Roll Circus*, Jagger dances and sings right into the camera, while Jones plays two maracas in each hand, standing near Rocky Dijon (b. Kwasi Dzidzornu, an African percussionist from Ghana) on congas. [54] The song ends with Jagger taking his shirt off and repeating "What's My Name?" over and over with tattoos of the Devil on his chest and arms answering that question.[55] In the June 1968 recording, Bill Wyman plays maracas, and Jones is part of the "devil's chorus" (also comprising Richards, Wyman, Pallenberg, and others) singing vocal "whoo-whoo"s inspired by Jimmy Miller.[56] When Robert F. Kennedy was tragically shot on June 5, 1968, Jagger changed his original line from "Who killed John Kennedy?" to "Who killed the Kennedys?" – suggesting the Devil was behind these and other killings.[57]

Within black American culture, the myth of the crossroads of Robert Johnson – who it was said made a deal with the Devil for prowess playing guitar – may have also inspired the theme of the Devil and satanic elements in several of the Stones' lyrics and titles, and obliquely resonated with the now-iconic lapping tongue logo, though John Pasche has indicated that the Hindu goddess Kali was actually the inspiration for this logo (*Exhibitionism*, "Iconic Logo"). Lust, sex, and drugs were countercultural and widely celebrated in the sixties, but may have retained some dark associations in Christian communities, especially of the older generation. Several drug busts throughout the decade furthered the image of the Stones as the "bad boys" of the British rock scene, an intentional and iconic image for them.

While Trynka portrays Mick Jagger as cold and calculating, pushing Jones out of the Stones for competitive or financial reasons, Norman offers some counter-images of Jagger (and Richards) supporting Jones, attending the court after his second drug bust and offering some money and a way out of the band that would maintain his pride. The Trynka and Norman biographies both depict a world of fame, greed, drugs, indulgence, and attempts to take the other lead band members' women, all of which causes the downfall of Jones and disintegration of his original vision of the band. In a telling response, when Jones saw the white goat being led to the sacrifice in Morocco, he said, "That's me. That's me"; and the others agreed.[58]

Still, Jones had his own dark side, clearly evident in his tendency to get lost in drugs and alcohol – even if it was prescription drugs, LSD, and alcohol and not heroin – and in his conflicted love and attachment to women countered by occasional bouts of devastating violence towards them that is also detailed in these biographies and no doubt played a significant role in his downfall as well.

In conclusion, vast audiences over many decades have recognized the creative contributions of Jagger and Richards. Jagger's creative lyrics, melodic style, charismatic dance moves, and expressive performances, and Richards' incisive melodies and guitar riffs, are emblematic of the Stones' output. Jones' distinct contribution was a subtle, sophisticated instrumental ability to add unusual sounds to the mix and fill gaps in the music with unexpected resonances and beautiful countermelodies on a significant range of instruments with varied historical and cultural associations. Beyond his early and extensive mastery of guitar, slide guitar, and blues-style harmonica, this assemblage of world music sounds constitutes the most distinctive musical contribution of Jones to the Rolling Stones.

From the founding of the band to the present, many fans of the Stones still express their love and appreciation for Brian Jones, often as their favorite in the first decade (see, for example, the piece on Stones fans in this volume by Philippe Puicouyoul, 194–205). YouTube videos such as "The Rolling Stones on the Ed Sullivan Show" include comments by these diehard Jones fans. One comment, by Kathy O'Neil from *c.* 2014, states, "Fact is, without Brian Jones, there wouldn't have been a Rolling Stones." A video tribute to Jones entitled "Brian Jones – The first Stone" offers a concluding statement by Dave Davies of the Kinks: "I'm not putting down anyone else in the Stones, but Brian was the true artist in that band … A lot of their early creativity was down to him."

I have discussed the assemblage aspects of Jones in both individual works and the musical events that traced some of the key world music influences and contributions of his life, as well as some of the challenges he faced. These musical events demonstrate the life of Jones as an assemblage of distinctive musical sounds and influences from diverse locations, cultures, epochs, genres, and instruments that he worked hard to master over decades, beginning with the guitar, slide guitar, and blues harmonica, and moving to his experiments with the dulcimer, marimba, sitar, and recorder. In the end, Jones' tragic downfall resulted from the emotional and physical consequences of the sex and drugs part of the equation, not the rock and roll and world music possibilities, which formed the basis for his extraordinary musical inspirations: his *courant d'air*.[59] Here, I have chosen to focus primarily on the musical events that contributed to the assemblage of Brian Jones in his relation to the Rolling Stones, but I have also indicated some of the other facets or life events that had an impact on the assemblage of his life. The last Rolling Stones concert with Brian Jones was on May 12, 1968, the *New Musical Express* concert for the Poll Winners Show.

This chapter demonstrates the three core pillars of ethnomusicology as defined in my book published in 2015, these being: musical content or sound, various forms of context (historical, biographical, conceptual, and/ or cultural), and a broader theoretical framework.[60] While one can choose to focus solely on musical elements in a given investigation, it is always more than just music that makes up the assemblage of "a life," a core interest of Deleuzean philosophy. Consequently, I have elected to include significant life events as well as the impact of musical events in this assemblage of Jones during his decade-long interactions with key players in the influential sphere of the Rolling Stones.

Notes

1 Jean Khalfa, ed., *An Introduction to the Philosophy of Gilles Deleuze* (London, 2003), 66.

2 *Ibid.*, 52.

3 Wyman*SA*, 172.

4 George E. Marcus and Erkan Saka, "Assemblage," *Theory, Culture & Society* 23 (2006), 102.

5 Khalfa, *An Introduction*, 1.

6 *Ibid.*, 3.

7 Khalfa relates this concept of events based on verbs not nouns to the Stoics, in opposition to the substantialism of the Platonists. *Ibid.*, 2.

8 *Ibid.*, 5–6.

9 Marcus and Saka, "Assemblage," 103.

10 Khalfa, *An Introduction*, 3.

11 The WOMAD festivals celebrated their 35th anniversary in 2017. Among other projects, Gabriel is known for his song honoring South African political freedom fighter Steve Biko on the album *Peter Gabriel III* (a.k.a. *Melt*) (1980), which he performed for two musical tours organized by Amnesty International: *Conspiracy of Hope* with other renowned artists including Sting and U2 in 1986, and *Human Rights Now!* in 1988. These musical efforts represent another significant and developing stream: the role music plays in underscoring important issues of social justice.

12 The Elizabethan influences and Jones' contribution in particular on "Lady Jane" (1966), for example, are noted in *RSCRS*, 72. See also *Ibid.*, 53 for similar influences in "Play With Fire" (1965), though perhaps less the result of Jones' input.

13 These emotional trials are described at length in several biographies of Jones and the Rolling Stones. See Trynka, and Philip Norman, *The Stones: The Acclaimed Biography* (London, 2002).

14 Interview with Charlie Watts in the documentary *25 × 5: The Continuing Adventures of the Rolling Stones* (Executive Producer Lorne Michaels). Transcribed by the author.

15 On the recorder playing for "Ruby Tuesday," see *RSG*, 244. An eclectic combination of styles is also evident in Jones' soundtrack for the German film *Mord und Totschlag* (1967), written in 1966–67 and starring Anita Pallenberg. Though uneven in quality, the soundtrack mixes together psychedelic, commercial pop, and pseudo-avant-garde, along with touches of the "early music" style featuring Jones on recorder, and the recording sessions were positively reviewed by legendary musicians Kenney Jones (Trynka, 210) and Jimmy Page (David Fricke, "Jimmy Page Looks Back," *RSt* [December 6, 2012]), who play on the soundtrack.

16 Norman, *The Stones*, 81. Lennon's quintessential wit and self-deprecating humor is evident here. A week after this initial meeting, the Stones received front-row tickets to the Beatles' first major London concert, at the Royal Albert Hall, and the Beatles supported the Stones in several key instances, for example they offered them a song to record early on in their career (the Stones recorded the Beatles' song "I Wanna Be Your Man," which rose to No. 13 in the pop charts), and it was George Harrison who suggested to Dick Rowe of Decca records that he should consider signing a group called the Rolling Stones (Norman, *The Stones*, 95).

17 One West Coast teenager exclaimed: "We'd have had no possibility of being exposed to Howlin' Wolf or Muddy Waters without them," that is, without the Rolling Stones, and in particular, Jones (Trynka, 147).

18 *Ibid.*, 146.

19 *Ibid.*, 275–6.

20 Trynka, 275. Jones' role in introducing open tunings to Richards is unacknowledged by Richards in the section of his autobiography pertaining to this issue (*Life*, 241–7), in which he states that he started playing open tunings in 1968–69, and that it was Ry Cooder who showed him open G-tuning. Richards' account notwithstanding, Jones' excellent slide bottleneck parts on the 1964 single "Little Red Rooster" clearly show that he was already familiar with open G-tuning several years earlier; Cooder's influence in this regard may have been in introducing Richards

to the different chord shapes (rather than soloistic bottleneck playing) that are possible in open G and E tunings, and that may be what Richards is citing.

21 Norman, *The Stones*, 59.

22 *Life*, 79.

23 *Exhibitionism: The Rolling Stones*: "Meet the Band" (n.p. [2016]); Norman, *The Stones*, 135.

24 Jack Hamilton, *Just Around Midnight: Rock and Roll and the Racial Imagination* (Cambridge, MA, 2016), 253.

25 Norman, *The Stones*, 74.

26 Hamilton, *Just Around Midnight*, 252–3.

27 *Ibid.*, 251–2.

28 Cited by Stanley Booth, "Cheltenham 1969–1970," in Dalton*FTY*, 117.

29 Mrs. Jones, "Brian Jones," in *ibid.*, 12.

30 Booth, "Cheltenham 1969–1970," in Dalton*FTY*, 117.

31 David Dalton, "Striking with a Spirit's Knife," in Dalton*FTY*, 113.

32 Tom Wolfe, *The Kandy-Kolored Tangerine-Flake Streamline Baby* (New York, 1965), 174.

33 Norman, *The Stones*, 91. Given his early take on the band, Oldham aligns himself with Jagger. Furthermore, Oldham seemed bothered by Jones' verbosity. In typical derogatory fashion, Oldham complained of Jones' "theories about 'subliminal themes in search of a juxtaposition'" and "the potential of half-finished melodies that by no means deserved completion." Andrew Loog Oldham, *Rolling Stoned* (Vancouver, 2013), 156.

34 "The elements that make up an assemblage also include the *qualities* present . . . and the affects and effectivity of the assemblage: that is, not just what it *is*, but what it *can do*." J. Macgregor Wise, "Assemblage," in *Gilles Deleuze: Key Concepts*, 2nd edn., ed. Charles J. Stivale (Montreal and Kingston, 2011), 92.

35 *RSG*, 106.

36 Trynka, 184–5.

37 *RSCRS*, 72.

38 Norman, *The Stones*, 197; *RSCRS*, 76.

39 Trynka, 186.

40 *Ibid.*, 187.

41 *RSG*, 220.

42 Wyman*RWTS*, 234. The first few songs the Stones wrote, including "Little by Little" and "Off the Hook," were credited to "Nanker Phelge," the name given to songs written collaboratively on Stones albums. In Trynka's account of the composition of "Paint It, Black" (187), he suggests that after "Brian fashioned a melody on the sitar, Mick added his vocals, *tracking Brian's sitar line* [emphasis mine], and the Jagger/Richards song partnership notched up one of its greatest songs, Paint It, Black." Unfortunately, these details about Jagger following Jones' sitar melody are not in Wyman*RWTS*, nor is the source cited. Confirming Jones' role in the authorship of the song, Elliott writes that "Brian Jones' virtuoso performance on the sitar was inspirational" (*RSCRS*, 74).

43 Faithfull, 88.

44 *Ibid.* It is not clear whether Faithfull has remembered this erroneously or whether it was indeed Jones who was mistaken, but the composer alluded to is the Elizabethan lutenist and songwriter *John* Dowland (1563–1626), whose galliard dedicated to the Earl of Essex (misquoted in Trynka, 201, as "Sussex") is based on his ayre "Can She Excuse My Wrongs," published in 1597.

45 *Ibid.*

46 Trynka, 202.

47 Trynka, 274.

48 Faithfull, 88–9.

49 Trynka, 285.

50 David Dalton, "Striking with a Spirit's Knife: A Shade of Blonde," in Dalton*FTY*, 113.

51 Dalton*RS*, 36.

52 Brian Jones, liner notes for *Brian Jones Presents the Pipes of Pan at Jajouka* (Polygram CD, 1995).

53 "The Devil is My Name" was the working title for "Sympathy for the Devil." The evolution of the song was captured on film by Jean-Luc Godard at Olympic Studios in London, the footage showing the extent to which Jones was now isolated from the rest of the band; see *RSCRS*, 105.

54 Kwasi "Rocky" Dzidzornu (1935–1993), famous for his percussion work with not only the Rolling Stones, but also Taj Mahal, Stevie Wonder, and many others.

55 While Jagger appeared to relish this Lucifer image, he actually had a more centrist approach. It is telling that after Jagger offered to write music for Kenneth Anger's film *Invocation of my Demon Brother*, with some exploration of black magic that this entailed, he quickly backtracked and wore a large wooden crucifix for nearly a year! (Norman, *The Stones*, 313).

56 *RSCRS*, 206.

57 As is well known, this song is based on the book Faithfull and Jagger were reading at the time, *The Master and Margarita* by Mikhail Bulgakov, written in the Soviet Union between 1928 and 1942, but first published in English in 1967, in which Satan reflects on the effects of the Russian Revolution (see, for example, *RSCRS*, 106). Apparently, Jagger did not want the band to be labelled as "satanists," though the powerful association stuck.

58 See Norman, *The Stones*, 309.

59 By the end of 1966, Jones was drunk in the studio and "barely functional" when Peter Whitehead went to film the Stones again (Trynka, 203). But the "fateful trip to Morocco" when he lost Pallenberg to Richards was March 1967. Jones went downhill after that, and drank so much that he was barely present in some of the later studio sessions, certainly a primary factor in the Stones asking him to leave the band so they could go on tour. While it is not clear if Pallenberg and Jones would have stayed together for a lifetime, it is clear that this "life event" caused a significant turn in Jones' will to live and his ability to create with the musical band he in fact founded. Trynka, citing Jones' friend Stash Klossowski, concludes that "it was the betrayal by his fellow Stones that was devastating. 'They didn't confront him . . . he was simply abandoned'." (Trynka, photo captions prior to 183.)

60 Brita Renée Heimarck, *Balinese Gender Wayang (Shadow Play) Music of Bapak I Wayan Loceng, from Sukawati, Bali, Indonesia: A Musical Biography, Musical Ethnography, and Critical Edition* (Middleton, WI, 2015), 4.

PART III

Stones on Film, Revival, and Fans

9 Shine a Light: The Rolling Stones on Film

MICHAEL BRENDAN BAKER

Songs by the Rolling Stones are used in the soundtracks of so many contemporary film and television productions that any attempt to count them would be a fool's errand. The group's role as the stars or principal subjects of documentary films concerned with popular music and culture is far easier to chronicle, however, but no less instructive in terms of demonstrating the central influence of the Stones within the world of motion pictures. It is not an exaggeration to suggest the Rolling Stones represent the most documented musical group in the history of cinema. It is explained, in part, as the result of their unrivalled longevity, but equally for the timing of their emergence on the scene and the ease with which they both invited and adapted to the presence of cameras in their professional lives. Looking at Dominique Tarlé's still-photography (1971) captured during the band's exile in France and the recording of *Exile on Main Street* at Villa Nellcôte, alongside home footage from the period (now available within the *Stones in Exile* DVD, Stephen Kijak, USA, 2010), it becomes clear that the band was surrounded by motion picture cameras – those of professionals as well as their own – to an ubiquitous degree. Over the course of their career, the Rolling Stones embraced documentary film-making and the opportunities made available through increasingly sophisticated, progressively mobile, synchronized sound film technology in a manner rivalled by few, if any, of their contemporaries. Early on, they understood the power of the moving image and the degree to which it could both secure and perpetuate the mythology of the band, collaborating with a range of innovative filmmakers and artists whose approaches would facilitate such a project of self-creation. However, after public controversies, personal turmoil, and diminishing financial returns, the Rolling Stones would begin to exert an increasing amount of control over their cinematic representation, which results in work through the 1980s, 1990s and 2000s that rarely, if ever, demonstrates the innovation and intimacy for which the first decade of their documentary appearances is so celebrated.[1]

If the theatrical première of the concert revue *T.A.M.I. Show* (Steve Binder, USA, 1964) marks the emergence of the rockumentary genre as we know it today – that is, those film and television projects recognized for their representations of live musical events, culturally important historic rock music gatherings, and, occasionally, behind-the-scenes tell-alls – we observed the fiftieth anniversary of the genre soon after the Stones celebrated their golden anniversary among rock's most cherished icons. And in that foundational film, revered by fans for career-defining performances by James Brown and the Supremes, we find Mick Jagger and Keith Richards participating in the birth of one of the documentary genre's most commercially viable and aesthetically rich categories. The history of the Rolling Stones in documentary film is, essentially, the history of the popular music documentary, and more specifically, the rockumentary genre. Several portraits of the Stones populate the first wave of rockumentaries, films that ultimately define the genre, including the aforementioned *T.A.M.I. Show*, *Charlie Is My Darling* (Peter Whitehead, UK, 1966), *Sympathy for the Devil* (Jean-Luc Godard, FRA, 1968), and *Gimme Shelter* (Albert Maysles, David Maysles, Charlotte Zwerin, USA, 1970). A survey of several key films spanning the first decade of film-making focused on the group (1964–74) illustrates the pivotal role non-fiction film played in their professional lives and in establishing their celebrity; across this body of work, the main currents and trends comprising the rockumentary genre are represented: the concert film, the artist biography, the festival film, and the "making of" or tour film.[2] The visual representation of the Stones in motion pictures is a central plank in establishing the iconography of rock performance (both onstage and off), and the structure and style of these films becomes a standard upon which other filmmakers and artists model their work. The diversity of approaches to documenting the creative work of the band and their persona is matched only by the diversity of ways in which they are revealed – or choose to reveal themselves – to the camera and filmmakers. The Rolling Stones, on film, are both canonized and contribute to the canonization of a documentary genre and a visual grammar of rock.

Roll Camera

Here they are, those five fellows from England, the Rolling Stones! JAN & DEAN (*T.A.M.I. SHOW*, 1964)

If the birth of rockumentary is foreshadowed by the 1960 concert film *Jazz on a Summer's Day* (Bert Stern, USA), the multi-artist revue film *T.A.M.I. Show* firmly establishes the basic features of the fledgling genre. The film is a record of the so-called British Invasion of American popular music as it was taking place (despite the absence of the Beatles, who had made their own big screen début several months earlier with *A Hard Day's Night*; "They wanted too damn much money," executive producer William Sargent told the *New York Times* on October 15, 1964). The Rolling Stones headline a bill alongside Gerry and the Pacemakers, Billy J. Kramer & the Dakotas, and established black crossover acts like Chuck Berry, the Supremes, Marvin Gaye, and James Brown. Originally conceived as the first of an annual film event featuring rock and roll artists, in support of music scholarships for teenagers, *T.A.M.I. Show* is a valuable document of the diversity of teen-oriented popular music at the time and a vivid illustration of the impact of the Civil Rights Act of 1964 – only months old at the time of the event – with its integrated cast of musicians and dancers as well as an integrated audience. Film director Binder credits producer and band leader Jack Nitzsche (who later appeared on several Stones albums as musician and arranger) for selecting the majority of the acts, most of whom went on to significant careers in pop music. Formally, *T.A.M.I. Show* is built upon the conventions of television, specifically the well-established variety show format (in many ways the film is a theatrically released compendium of awards show-style musical performances still common today) and broadcast television contemporaries *Shindig!* (ABC, 1964–66) and the Binder-directed *Hullabaloo* (NBC, 1965–66). The film is composed primarily of three- or four-song medleys from each artist, with edits limited to the transitions between acts, and introductions by teen pin-ups Jan & Dean serving as bumpers. Most artists appear alone on stage and receive off-screen musical support from select members of the Wrecking Crew – the famed LA session musicians, including Hal Blaine (drums), Tommy Tedesco (guitar), and Lyle Ritz (bass), whose work appears on a dizzying assortment of classic recordings ranging from Frank Sinatra and Herb Alpert to the Beach Boys and Simon & Garfunkel. The Stones are among a small number of artists who perform without accompaniment by the Wrecking Crew, and their segment features more camera movement, crowd-reaction shots, and close-ups than any other in the film. It is important to recall the threat to common decency and conservative morality rock and roll music, and the Rolling Stones in particular, was perceived to present mainstream Western society upon its arrival in the mid-twentieth century. As such, we cannot take for granted the impact of even the most benign performative gestures exhibited by the band. Describing the potency and the rebellious qualities of Jagger's performance style from the outset, David James writes,

> Both spontaneous and calculated, the sexual instability of his body was matched by the dualities in his voice, the combination of the vowels and phrasing learned from blues records with the Cockney affectations becoming one of rock 'n' roll's seminal amalgamations of conflicting racial, national, and sexual characteristics, all paraded on a similarly ersatz working-class attitudinizing.[3]

The physicality of Jagger's performance and the slow build from his reserved vocal delivery and stationary position during the opener "Around and Around," to the prowling, crowd-provoking dynamism exhibited during the set's penultimate song, "I'm Alright," proves foundational to subsequent cinematic representations of the Stones as performers and central to fan expectations. In this first of many documentary portraits of the group as live performers, the sheer force of Jagger's musical energy and endless charisma suggests *seeing* the Rolling Stones is perhaps just as important as hearing them, and that their persona as a group is not discernible solely by way of their sonic identity.

Collaborations with the Avant-Garde

[*Charlie Is My Darling*] brings out a pathetic sadness about the teenage idolatry about pop singers, and the effect it has on the Stones who emerge from the film as basically very talented musicians who would be completely destroyed once they lost their own individual personalities. ROBIN BEAN (*FILMS AND FILMING*, DECEMBER, 1966)

The Rolling Stones' first starring role in a documentary film exemplifies their relationship with the emergent British arts scene of the 1960s. Moreover, it highlights Jagger's early investment in cultivating an image of himself and the band that exists outside the perceived triviality of pop music. Nine months after the release of *T.A.M.I. Show* arrives a tour movie following the band about to explode onto the world stage. Peter Whitehead, trained in film-making during his time at the Slade School of Fine Art in London, was commissioned by the Stones' then-manager Andrew Loog Oldham to produce a documentary of the band's September 1965 tour of Ireland, with the hope that it would attract financiers for a feature-length vehicle similar to that of *Hard Day's Night* (Richard Lester, UK, 1964) released a year earlier.[4] The result, *Charlie Is My Darling*, is a fifty-minute blend of life on the road, backstage moments, and public appearances alongside several brief musical sequences. Structurally, the film offers viewers no sense at all of the itinerary of the tour, the venues, the scale of the performances, or the audiences themselves; the material is only truly meaningful when refracted through the lens of the Stones' long history. Unreleased until 2012 as a result of litigation between the band and their former manager (which is to say nothing of the many different unlicensed music sources that appear on the soundtrack, all serving as a major impediment to any official release), the film was nonetheless widely available on bootleg videocassette for many years and would screen at retrospectives of Whitehead's work when the director was in attendance.

Charlie Is My Darling serves as a counterbalance to the overwhelming number of rockumentaries that adopt a strictly observational mode of address, wherein filmmakers serve as witness to events for the absent viewing audience, oftentimes crafting the illusion of unmediated access to those events.[5] Adopting the mobile 16 mm motion picture camera and then-new wireless synchronized sound recorder favored by so many of his contemporaries (a 16 mm Éclair NPR camera matched with a Kudelski Nagra III recorder; see Figure 9.1), Whitehead is an active participant in the events he photographs. At times, his voice is heard off-screen asking questions of those on-screen and directing the action. Recurring images of youthful fans and synch-sound interviews with members of the public feature Whitehead's insistent queries, "What do you like about them? Why? What is it? When did you first grow your hair long?" Meanwhile, several extended exchanges between Whitehead and band members directly address the hysteria surrounding the group and the dilemma facing young musicians recognized more for their behavior than their music. Guitarist Brian Jones explains he is satisfied with the success of the Stones but creatively unfulfilled by life as a pop star; at Whitehead's prompting he discusses an unrealized film project based on the principles of Surrealism. Drummer Charlie Watts, after whom the film is named, feels humbled by

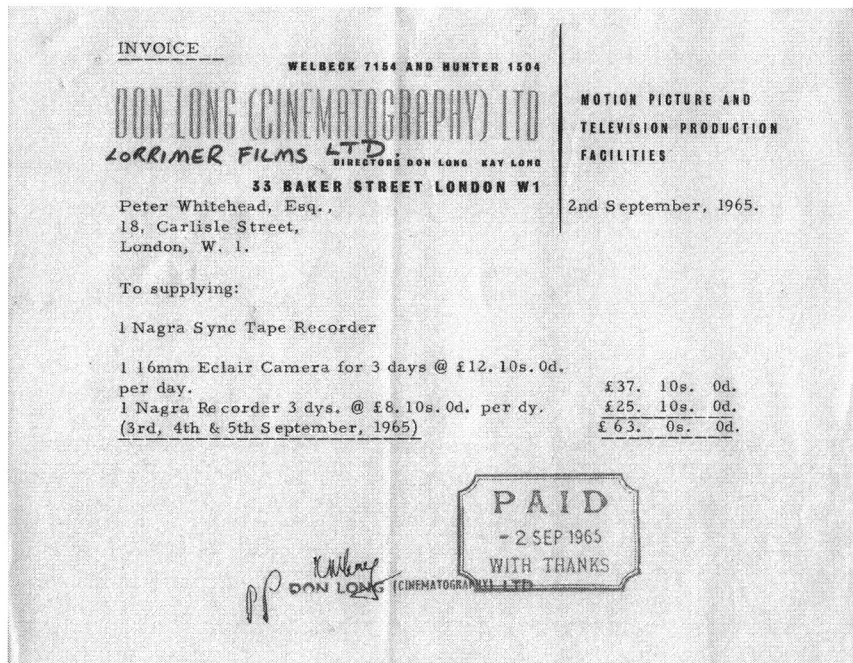

Figure 9.1 Invoice for the rental of camera and recorder used by Whitehead for the filming of *Charlie Is My Darling*. Courtesy of Peter Whitehead.

his experience in the Rolling Stones and plainly states he is not yet an artist, simply a musician in a successful band. These weighty moments clash with scenes of bored band members prepping for the stage and jockeying for a turn in front of the mirror – all appear to be blotting cold sores and other blemishes with cover-up, an image later played for laughs in the classic music mockumentary, *This Is Spinal Tap* (Rob Reiner, USA, 1986) – but all leave viewers with the same impression that the most powerful acts of revelation in the film are those that suggest the Stones have let down their guard.

Stylistically, there is little of note apart from a brief step-printed sequence focused on Jagger's acrobatic stage persona. "All of it's acting," Jagger explains in a voice-over, "But there's a difference between acting and not enjoying it, and just doing what you want to do. It's like getting into a part." Images of the band travelling in cars, waiting in airport lounges, and racing through crowded train stations as enthusiastic fans clutch and grab the Stones seem to fascinate Whitehead more than the music and occupy a large portion of the film's running time. As Coelho has written,

> Blurring the distinction between the "center" and the "periphery" of his subject by training his camera on just about everything – entrances and exits of the band, policemen, bystanders, street life, curious onlookers, rioters, impromptu backstage music – Whitehead prioritizes the mundane, improvised, sometimes vapid offstage culture, as opposed to the frenzy of the more scripted live show.[6]

There is the customary backstage-to-front-of-house tracking shot now so common to the genre, a feature *Charlie Is My Darling* shares with the more widely copied shot from D. A. Pennebaker's Dylan film, *Don't Look Back* (D. A. Pennebaker, USA, 1965) produced in the same year. The soundtrack is a mélange of clips from Stones recordings with preference given to "Play With Fire" (a track recorded and released shortly after the conclusion of the Irish tour), instrumental versions of Stones songs recorded by other acts, and candid audio interviews with band members in a manner quite similar to *The Beatles at Shea Stadium* (ABC Television, USA, 1965). There is not, however, a single musical performance sequence featuring synchronized sound apart from brief moments of the group warming up and jamming backstage. There is an extended performance segment in the middle of the film featuring a number of songs, but the soundtrack appears to be a separate audio recording of the event (poorly) post-synchronized with the image track. The sequence concludes with a stage invasion that completely disrupts the performance and ends the show; the band makes a hasty retreat from the venue with the assistance of police officers as the crowd of screaming girls chants, "We want the Stones! We want the

Stones!" It is an eerie portent of the events captured in *Gimme Shelter*, which serves to document the end of the 1960s idyllic dream of free love and non-violence.

According to Whitehead, *Charlie Is My Darling* received a Gold Medal at the 1966 Mannheim Film Festival (records suggest it was, in fact, Whitehead's *Wholly Communion* that won the prize); it was screened in a truncated version on German television, while the BBC and Granada refused to put it on the air. Joseph von Sternberg, acclaimed filmmaker and director of the festival that year, reportedly said of the film, "When all the other films at this festival are long forgotten, this film will still be watched – as a unique document of its times."[7] Von Sternberg's prediction, however, would not come to pass for many years as a result of prolonged legal battles and business maneuvering between Whitehead, manager Oldham, and ultimately Jagger himself that kept the film from public exhibition as ownership and commercial rights remained in dispute.[8] The film would only become widely available in 2012 when Allen Klein's ABKCO – owner of most audiovisual materials dating to that period of the band's history – released a version containing new material (re-edited by Nathan Punwar) dubbed, *Charlie Is My Darling – Ireland 1965*. The highlight of the film is undoubtedly a step-printed sequence featuring stage invasions at Rolling Stones concerts set to the slow tempo of the Jagger/Richards ballad, "Lady Jane," from *Aftermath* (1966). Whitehead's marriage of the glacially paced acts of violence to the gentle instrumentation of the song – a not-so-subtle commentary on youth culture and fan worship at a transformative moment in popular music history – is ahead of its time in anticipating a recurring trope of contemporary music video, namely an investment in abstraction and expressionistic devices at the expense of conventional portraiture of the performance.[9]

Oldham, Jagger, and the Stones continued their flirtation with cinema's avant-garde with the film-making partnerships that followed their work with Whitehead. French filmmaker Jean-Luc Godard's foray into the emerging rockumentary genre is in many ways influenced by Pennebaker and occurs during a period of collaboration between the French New Wave *auteur* and the American on another project – the alternately abandoned, disowned, and adopted *One P.M.* (1972). Godard's curious portrait of the Rolling Stones, *One Plus One* (later, *Sympathy for the Devil* [FRA, 1968]), features camerawork and backstage footage that is not dissimilar from Pennebaker's largely observational work, but Godard's methods and philosophy are something entirely different. Focused entirely (musically, that is) on the recording of what became the title track of the film, Godard alternately builds upon and undermines rock's political potential with a series of digressions that take the viewer far from the recording studio and instead to fictional sequences featuring Black Panthers stockpiling arms for an impending revolution, feminists, and Marxist revolutionaries spouting political slogans, prose from romantic novellas, and long passages from central texts by LeRoi Jones (Amiri Baraka) and Eldridge Cleaver. It is fair to say that no other example of this bricolage exists in rockumentary history, though Godard's radical influence is felt in arts documentaries and biographies of avant-garde musicians, all of which share a kinship with the more commercially successful documentary genre. It is a testament to Godard's talents (and patience as a filmmaker) that the in-studio footage of the Stones remains one of the most comprehensive and illuminating documents of rock songwriting and record production ever captured on film, but it is in no way conventional. Shaun Inouye writes,

> the Stones appear more like actors on-set than documentary subjects on-location, ambling through rehearsed material under stage-lights and boom-mikes while Godard's camera, casting bouncing shadows across the room, ostensibly films its own participation in the recording process. With each tracking pass, Godard seems to suggest that the reality "captured" by the documentarian is no more real than the reality fabricated by a movie studio, and its "real-life" subjects, no more authentic than the actors' best roles.[10]

Godard's in-studio rehearsal footage is beautifully composed and photographed by cinematographer Tony Richmond, who made vital contributions to the rockumentary genre in films such as *Let It Be* (Michael Lindsay-Hogg, UK, 1970) and *The Kids Are Alright* (Jeff Stein, USA, 1979) over a career of forty-five years and counting. Completed two years before its 1970 North American release, it is a complex film befitting Godard's temperament and the Stones' desire to be validated artistically, and it challenges the conventional representation of musical performance in non-fiction film. As a portrait of the Rolling Stones, however, it remains a difficult film with which to engage and is no doubt the most perplexing entry in the group's filmography, its importance in chronicling the compositional process of "Sympathy for the Devil" notwithstanding.

Gimme Shelter

There is quite a lot of music and performing in *Gimme Shelter*, some of it beautifully recorded, but it is not a concert film, like *Woodstock*. It is more like an end-of-the-world film, and I found it very depressing. VINCENT CANBY, *NEW YORK TIMES*, DECEMBER 7, 1970

With the December 1970 release of *Gimme Shelter* arriving as it did eight months after the blockbuster success of *Woodstock* (Michael Wadleigh, USA, 1970) and only weeks after the première of *Elvis: That's the Way It Is*

(Denis Saunders, USA, 1970), the box office future of the rockumentary genre seemed assured (despite the unexpected failure of the Beatles' *Let It Be*), with the Stones playing a major recurring role in its evolution and emergence. Recognized as one of the great achievements of the rockumentary genre and American documentary history as a whole – in large part the result of its serendipitous murder sub-plot and Altamont's symbolic standing as the definitive end of the 1960s peace-and-love movement – *Gimme Shelter* is a structurally complex film that ultimately transcends the genre with its appeal to a general audience. For better or worse, the bedlam and the beauty captured by pioneering American documentarians Albert and David Maysles during the 1969 American tour rank among the most iconic in the band's history and trap in amber the image of a band at once reckless, composed, and creatively ahead of their peers.

Mick Jagger and new manager Allen Klein discussed the possibility of contracting D. A. Pennebaker to produce a film about the 1969 Stones tour prompted by the knowledge that the Woodstock festival would be filmed and released by a major Hollywood studio; it is said Pennebaker declined to participate because of concerns about the scene developing around the group.[11] Ultimately, filmmaker Haskell Wexler (who also passed on the project after a meeting with Jagger) recommended the Maysles brothers and their partner, Charlotte Zwerin, on the basis of the trio's central place in the American New Documentary movement and their groundbreaking approach to portraiture, including *With Love from Truman* (1966) and *Salesman* (1968). Filmed over the course of several weeks in November and December 1969, *Gimme Shelter* features four distinct areas of action: on-stage and on-the-road sequences shot during the Stones' US tour in advance of the Altamont Speedway Free Festival (which took place on December 6, 1969 – the film premièred on the first anniversary of the event); scenes of the group recording tracks at Muscle Shoals Sound Studio in Alabama for their forthcoming *Sticky Fingers* LP (1971); observational footage of the band's managers, lawyers, and allies making arrangements for the one-day festival event; and performances from the Stones, first at Madison Square Garden, and subsequently alongside other artists at the Altamont concert (shot with the assistance of a team of cinematographers including local film studies graduates George Lucas and Walter Murch). Framing all of these elements are scenes of the band reviewing the Maysles' rough-cut of the film and commenting upon the unfortunate events of Altamont. It is not a comprehensive portrait of the concert itself: performances by Santana and Crosby, Stills, Nash & Young are not featured (the musicians do not appear in the film at all), while sets by Jefferson Airplane and the Flying Burrito Brothers are represented by single songs. Continuing a trend established with *Woodstock*, the filmmakers collaborated with an outside sound engineer for the recording of the concert audio tracks. Glyn Johns' (Bob Dylan, the Beatles, the Who) multi-channel audio recordings of the Madison Square Garden performances of November 27–28, 1969 were edited and mixed for use in *Gimme Shelter* before serving as the source for the band's seminal live LP, *Get Yer Ya-Ya's Out! The Rolling Stones in Concert* (1970); the album was released in advance of *Gimme Shelter*'s theatrical première.

The death of eighteen-year-old Meredith Hunter at the hands of the Hell's Angels during the Stones' headlining set becomes the organizing element that structures the entire film. The death also brings to the fore issues of collaboration and responsibility that run throughout the rockumentary genre (and documentary in general) by forcing viewers to question the role played by filmmaker and subject in the horrible attack. Pauline Kael famously described the film as akin to "reviewing the footage of President Kennedy's assassination or Lee Harvey Oswald's murder," and laid the blame at the feet of the filmmakers themselves in a controversial piece published in the *New Yorker* (December 19, 1970). Popular music scholar Sheila Whiteley offers a more nuanced analysis of the event:

> Whilst the arrogance and brutality inherent in [the Stones'] songs suggest a certain correlation with the events at Altamont it would, nevertheless, seem somewhat simplistic to posit an unproblematic stimulus/response interpretation. Jagger might introduce himself as Lucifer, as "the Midnight Rambler," but overall it is suggested that his role was more that of the symbolic anarchist, expressing the right to personal freedom, the freedom to experience. As such he provides an insight into degeneracy rather than an incitement to a pseudo-tribal response.[12]

As a result of the festival's disorganization and the fatal final act, the Altamont Speedway Free Festival and its filmed record are considered by many to be the symbolic conclusion to the 1960s and the shadowy counterbalance to the idealism of Woodstock (and its film). Robert Christgau argued in 1972 that "writers focus on Altamont not because it brought on the end of an era but because it provided such a complex metaphor for the way an era ended."[13] The spirit of collaboration and the sense of community that has come to define Woodstock and the era as a whole is overturned by Altamont's entanglement of complex business concerns and the Stones' cultivated egotism, revealing fissures in a youth culture so often identified as unified and single-minded. That the event concludes with a senseless murder only seems to confirm the film's status as an eschatological statement of 1960s utopian youth culture.

Gimme Shelter is not the first rockumentary to focus on the off-stage personalities of the performers – *Lonely Boy* (Wolf Koenig and Roman

Kroitor, CAN, 1962), the Beatles documentaries, and *Don't Look Back* were pioneers in that regard – nor is it unique in documenting the act of making records. But unlike earlier rockumentaries and the current concert film genre, *Gimme Shelter* foregrounds the role cinema plays in the act of recollection; the film is a meditation on the act of documentation and becomes something more than an exercise in representing a singular musical event or experience. Moreover, it accents the role of the film-makers as complicit in the process of mythologizing the event. In his 1970 review of the film, Vincent Canby wrote:

> As was the movie about the Woodstock festival, *Gimme Shelter* was a part of the event it recorded, being, in fact, a commissioned movie, the proceeds from which are to help the Stones pay the costs of the free concert (although they grossed a reported $1.5-million from the other, nonfree [*sic*] concerts on their tour). Thus, the movie that examines the Stones, and the Altamont manifestation, with such a cold eye, seems somehow to be examining itself. (*New York Times*, December 7, 1970)

The film presents viewers with a flow of performances, conversations, arguments, and incidents from before, during, and after the concert that come together as a recollection of, and conversation about, Altamont, leaving a foreboding sense that the Rolling Stones are particularly ill suited to managing and containing the aggression and violence demonstrated at the event (a feeling underscored by their ill-advised decision to employ the Hell's Angels as protectors); the Maysles and Zwerin foreshadow these events by employing audio recordings of callers to a KSAN radio show after the festival concludes as an expository device throughout the film. Through extensive scenes involving the business behind the production of the event, the presence of band members during the editing of the film, and the incorporation of the KSAN broadcasts, the Maysles and Zwerin contextualize the events of Altamont and encourage interpretation and critique. It is a rare example of a rockumentary film engaging in the ethical debates concerning the relationship between filmmaker and subject, which were crucial to the development of the New Documentary of the 1960s and 1970s.

Gimme Shelter regularly employs a reflexive mode of address during those scenes involving the band screening rushes (daily footage) of the film-in-progress and footage of Hunter, prompting the band members and film audience alike to question the filmmakers' role in creating the experience; it is a representational strategy not yet explored within rockumentaries at this point in their evolution but employed here with striking effect as the filmmakers highlight the form of the text itself.[14] Much has been written about the passive, almost dismissive response of Jagger to the violent footage captured by the Maysles (and Kael was particularly damning in her evaluation of Jagger's behavior), but less has been said about Watts, who serves as the Maysles' true object of interest during these passages precisely for his humane response to the events. Watts views the footage and tries to understand how things arrived at such a point, remarking, "Oh dear, what a shame." Whether or not the Maysles and Zwerin consciously construct Watts as sympathetic figure and a surrogate for the audience is debatable, but there is no denying his appearances convey none of the antagonism demonstrated by Jagger and his dismissive responses to the material he screens in the company of the Maysles (including his evaluation of Tina Turner's searing performance as an opening act for the Madison Square Garden shows: "It's nice to have a chick occasionally."). One might say Watts' naturalistic behavior casts unfavorable light on Jagger's inauthentic performance in the company of the filmmakers; his off-stage persona is no less constructed than the one he adopts during live performances.

Gimme Shelter refines many of the basic shooting strategies introduced by earlier works of this classical period of the rockumentary genre. While there are fleeting lyrical elements on display during musical sequences – the slow-motion and superimposition employed during the "Love in Vain" performance, which recalls the "Lady Jane" sequence from *Tonite Let's All Make Love in London* – on-stage performances are overwhelmingly shot in a journalistic style. It is worth asking the question whether or not these impressionistic elements were prompted by the likelihood of poor synchronization if the filmmakers proceeded with their decision to include "Love in Vain" in the finished film; the audio recording of the song available on *Get Yer Ya-Ya's Out!* – and presumably the one available to the filmmakers during post-production – may have come from a performance in Baltimore preceding the New York City concerts. The cameras are positioned at the front and side of the stage and focus on Jagger at the expense of the rest of the band (particularly during the Madison Square Garden performances), and there is an assuredness and clarity to the framing and pictorial quality that dimly sets the film apart from earlier work in the genre, including that of Maysles. What is noteworthy is a higher rate of cutting adopted by the Maysles and Zwerin during performance sequences relative to earlier examples from the genre. The reduction in the average shot length imbues these sections of the film with a particular rhythmic quality, and reflects the dynamism of Jagger's expressive performance style in a manner that is clearly differentiated from non-musical sequences of observation, interactivity, and reflexivity elsewhere in the film. Also of interest is the way in which the filmmakers accent moments away from the action that nonetheless communicate the decadence and mystique of life on the road and life on stage. The film is peppered with sequences concerned with the mundane moments of a rock star's routine, but these passages are invigorated by Albert Maysles' wandering eye and his trademark attention to the quirky details of his subjects. His fascination with Jagger's flowing red scarf (both backstage and caught in the car door of his chauffeured ride) and Richards' scuffed and scarred snakeskin boots in Muscle Shoals (while reclining in the studio listening to an early playback of "Wild Horses") comprise the two most memorable images among Maysles' inventory of rock iconography, particularly in that they are captured far from the action. Such moments become central to conveying the sense of access that is central to later works within the tour film and "the-making-of" categories, as documentary filmmakers work to carve out the off-stage personalities of rock performers from their outsized celebrity and on-stage personae.

Moving Forward, Moving Backwards

"It's vérité," [Frank] said.
"Never mind vérité," [Richards] reportedly replied, "I want poetry."
JOHN ROBINSON, *THE GUARDIAN*, OCTOBER 9, 2004

Two additional feature-length films starring the Rolling Stones appeared in the years immediately following *Gimme Shelter* and did little to shed the aura of danger surrounding the band. Both films were made during the American tour in support of *Exile on Main Street* (1972) under the guise of a single production. In the end, two very different films resulted, with the first focused entirely on backstage affairs, reinforcing the veneer of irresponsibility that followed the band after the events of Altamont. *Cocksucker Blues* (Robert Frank, USA, 1972) is a portrait of excess and debauchery so raw and unflattering that the band immediately filed an injunction against its release, and came to the unheard-of agreement that it could only be screened on a limited basis within the context of a retrospective of the artist's work and only if the filmmaker was in attendance at the screening.[15] The artist in question, celebrated postwar photographer Robert Frank, was approached by Jagger to create the sleeve for *Exile on Main Street*. Instead, Frank counter-proposed that he design the sleeve as part of a larger project of documentation that would highlight his adoption of 8 mm motion picture photography. Assisted by his friend and protégé, Danny Seymour, Frank would enjoy access to the band and their entourage to a degree previously unheard of in the world of popular music. Frank's standing in the American art world as a photographer and experimental filmmaker has resulted in the banned film appearing in special engagements at major institutions, including the Whitney Museum of American Art (where it publicly premièred in 1980), Tate Modern

(2004), Metropolitan Museum of Art (2009), Museum of Modern Art (2013), and in a touring retrospective in 2016, but it is otherwise only available in various bootleg formats.[16]

Less interested in musical performance than in the seamy side of the rock lifestyle with its drugs, adoring fans, and celebrity hangers-on (including Andy Warhol, Truman Capote, and Dick Cavett), together with the monotony that quickly comes to define life on the road, Frank leverages the mobility and discrete nature of the Super 8 mm and 16 mm motion picture film formats not only to capture images off the cuff and when the band is most vulnerable, but to hastily conceive and direct sequences that will capture the attention of audiences. How else can we explain images of Keith Richards strung out on heroin, the scene purportedly depicting roadies sexually assaulting groupies on the Stones' private jet, or Jagger with his hand down the front of his jeans masturbating for the camera? Frank structures footage of tour rehearsals, listening sessions, travel time, backstage prep, and recreation in a stream of consciousness flow with no clear chronology or context for the images. A title card introduces the content of the film as "fictitious" in what can only be presumed to be a legal maneuver to protect the band. *Cocksucker Blues* represents a level of access never seen before or since, and contributes to the development of the tour film current established by *Don't Look Back* and *Elvis on Tour*, wherein the personalities and lifestyles of the musicians are framed by their backstage routines and lives away from the spotlight, often at the expense of performance footage. Ultimately, the Stones' sensitivity to their portrayal in this material – so soon after their featured role in *Gimme Shelter* – deepened their resolve to control its availability, a position further reflected in their selective use of Frank's material in the contemporary, Stones-produced *Stones in Exile*, chronicling the making of the album. *Cocksucker Blues* remains unavailable outside of the original screening agreement struck with Frank, and it isn't beyond the realm of possibility that whatever quality prints of the film still exist will go to the grave with the director unless the Stones acknowledge the historical significance of the film and accept that it plays a major role both in the evolution of the rockumentary genre and their legacy.

Ladies and Gentlemen: The Rolling Stones, the second film produced during the 1972 US tour, is a relatively bland corrective to the portrayal of excess, abuse, and disaster that follows the band throughout *Gimme Shelter* and *Cocksucker Blues* (while nonetheless demonstrating the negative impact the band's infamous alcohol and drug use had upon their stage performances at this pivotal point in their career). Shot on 16 mm by cinematographers-for-hire Steve Gebhardt and Bob Fries over four nights in Texas, then optically processed to 35 mm for theatrical distribution, stylistically – with its static camera positions and conventional framing and editing – *Ladies and Gentlemen* ... represents a step backward from the sophistication of *Gimme Shelter*. Many Stones fans regard this period as a high point in the band's history, yet the absence of any framing material for the performances captured here leaves the film floating free of any historical context with which a casual viewer could properly place the performance within the band's career.

Frank and his close friend and collaborator Danny Seymour originally intended to focus on the 1972 North America tour in its entirety, but the backstage footage captured by the pair, ultimately crafted into *Cocksucker Blues*, was deemed inflammatory and uncommercial, and was cast aside. It was at this point that director Rollin Binzer, a highly respected figure in the world of advertising, was brought in to shape Gebhardt and Fries' concert footage into a feature-length film and market it as a major event. In lieu of a conventional theatrical release, the band opted to "four-wall" the film and present it as a special engagement through 1974 with a multitude of city-by-city promotional stunts, showing it using a customized projector and screen, branded Stones stage curtain, and – most importantly – state-of-the-art quadraphonic sound system.[17] Fries and Keith Richards worked on post-production audio for four months at both Twickenham Studios in England and the Record Plant in Los Angeles in an effort to perfect the quadraphonic soundtrack, which was marketed as the first of its kind. In this regard, the Stones consciously enhanced the soundtrack of the film as the spectacular feature of the presentation, and did so with a commitment to leading-edge sound reproduction technology that foreshadows the theatrical concert film of the 1980s and 1990s. While individually the limited-engagement screenings were successful, they didn't occur in any significant numbers and never outside of major North American centers. Like several other Stones films before it, *Ladies and Gentlemen* ... was officially unavailable for many years after its original release and suffused with some mystique by fans of the band and film collectors; in early 2010 it was briefly rereleased to theatres and finally made available on home video after the band successfully regained various international rights to the film. Importantly, the project as a whole provided the band with a degree of control over the presentation of the event and their image that they had not previously enjoyed, and this set a precedent for the Stones' participation in future documentary productions.

***

> The band, in short, has gone from a threatening R-rated attraction to something in the nature of a PG-rated one, which is not simply that the Stones have gone soft; it's simply a different approach.[18]

In the 1970s, the floodgates for the feature-length theatrical rockumentary opened and a torrent of work appeared in the first half of the decade, establishing the genre as a serious box office and record-selling concern. The public's imagination was captured with chronicles of large-scale cultural events such as Woodstock and Isle of Wight, spectacles based upon elaborately produced stadium tours, and portraits of larger-than-life rock celebrity, all at a time when both record sales and the overall growth of the North American entertainment industries were expanding exponentially. The Rolling Stones, with their featured performance in *T.A.M.I. Show*, the intimate portraiture of *Charlie Is My Darling*, the postmodern turn of *Sympathy for the Devil*, the dark reckoning of *Gimme Shelter*, and the divergent documentation of the 1972 North American tour as presented in *Cocksucker Blues* and *Ladies and Gentlemen: The Rolling Stones*, were a central force in the evolution of this documentary category and used these films to craft and reinforce their public image. Not even the Beatles, featured as they were in a number of key early popular music films and documentaries, kept pace with the Stones on-screen during their brief tenure before their dissolution in the early 1970s. Perhaps both the Stones' acceptance of, and regular participation in, non-fictional projects was a tactical decision that allowed them to cultivate and more deeply entrench the bad-boy image that served as one of the clearest points of differentiation between themselves and the Beatles within the popular imaginary. Whereas the Beatles were controlling and buttoned-up, removing themselves from both the rigors of touring and the scrutiny of life in the public eye, the Stones toured relentlessly and invited filmmakers to document both their performances and their creative lives offstage. It is then curious that at precisely this moment in the genre's development, in the wake of *Ladies and Gentlemen . . .* and facing a series of personal and professional obstacles, the group would withdraw from cinema's spotlight. The band would not participate in another theatrical documentary project for nearly a decade, finally returning to the screen with the feature-length concert film *Let's Spend the Night Together* (Hal Ashby, USA, 1983). The project was met with mixed reactions, celebrated by some for Ashby's ability to capture faithfully the pastel-soaked gigantism of the tour's stage design and enormity of the stadium crowds that the band now commanded ("It's just a concert," wrote Janet Maslin for the *New York Times*, "a beautifully crafted record of the Stones' performing style at this stage of their career, and Mr. Ashby hasn't tried to make it anything more."). It was attacked by others for its complete lack of creativity and several poor editorial decisions; Roger Ebert in the *Chicago Sun-Times* admonished the band and Ashby for including images of famine victims and decapitated political prisoners in a regrettable montage sequence set to "Time Is on My Side," images that the band excised from the film upon its release on home video in 2010.

Currently, the Rolling Stones remain ever present in popular music documentaries and committed to non-fictional portraits of their creative process and live performances as key to their artistic personae. With almost each album release, a making-of documentary is included in the album package, while a made-for-home video tour documentary or concert film often follows in the album's promotional cycle. As Coelho has written, it is the continuation of a practice adopted in the wake of *Cocksucker Blues* that finds "the Stones [taking] increasing control of their concert footage as a way to rectify, reify, and even deify their historical position within popular music."[19] Occasionally, the investment is made in a production intended for theatrical release or pay-television. *Shine A Light* (Martin Scorsese, USA, 2008), shot at New York City's Beacon Theatre during the course of the 2006 *A Bigger Bang* tour in observance of the band's 45th anniversary and released theatrically in standard and IMAX formats, was celebrated by fans and critics alike and prompted numerous articles on the resurgent popularity of "rock docs." It was a box office success, grossing $15.8 million worldwide, ranking it among the highest-grossing documentary releases of 2008 (and for a time in the top ten highest-grossing concert documentaries ever), and the most successful Stones film in their history.[20] Nonetheless, for some it was a timid portrait of a rock act in decline. More recently, the fiftieth-anniversary retrospective project for HBO, *Crossfire Hurricane* (Brett Morgen, USA, 2012), commemorated the first twenty years of their career and did so by accenting the central place the Rolling Stones occupy in the rockumentary canon, explicitly privileging the cinematic record to give visual form to the audio interviews recorded exclusively for the project. The history of the Rolling Stones on film has become the history of the band itself. And so we might playfully ask, were the Rolling Stones the authors of these filmic images that now stand as iconic of the group and representative of rock culture at large, or did the films create the Stones and cement our impression of the group as popular music's most authentic purveyors of the ideals and rebellious nature of rock and roll?

Selected Filmography

Binder, Steve. 1964. *T.A.M.I. Show*. USA.
Whitehead, Peter. 1966. *Charlie Is My Darling*. UK/USA.
  1967. *Tonite Let's All Make Love in London*. UK.
Godard, Jean-Luc. 1968. *Sympathy for the Devil* [*One Plus One*]. UK/FRA.
Woodhead, Leslie. 1969. *The Stones in the Park*. UK: Granada Television.
Maysles, Albert, David, and Charlotte Mitchell-Zwerin. 1970. *Gimme Shelter*. USA.
Frank, Robert. 1972. *Cocksucker Blues*. USA.
Binzer, Rollin. 1974. *Ladies and Gentlemen: The Rolling Stones*. USA.
Lenau Calmes, Lynn. 1981. *Some Girls: Live in Texas '78*. USA.

Ashby, Hal. 1983. *Let's Spend the Night Together*. USA.

Michaels, Lorne. 1989. *25 × 5: The Continuing Adventures of the Rolling Stones*. USA.

Kroitor, Roman, and Noel Archambault, and David Douglas, and Julien Temple. 1991. *Rolling Stones: Live at the Max*. IRE/CAN/USA.

Gable, Jim. 1995. *Stripped*. USA.

Lindsay-Hogg, Michael. 1996. *The Rolling Stones Rock and Roll Circus* (1968). UK.

Scorsese, Martin. 2008. *Shine A Light*. USA.

Kijak, Stephen. 2010. *Stones in Exile*. USA.

Morgen, Brett. 2012. *Crossfire Hurricane*. USA.

Dugdale, Paul.
   2016. *The Rolling Stones: Havana Moon*. USA
   2017. *Olé Olé Olé!: A Trip Across Latin America*. USA.

Notes

1 For a comprehensive listing and discussion of films, television appearances, and promotional films and videos focusing on the Stones up through the mid-1990s, see Karnbach & Bernson, 313–91. For a survey of the Stones' appearances on radio and television during the 1960s, see Richard Havers, *Rolling Stones On Air in the Sixties: TV and Radio as it Happened* (New York, 2017).

2 For a study of the rockumentary, see Michael Brendan Baker, "Rockumentary: Style, Performance, and Sound in a Documentary Genre," Ph.D. diss., McGill University (2011).

3 David James, *Rock 'n' Film: Cinema's Dance with Popular Music* (New York, 2016), 257.

4 It is likely that *The Rolling Stones Rock and Roll Circus*, produced for the BBC in 1968 but not broadcast and unavailable until a home video release in 1996, was one such project.

5 Bill Nichols, *Representing Reality: Issues and Concepts in Documentary* (Bloomington, 1991), 38–42.

6 Victor Coelho, "Through the Lens, Darkly: Peter Whitehead and The Rolling Stones," *Framework: The Journal of Cinema and Media* 52 (2011), 181.

7 Peter Whitehead. "Those Crazy, Joyous Days," *The Guardian* (November 22, 2002): www.theguardian.com/culture/2002/nov/22/artsfeatures7 (accessed February 27, 2019).

8 Using previously unpublished correspondence and materials, Victor Coelho ("Through the Lens") chronicles Whitehead's attempts to engage with Oldham and Jagger as a creative partner, and the Stones' efforts, in turn, to acquire outright ownership of Whitehead's footage of the band.

9 Whitehead ultimately went on to a successful career in alternative cinema, directing several films with a strong interest in popular music culture. Of note is his document of the late 1960s political counterculture and the nightlife of "swinging London," *Tonite Let's All Make Love in London: Pop Concerto for Film* (1967), which largely abandons the quasi-journalistic approach of his earlier Stones film and instead relishes in a stream of consciousness montage aesthetic punctuated by step-printing, strobe effects, and superimpositions. Volume 52/1 (2011) of *Framework: The Journal of Cinema and Media*, is devoted entirely to the life and work of Whitehead.

10 Shaun Inouye, "Indicting Truth: Jean-Luc Godard's *Sympathy for the Devil* and 1960s Documentary Cinema," *Studies in Documentary Film* 7 (2013), 150.

11 Joel Selvin, *Altamont: The Rolling Stones, the Hells Angels, and the Inside Story of Rock's Darkest Day* (New York, 2016).

12 Sheila Whiteley, "Little Red Rooster v. The Honky Tonk Woman: Mick Jagger, Sexuality, Style and Image," in *Sexing the Groove: Popular Music and Gender*, ed. Sheila Whiteley (New York, 1997), 86–7.

13 Robert Christgau, "The Rolling Stones: Can't Get No Satisfaction (1972)," in Robert Christgau, *Any Old Way You Choose It* (New York, 2000), 219.

14 Nichols, *Representing Reality*, 60–3.

15 Owen Gleiberman, "The Rolling Stones in 'C—sucker Blues': A Verité Gas, Gas, Gas," *Variety* (July 21, 2016): variety.com/2016/film/columns/the-rolling-stones-robert-frank-1201819197/ (accessed February 27, 2019).

16 In our contemporary age of online video, streaming, and sharing, unofficial copies of the film are now readily available on platforms such as YouTube and Vimeo. In 2013, a private collector publicly auctioned one of the only known 16 mm prints of the film; it quickly sold for over £25,000 to an unnamed collector.

17 In the film business, "four-walling" refers to the practice of filmmakers or distributors renting theatres and event spaces outright, covering the costs involved in promoting and exhibiting the work, and taking 100 per cent of the box office gross; it represents a risk mitigated by the complete control the promoter has over the event and the likelihood that such an exclusive engagement will be well attended and create strong word-of-mouth for any subsequent screenings.

18 Robert Hilburn, *Los Angeles Times* (June 3, 1975).

19 Coelho, "Through the Lens," 176.

20 Baker, "Rockumentary," 1; see also Michael Brendan Baker, "Martin Scorsese and the Music Documentary," in Aaron Baker (ed.), *A Companion to Martin Scorsese* (Hoboken, 2014), 239–58.

10 Second Life and the Dynamics of Revival: The Stones after 1989

VICTOR COELHO

1989 marked the end of one career and the beginning of another for the Rolling Stones. The year capped almost a decade of disharmony and uneven musical production – "Giants Enter a Deep Sleep" is how Elliott describes this period[1] – and witnesses the most acrimonious chapter in the venerable Jagger/Richards partnership, one of the most creative collaborative musical relationships in popular music history. Although the decade began with a successful tour in 1981–82 to promote the album *Tattoo You*, memorialized in the pastel-heavy Hal Ashby-produced film *Let's Spend the Night Together*, the animosity within the entire band continued into the mid-1980s. With Richards' addictions and resultant legal troubles reaching a critical stage, control of the group tilted decisively (and understandably) in the direction of Jagger, who remained resolutely in charge. As producer Chris Kimsey remembers from the recording sessions of their grunge- and funk-influenced album *Undercover* (1983),

> When we got to making *Undercover*, that was the worst time I'd ever experienced with them . . . We recorded a lot of it in Nassau [Bahamas], then mixed it in New York, at the Hit Factory. I would get Mick in the studio from like, midday until seven o'clock, then Keith from like, nine o'clock till five in the morning. They would not be together. They specifically avoided each other. Mick would say, "When's he coming in? I'll be there later." After about a week, it was killing me. And it was such silly things, like one would say, "What did he do?" And I'd play a bit, and the other would say, "Get rid of it."[2]

Nevertheless, in a decade dominated by the emergence of new platforms for accessing music in sound and image – the rise of the compact disc, Blockbuster, MTV, cable networks, the personal computer – the Stones remained in business, and, to be sure, *a* business (anticipating Jay-Z's famous declaration that "I'm not a businessman; I'm a *business*, man"). 1981, for example, sees many enquiries about Stones-related projects by Showtime, HBO, home video providers, and even for tie-ins with hotels, along with proposals for concerts to be shown on pay-per-view offerings, which had already proved to be successful in broadcasting high-profile sporting events such as championship boxing matches.[3]

A flood of licensing requests came to the group's attention: MCA wanted to use "Start Me Up" and "Miss You" in their TV show *Miami Vice*; the Ed Sullivan show asked for footage of the Stones' famous performances during the 1960s for use in the *Best of Sullivan* broadcasts; and representatives for Jerry Lewis inquired about airing videos of "Miss You," "Respectable," and "Far Away Eyes" for broadcast on the annual Muscular Dystrophy Telethon.[4] Noting that club dance music was once again dominating the pop charts along with the emergence of rap, sampling, and remixing, Atlantic decided to release 12" dance product of "Too Much Blood" (from *Undercover*), remixed by producer Arthur Baker to create three versions: dance, album, and dub. Although touring was on hold and band relationships were chilly, requests to perform in Eastern Europe and China were considered.[5] In 1982, there were meetings to discuss ideas about a Rolling Stones merchandising and sportswear line, with a possible test market being Italy, "where the Rock and Roll concept [can be translated] most effectively."[6] By the mid-1980s, tensions between band members became further strained when first Jagger, and then, finally, Richards, Wood, and even Watts, decided to pursue solo projects or collaborations with other artists, and in general reassess their own frayed relationships and overall concept of what the Stones were as a band.[7] Their contractually obligated inaugural album for CBS, the aptly-titled *Dirty Work* (1986), and the promotional video of the opening track, "One Hit to the Body," in particular, demonstrated for all to see the raw (but visually dramatic), adversarial relationship that had opened up between Jagger and Richards. The album was certified Platinum, but the songwriting is at best compliant and uncompelling. The writing on the wall did not forecast a return to greatness.

But the next few years saw a lasting and brilliant solution to these problems. In 1989, with considerable financial backing and an enormous fanbase with disposable income emerging from the Reagan years, the group mounted a full-fledged return as a living, touring, and recording group, initiating a formidable revival, now going on thirty years, that has helped to stimulate virtually every sector of the rock industry and allow the Stones to take control of their own history, rather than have it managed for them. When Bill Clinton was elected President of the United States in November, 1992, to the soundtrack of Fleetwood Mac's "Don't Stop Thinking About Tomorrow," Baby Boomers, classic rock, the nascent internet, Al Gore's dual call to care for the environment as well as accelerate the use of technology, and rock's first adult generation all converged on the podium. The Rolling Stones would soon occupy the center of this new world. Rock has always functioned as an important source of youth identity, but the "second life" revival of the Stones forced a

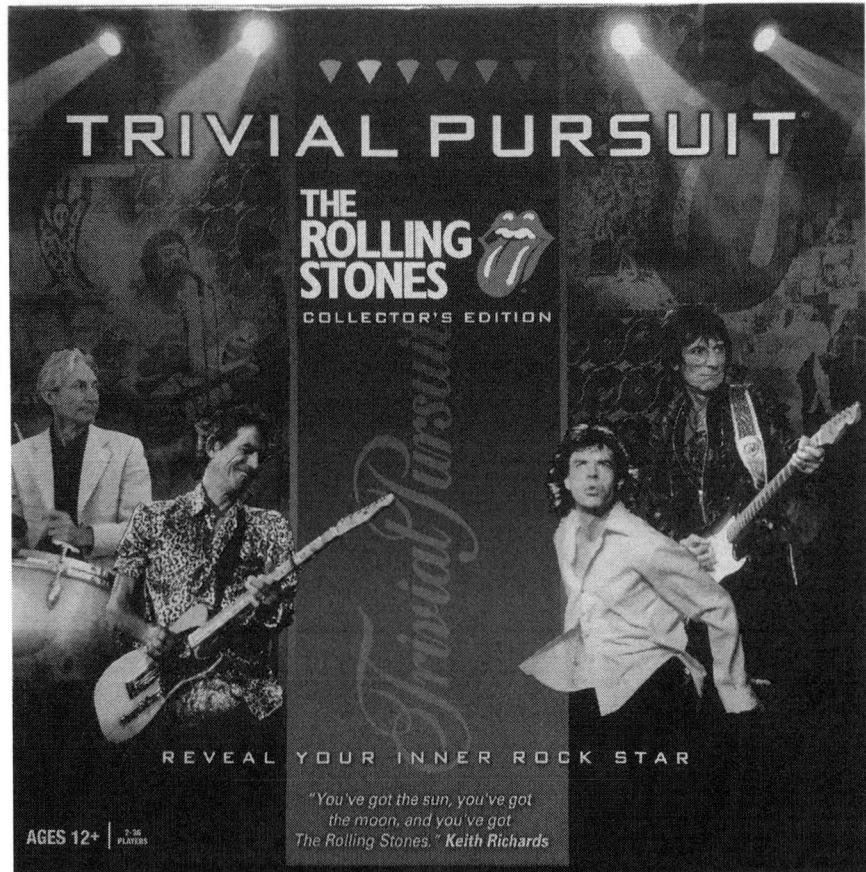

Figure 10.1 Hasbro "Rolling Stones Trivial Pursuit" (*c.* 2010). Photo by author.

reconsideration of who rock's fans and consumers were. The Stones clearly understood that rock was no longer the language *only* of youth.

The Stones' revival capitalized on the musical and economic opportunities made possible by a new business model of the rock industry: corporate sponsorship, and promoters guaranteeing enormous artist fees in return for revenue streams from licensing and the sale of official merchandise – not just T-shirts and tour posters, but intimate apparel, high-end Globetrotter luggage, and even a franchise of the Trivial Pursuit Collector's Edition board game (see Figure 10.1).[8] Just as important in this revival was the recognition of the Stones as culture, and by extension, the validation of rock music as part of history, in which the Stones, along with the Beatles, Clapton, and others, occupied an aristocratic and privileged position. This history was institutionalized by several factors: the construction and programming of the Rock and Roll Hall of Fame, of which the Stones became laureates in 1989; the academic inclusion of rock music within the university curriculum and the production of scholarly research; authorized film documentaries such as Lorne Michaels' *25 × 5* of 1989 – which was even deployed for annual funding drives by the Public Broadcasting Service (PBS) – tracing the history of the group and released to coincide with the 1989 tour; curated rock exhibits at major museums that revalued rock instruments as *objets d'art*; and, of course, the latent economic power contained in their output of almost 400 songs that eventually became the first major rock catalog available on iTunes (years before the Beatles), and is now, of course, part of the streaming libraries of Pandora, Spotify, Amazon, and Apple Music.[9] In terms of their fan base, the Stones succeeded not only in sustaining their original "Nation" of fans, but in reaching new audiences globally, with shows in Latin America, India, and Russia, and no doubt aided by the cameo appearances of more contemporary artists on stage with them. Tightly bound into their "Nation" are allegiances that define social politics, lifestyles, worldviews, and communities. Even the use of their trademark lapping tongue, an image that is both sexual and cheeky, has evolved into a strong symbol of identification and an instant branding of the group for their formidable merchandise enterprise.[10] For their fans, the Stones seem to provide a modern sanctuary, an escape from a world often obsessed by the cultural and puritanical politics of correctness, sex, and language, and an antidote of authenticity to the puerility of many synthetic, trend-driven, and rootless pop genres.

In short, over the last thirty years the Stones have carefully curated their musical legacy as a way to memorialize their historical position within popular music. With the *Steel Wheels/Urban Jungle* tour of 1989, a venture that sparked the major resurgence of the band, the Stones seized upon the possibilities offered by new technologies in video (such as the IMAX film *Stones at the Max* [1991]) and the growing retail videocassette/DVD market (producing concert films of all of their tours) towards carefully constructing their historical image, a method of representation that was more immediate and visually affirmative than through new recordings. Five years later, during the retro *Voodoo Lounge* tour of 1994–95, which marks the arrival on the scene of bass player Darryl Jones as a replacement for Bill Wyman, the Stones issued two concert films, appearing both as Renaissance aristocrats in *Voodoo Lounge* (1994) and as a tough, leather-and jean-clad club band for the mainly acoustic project *Stripped* (1995), much of it filmed in grainy black-and-white, a look that aligned with their first cover ever of a Bob Dylan song – naturally, "Like a Rolling Stone" – of which the group's version and promotional video are stunningly good. The *Stripped* project also capitalized on the very popular format of MTV's "Unplugged" series that was critical in the mass resurgence of Eric Clapton (and the Martin Guitar Company) in 1992, featuring his acoustic renditions of his most famous songs. Beyond the films, the colossal dimensions of the architectural design and stage production of their live shows, particularly for the *Bridges to Babylon* tour of 1997–98, allowed the group to create a full retrospective of their career through the projection of a vast archive of digital imagery and props, while also "returning" them to their origins as a club band through the use of a secondary "club" stage that was set up towards the back of the stadium or arena, on which the group played a short selection of famous singles in close proximity to fans. The Rolling Stones show became a lesson in history.

***

In a widely circulated story about Neil Young, the singer performs a concert in which he plays only his newest – and, therefore, unfamiliar – material from his latest album. As the new songs begin to pile up, one after another, longtime fans who came to hear his greatest hits begin shouting for him to play his classic older songs: "Heart of Gold!" "Southern Man!" etc. Finally, Young announces to the audience that he is going to play "a song you've heard before," and as the crowd cheers in appreciation, he repeats the first song he played that night. This tale illustrates the difficulty faced by artists whose canonic repertory – for the Stones this would be their music generally through *Exile* with the addition of another half-dozen singles – has defined and complicated their own historical position and the close relationship with their fanbase(s). The Neil Young story underlines the irony of how the classic rock format, tribute bands, and the predictable economic certainty of releasing greatest hits packages over new product, has both sustained the Stones and limited their creativity.[11] The group released two greatest hits anthologies after 1989: *Forty Licks* in 2002, to commemorate their 40th year and kick off a tour of the same name, and *GRRR*, in 2012, to mark the band's golden anniversary and the *Fifty and Counting* tour. This album, naturally, contained fifty songs, thirty-two of which had appeared earlier on *Forty Licks*, along with a few pieces of newer material. To justify the considerable duplication of songs contained on previous anthologies, some of the older tracks were remastered, often – but not always – resulting in an enhancement of the originals.

But the fact remains that if tours are traditionally linked to the release of new product – "product" today can be expanded to include EP, single, and album formats, as well as video and film scores – and the products in these cases consist of two greatest hits packages that are central to the branding, merchandising, and publicity of the tours, it is only natural that the last remaining variable (and hopefully still the most important!), *the set list*, will be determined by greatest hits programming. And given the many concordances between *Forty Licks* and *GRRR*, this results in almost two-thirds of the set lists being identical for tours that are a decade apart.

A more historically and musically compelling solution of presenting earlier material was achieved through a marvelous Stones pre-tour show in 2015 at the Fonda Theatre in Los Angeles, in which they gave a complete performance of a single album, *Sticky Fingers* (though not in the same running order as on the record). The concept has recently been used by U2 (performing all of *The Joshua Tree* [1987] in 2017) and Van Morrison (all of *Astral Weeks* [1968] at the Hollywood Bowl in 2009), among others. Of course, complete concept albums like *Tommy*, *Quadrophenia*, and *Dark Side of the Moon* were regularly performed live during the 1970s from beginning to end.[12] As an album, *Sticky Fingers* is dark, replete with references to addiction and withdrawal, and containing some of the Stones' greatest work, with two of the central songs on the album, "Wild Horses" and "You Gotta Move" both recorded much earlier in the famous Muscle Shoals studio in Alabama during their well-documented 1969 tour. The album comes right at the moment of their exile and narrates the closing darkness from the shades being drawn on the sixties. But it is also a *musician's* album: The Stones demonstrate so many different roots techniques (bottleneck, Delta strumming, country idioms), tunings (standard, E, "Spanish" [or G], and "Nashville" [playing without the lower octaves on a 12-string]), vocal dialects, and lyrical images, as well as mastery of the stylistic idioms in country, folk, Mississippi Delta, rock and roll, Latin-jazz, and R&B. The album is also the first to feature the full contribution of Mick Taylor, and there is no question that his stylish playing and deep knowledge of styles are critical to the group's sound. With two further personnel changes to come (Taylor to Wood and Wyman to Jones), it is no wonder, then, that many of the songs from *Sticky Fingers* have been performed live only infrequently since they originally appeared in 1971: While "Brown Sugar" and "Bitch" had been in the live set for decades, "Sister Morphine" was not played live until 1997's *Bridges to Babylon* tour, with "Sway" receiving its first live performance during the *Bigger Bang* tour in 2005. Similarly, "Can't You Hear Me Knocking," which brought Taylor's deft improvisational skills out of the shadows, was performed once in 1971, but not again until three decades later, long after Taylor left the band; "Moonlight Mile" was finally given a performance only in 1999. Thus, there has been no continuous performing tradition for most of the songs on *Sticky Fingers* or *a priori* notion of how they should go, how they will be received, and how well they are known, other than how audiences basically remember them. It will be surprising to know that "Wild Horses" (despite its popularity as one of the group's most exquisite ballads) is not even one of the thirty most-performed songs by the group, and has been played live only slightly more than "Saint of Me" (*Bridges to Babylon*, 1997) and "I Go Wild" (*Voodoo Lounge*, 1994).[13]

The Stones' fresh and historical approach in the *Sticky Fingers* performance at the Fonda Theatre is clear from the start. Ron Wood is outstanding through his versatility and commitment to the poetic aspect of the music, particularly evident in his remarkable playing on "Sister Morphine," clearly referencing Ry Cooder's original slide parts on the album, and transforming this folk song of despair to one of trauma. Indeed, his conscious use of the original and iconic threads of *Sticky Fingers* is a crucial aspect of revival and the Stones' ability to stitch the present onto the past. This is one of the finest performances of the Stones ever captured on video.

Some of the new material from the last thirty years has achieved familiarity in the Stones' vast song catalog and received critical acclaim. This is because in *Steel Wheels*, their 1989 "comeback" album recorded at Sir George Martin's AIR Studios in Montserrat, the Stones "sound" like the Stones. Unlike their efforts in *Undercover* (1983) and the appropriately titled *Dirty Work* (1986), their riff-based sound and their musical instincts return in songs like "Sad, Sad, Sad" and "Mixed Emotions."[14] Other songs, like "Slipping Away" from *Steel Wheels*, a beautiful ballad written and sung by Richards, along with the later "Saint of Me" and "I Go Wild," cited above, "Out of Control" (*Bridges*), and "You Got Me Rocking" (*Voodoo Lounge*), all became staples of their live set for many years. As the Stones' revival quickly became a monumental financial success, for *Voodoo Lounge* of 1994 – the second album of new material, coinciding with a tour on an even larger scale than *Steel Wheels* – the Stones brought in famous rock producer and bass player Don Was, a fan of the Stones since he was twelve. Was' creative philosophy in producing this album was to push the group towards recapturing their iconic sound and hit singles of the sixties and early seventies – in short, to make a retro album, a decision accepted only reluctantly by Jagger and Richards. Nevertheless, *Voodoo Lounge* contains some of the most consistently high quality and compelling original compositions by the Stones of the past thirty years. The album has the classic riff-driven Stones presence; but it is not just a riff for the sake of a riff (as is sometimes the case on *Steel Wheels*), but rather the riff becomes a point of reference to the great Stones compositions of the past. Almost every song on *Voodoo Lounge* seems to have a "parent" composition in the Stones' past catalog: The dark opening song "Love is Strong" is allied with "Gimme Shelter" or "Dancing with Mr. D," themselves opening songs on *Let It Bleed* and *Goats Head Soup*, respectively. The dizzying "Sparks Will Fly" channels "All Down the Line" from *Exile*, but also employs a wonderfully "retro" refrain that seems right out of "Let's Spend the Night Together." The ballad "Out of Tears" brings to mind "Angie," and the use of harpsichord and Baroque overtones on "New Faces" echoes the sixties London of "Play with Fire" and "Ruby Tuesday." One of the most successful Stones albums after 1989, *Voodoo Lounge* débuted at No. 1 and No. 2 in the UK and USA, respectively, and won the 1995 Grammy Award for Best Rock Album.

Dissatisfied, however, with the retro result of *Voodoo Lounge*, and with a unified approach to recording far from being assured with Jagger and Richards at different ends of the creative spectrum, the group opted for a contrasting, contemporary, sound for their next release, *Bridges to Babylon* (1997). Although this project saw the return of Don Was as producer, he mostly worked in Richards' camp; Jagger, on the other hand, was keen to experiment with loops and samples and engaged the Los Angeles team, the Dust Brothers, who had previously worked with Beck (*Odelay*, 1996) and the Beastie Boys (*Paul's Boutique*, 1989), as well as producer and DJ Danny Saber, to work on several tracks. With regard to Jagger and Richards, each had his own studio, so they could record their own songs how they wanted. Not surprisingly, the end result on *Bridges* is mixed. The samples, loops, and synthesized sounds were not compelling for Richards, though the main single from the album, "Anybody Seen My Baby," and its dozen remixes show that the experimentations by Jagger had both artistic merit – and tangible results. The best song on the album is "Out of Control," a dramatic, theatrical, and episodic piece that draws its bass line, self-referentially, from the Temptations' "Papa Was a Rolling Stone." The Stones, of course, had already covered the Temptations' "Just My Imagination" on *Some Girls*, and "Ain't Too Proud to Beg" on *It's Only Rock 'n Roll*; a later remix of "Out of Control" seems to confirm the connection between the two songs by including some Temptations samples.[15] "Out of Control" became one of the highlights of the live show, with the stage and Jagger's dancing flooded by white strobe lights with each return of the refrain.

The last two studio albums, *A Bigger Bang* (2005) and *Blue and Lonesome* (2016), return to music for the core band, are devoid of horn sections and many extra musicians, and instead are dedicated to producing what is largely understood by fans as the "classic" Rolling Stones sound. It is difficult, however, to reconcile what is on these albums with anything resembling "authentic" Stones, and despite the fact that the material on *Blue* consists entirely of blues arrangements, they are hardly "covers" in the sense of duplicating a previous record, as the Stones did on their earliest albums. As true bluesmen themselves since their exilic period, for the Stones the blues repertory is a retelling of a story in the venerable oral tradition, not a mimicry or a photocopy on thicker paper. Indeed, *A Bigger*

Bang delivers mainly a raw, urban sound – a distant echo, perhaps, of *Some Girls* – live off the floor with natural overdrive, but light on technology or studio effects as on *Bridges*.[16] With the absence of Charlie Watts (recuperating from radiation treatment for throat cancer – thankfully, in remission) and Ron Wood (working his way successfully through rehab), the album was begun by just Jagger and Richards, leading to a welcome *déjà vu* camaraderie that is evident in the singular approach to both the sound of the album and the composition of the songs. On the whole, though, the final product is uneven. And no matter how good some of the songs are – "Rough Justice," "Let Me Down Slow," and the sinister "Back of My Hand" blues – in live performance they assume a subsidiary role to the older material. By contrast, the core works from the large Stones catalog are given grand, theatrical stagings in performance. "Gimme Shelter" has turned into a virtuoso, show-stopping operatic duet between Mick Jagger and Lisa Fisher that creates a tremendous surge in the emotional and dramatic level of the show. Both "Sympathy for the Devil" and "You Can't Always Get What You Want" are planned on an even grander scale; they use the entire multi-tiered stage, the works broadening out into symphonic proportions of sound, gesture, numbers of musicians, imagery, choristers, and staging.

Since their "return" with *Steel Wheels* in 1989, followed in 1991 by an IMAX film that monumentalized their presence in the public square of rock and roll, the Rolling Stones have created a massive second life through the creative and innovative leveraging of their enormous repertory of musical assets. Aware of the cultural and economic value of their past and fiercely opposed to the cheapening of pop music as a result of pandering to fleeting musical tastes, they have been able to curate a living museum in which their history is represented live, digitally, on film, and as merchandise.[17] They have tapped into the desires of a fan base they have cultivated for over fifty years, and they accept their role as a rock *cicerone*, leading listeners to the roots of popular music, as well as by revealing the magnitude of their own influence in music history through their many live song collaborations with artists of later generations. It is the reason why their music persists over time.

Notes

1 Elliott, *RSCRS*, 235.
2 Quoted in Rich Cohen, "Inside Mick Jagger and Keith Richards's Five-Decade Bromance," *Vanity Fair* (April 1, 2016). For a frank chronicle of some of the dysfunctionality of the group at this time, see *Life*, 431–5.
3 Rock Hall, Jeff Gold Collection, Art Collins Correspondence, 1978–85.

4 *Ibid.*

5 *Ibid.*

6 Rock Hall, Jeff Gold Collection, Alvinia Bridges/Rolling Stones Documents, 1981–83. Memo from Joyce Moy to Mick Jagger, November 1, 1982.

7 See *Life*, 453–64, for one side of the Jagger/Richards relationship during this period.

8 On the business model used to market the tours by promoter Michael Cohl, see Andrew Serwer, "Inside the Rolling Stones, Inc.," *Fortune* (September 30, 2002): money.cnn.com/magazines/fortune/fortune_archive/2002/09/30/329302/ (accessed February 27, 2019).

9 On rock's position in music history and the electric guitar as an *objet d'art*, see Victor Coelho, "Picking through Cultures: A Guitarist's Music History," in *The Cambridge Companion to the Guitar*, ed. Victor Coelho (Cambridge, 2002), 1–14.

10 A clear example of the identification of the Stones' lapping tongue logo with the band's image in popular culture is illustrated by a character in the HBO series, *The Sopranos*. Janice Soprano (played by Aida Turturro) is the wayward, rebellious, and troubled sister of mob boss Tony Soprano. Janice sports a tattoo of the tongue logo on her breast. When Turturro was asked if the tattoo was real, she replied, "No, it's not real. But when I met Keith Richards, I think he was disappointed. I said, 'But I wear it a lot!'" The addition of the logo was clearly a conscious choice by producers of the show. See "The Sopranos' Aida Turturro Talks About Fighting Hunger and Her Hit Show," CNN.com (March 20, 2001): www.cnn.com/chat/transcripts/2001/03/20/turturro/ (accessed February 27, 2019).

11 For an account of life in a Stones tribute band, see Steven Kurutz, *Like a Rolling Stone: The Strange Life of a Tribute Band* (New York, 2008). For a study of tribute bands more broadly, see Georgina Gregory, *Send in the Clones: A Cultural Study of the Tribute Band* (Sheffield, UK and Bristol, CT, 2012).

12 Other notable examples include 1970s progressive rockers Yes, who toured widely in 2013 performing three albums in their entirety (*The Yes Album, Close to the Edge*, and *Going for the One*), and Jethro Tull's Ian Anderson, who performed *Thick as a Brick* on tour in 2012, coupled with his recent release, *Thick as a Brick 2*.

13 These data, compiled at www.setlist.fm/stats/the-rolling-stones-bd6ad22.html (accessed February 27, 2019), are inclusive of concerts through October, 2018 and comprise, admittedly, a purely quantitative approach without a description of the data collection methods, but the filters do allow for many types of revealing searches, and the results can be verified elsewhere.

14 Shortly after the *Steel Wheels* sessions, Air Studios, along with most of the island, was totally destroyed by Hurricane Hugo in 1989, followed by the further devastation caused by the eruption of the Soufrière volcano in 1995. For a fascinating archaeological study of the site and its rock (and roll) artifacts, see J. F. Cherry, K. Ryzewski, and L. J. Pecoraro, "'A Kind of Sacred Place': The Rock-and-Roll Ruins of AIR Studios, Montserrat," in *Archaeologies of Mobility and Movement: Contributions to Global Historical Archaeology*, ed. M. Beaudry and T. Parno (New York, 2013), 181–98.

15 See Elliott, *RSCRS*, 316.

16 See *RSG*, 610–13.

17 Indeed, two recent exhibitions dedicated to the Stones have examined the group's entire body of work in this context: the *Rolling Stones: 50 Years of Satisfaction* exhibit at the Rock and Roll Hall of Fame Museum (2013), and the more instrument- and amp-heavy traveling show *Exhibitionism* (2016–), with full participation by the group.

Postlude: Being a Rolling Stones Fan is Not a Choice But a State of Mind

PHILIPPE "PHILFAN" PUICOUYOUL

Translated from the French by Matthew Schuster

It's now, now! Jump in a cab, there are already thirty people!

No, really?

Yes! You don't have time to take a shower, do what I'm telling you!

OK, coming quickly. And thanks, eh!

Come on, come on!

I put the phone down, dress up in nothing too special and call up a taxi. Then I look at the time. It's six in the morning. Bertrand just called me from his cell phone at the Champs-Élysées. I jump in the cab heading for the Virgin Megastore. I'm en route to wait in line for hours to get a pass for the ultimate joy. Tonight, with a little patience and a little luck, once again I'll see the Rolling Stones – for the thirtieth time in my life. On to the

Figure P.1 Rolling Stones concert at the Berlin Waldbühne: audience in front of the stage, September 15, 1965. Photo: Alexander Enger, Preußischer Kulturbesitz; bpk Bildagentur/Art Resource, NY.

Trabendo. Not far now. Sinking into the soft leather of the Mercedes, I breathe a sigh of happiness. I am sixty years old.

***

What better name could have been given to this group that represents all we wanted to be: free as vagabonds or as a rolling stone, without attachments to a society that seemed to compromise our soul?

The world of the Rolling Stones is filled with colorful characters who have crossed the group's path for almost sixty years: influential women and musicians, producers and artists, photographers and filmmakers, dealers, and just plain pests. Some remained their friends, others disappeared, but their most reliable friends – the ones they didn't think about every day, the ones who create their glory in the shadows – are the fans themselves.

The planet is Stones and only the fans know it. The parallel world of fans is vast, complex, messy, organized, silent or brash, and always present. For over fifty years, the Anonymous have supported this virtual concept of the Rolling Stones. They like what they represent, what they *imagine* they represent. They would like to be them, of course – it is the classic story of the defector, from nothing to everything, from the shadow to the light, from envy to action – but because of this, or in spite of this, they have immense respect for their idols, for their paths, for their attitudes, and for the nonchalance they display. These idols that are the mirrors of our desires (see Figure P.1).

The Rolling Stones had fun giving their admirers what they wanted (this is a business, after all), but no human being can go on pretending forever. The history and legend of the Stones are thus inevitable. Oldham could not invent Jagger or Richards entirely; he only shaped the ingredients he had at his disposal. One was born to be the frontman, the other to play the villain, and the story did the rest. The tale, however, continued beyond anything we could have imagined, and their longevity has turned against them. They were caught in their own trap and the Rolling Stones became much more than Mick, Keith, and Charlie. The group has become a separate entity unto itself.

***

Let's Spend Life Together, or "Fanlife" as Therapy

What makes them different from other idols is that the Stones are a multi-headed monster. Celebrities like Michael Jackson, Bruce Springsteen, or

Elvis Presley represent only themselves: There is no interaction of personalities. The Stones represent, by virtue of their plurality, a whole. A whole of which every fan wants to be a part, as every wolf has always wanted to be part of the pack – not in the pejorative sense of Panurge, but in the idea of belonging to something, for those who, consciously or unconsciously, need it.[1] And the extraordinary longevity of the Stones gives those who love them a sense of eternity. Nothing can disappear; the Stones were there when we were twelve years old, they were there again when we were twenty-two years old, again when we were thirty-two, then forty-two, then almost fifty-two – incredible – then almost sixty-two – unimaginable! And they were already there in 2012, to scramble with Lady Gaga for a raucous, exhilarating, rock and roll "Gimme Shelter!" Could it be that nothing could happen to us either? It is an illusion, of course. But it is both amusing and soothing to play with this idea of eternity, against all logic, against all rationalism, against everything. "Amazing," as Jagger said that same evening between "Going Down" and "Dead Flowers," two titles that evoke an entire psychoanalytical program in themselves: the end that inevitably awaits us, from the descent to the tomb to the faded flowers that will remain alone above, when family and friends have left to resume their lives.

With the Stones, one becomes in the first place a fan of their imaginary personalities. It is a game that is obviously rigged, but to be a real fan, and to know why, is to admit it once and for all. We love the image, we care less about the truth, and let no one come to disturb us behind the walls of this world that some of us have put so much time into building. We then become a fan of the group as a human association, an association that produces something that makes us feel good – the music – and especially something that lasts, which is, again, very reassuring. You become a fan of the phenomenon itself, you place it in the light, you sprinkle it with your own delusions, you play with it, you look at it; you look at yourself.

And finally, if the therapy has worked – and that is the purpose of the game – we realize some day that our fidelity has brought us happiness, and we become fans of ourselves. We love ourselves for having been able to manage for a long time this protection that the Stones, a virtual entity, offered us if only we knew how to use it. We love having been able to read between the lines, having been able to belong to a particular kind of universal tribe of troublemakers, indispensable puppets who mock a world that takes itself so seriously.

Whether it is the very first generation of fans of the Rolling Stones at the beginning of the sixties or the fourth and last generation of twenty-year-olds who queue at ticket booths and stadium entrances, it is nice to see that music can generate gatherings other than those involving religion, strikes, or wars. It is a new epic that began in the fifties, after World War II, just as religion in the West was going through the worst crisis of faith in its history. This epic is ours. Salman Rushdie, interviewed a few years ago about the Rolling Stones, about the massive scale of their tour, about all those people who work for them to mount shows on various stages around the world, on these kilometers of cables, on all these trucks, on all this Caravan in motion, said a very wise thing: "It is good to know that pleasure also has its army."

From 1965 on, the first generation, to which I belong, began to worship the Stones not only for their natural savagery and for what it represented in the way of generational liberation, but also for their critical "commitment." "(I Can't Get No) Satisfaction" did not become the anthem of an entire generation for nothing. Young people who wanted to escape the parental or school shackles found themselves there. "Let's Spend the Night Together" had primed the bomb: The Stones and their arrogance heralded a change of era, a true relationship change between generations. Young people were about to be taken for what they really were, namely a marching, creative, and artistic force – but also a purchasing power. For the first time, the desires of young people would be taken into account by the producers of consumer products; they had to be taken into account if the producers wanted to survive.

The cultural prohibitions made obsolete by the Stones are numerous, from the abuse of alcohol to that of drugs, from provocative attitudes to forbidden songs, from trials of resounding implications to declarations of war on the part of a society that was desperately trying to respond to the devastating phenomenon. In 2019, young people who love the Stones have only a vague notion of all these ingredients that made their reputation and which have made them loved by millions of people; they have only the love of their music. And as they live mostly in their own virtual world, made up of social networks and texted conversations, perhaps they finally like the concept of *legend*.

***

The Frame of Time

I have lived my "fanlife" in several stages: by myself at first, in front of my Teppaz (a very popular French record player of the time) in the sixties, then in a small youth community, free as we believed we were free during the seventies. I survived as best I could during the eighties, faced with the animosity and discord between Jagger and Richards. Then in a group, discovered by chance at the exit of a concert by Richards at the Zenith in the early nineties. And, finally, as part of an international community, strongly helped in this by the advent of the internet. This is *my* whole story.

The calendar of my life is structured by Stones events. In the spring of 1965, where was I? In the high-school courtyard with "Heart of Stone" in my hand. In June 1968, where was I? In Château-Thierry, where I had just bought the "Jumpin' Jack Flash" single, when one of my buddies broke his copy saying it was crap and that the Stones were over! In August 1973, where was I? In Italy, where I heard "Angie" for the first time near the showers on a campsite in Verona! In May 1976, where was I? In Paris, where I had just moved into an unappealing, noisy apartment in which I had fun with "Crazy Mama," with the headphones over my ears! In August 1977, where was I? Driving across California, where my eyes came across a huge highway billboard announcing the release of *Love You Live*! In September 1986, where was I? With buddies in a car returning from Normandy with a heavy heart because of my recent divorce and my brain filling up with *Dirty Work*. In July 1995, where was I when I could not go to see them at the Olympia? Busy as a father, taking care of my three-year-old twins in a garden in the Loiret.

Yes, *my* whole story. But a story that could well be that of all the fans.

Let Me Introduce Myself

In September 1964, my older brother returned from England with a few records in his suitcase. There were the legendary Beatles that he adored, the Kinks and their so-British "You Really Got Me," the Moody Blues in their first line-up, with Denny Laine screaming more than singing a fabulous "Bye Bye Bird," the Animals' huge hit "House of the Rising Sun," and two singles by the Rolling Stones, "Not Fade Away" and "It's All Over Now." Something happened while I was listening to these two songs. In the space of a few minutes I had become a fan of the biggest rock and roll band in the world, but I didn't yet know it. I was twelve years old. I had fallen into the magic cauldron.

In June 1969, my parents decided to send me to England, too. On Sunday, June 29, at Orly Airport, I took off for the first time in my life, and three-quarters of an hour later, I arrived at Heathrow. Using my very poor English, I managed to catch the No. 55 double-decker, which took me to the Blackheath high school that was my destination. On the Thursday following my arrival, we were given permission to go to London. I did not miss the opportunity, and off I went – still aboard the 55 – meandering through the London suburbs. Arriving at the edge of the city, the shock hit me right away. On the wooden panels that people in England use to tack their headlines, I read these four fateful words:

BRIAN JONES IS DEAD

I was overcome by stupor, incomprehension, a feeling of horror, frustration, doubting my English – could there be a tiny chance that I have translated incorrectly? – and finally infinite sadness. Because instantly, as someone who knew nothing of the internal problems of the Rolling Stones and who did not yet know that Brian was no longer part of the group he himself to a very large extent created, I think I understood the magnitude of the disaster: The Stones were over! Lost, I wandered about the entire evening, trying to read as many newspapers as I could in the hope of learning more.

The next morning, it was announced on the radio that the Stones would give a free concert on Saturday in memory of Brian. I will never forget the vertigo that overwhelmed me then, sitting on my boarding school bed. But luck was on my side. At around 11:00 a.m., a teacher asked who wanted to attend the changing of the guard that took place every Saturday in front of Buckingham Palace. I had spent two hours devising a thousand stratagems to escape from high school and go to the concert, and bingo, this teacher suddenly granted my deepest wish. Imagine, the changing of the guard! It was too good to believe.

That Friday night, July 4, 1969, I slept very badly. Excited at the idea of seeing my idols in flesh and blood, and overwhelmed with sadness because of the loss of Jones. I think it was that night that the Devil seized me. On Saturday, July 5, I awoke normally, but I was shaking while I got dressed. There was nothing special about the departure from the high school. The No. 55 was more expensive – and slower than ever. I had no specific plan in mind, not knowing very well how the organized visit would unfold.

Then it was 10:30 a.m. The group of school pupils was now walking into the Underground station. Suddenly the name of Hyde Park Corner jumped out at me: Hyde Park, that's where they were supposed to play! I did not think long. I immediately took action. At the next junction I managed to find myself at the back of the pack, and took a left turn into a corridor leading to freedom while my little companions continued their journey straight to Buckingham Palace. Goodbye, see you later. I lost them . . .

I struggled with the blasted London Underground, but at 11:00 a.m. I managed to reach the corner of Hyde Park. It was late in the morning and sunny, and a crowd of people was heading towards the center of the park; I only had to follow the movement. After walking for two or three minutes, I arrived at the scene and was amazed: Although I thought I would be among the first to arrive, I realized that thousands of people were already there. The turf between the stage – so far away – and me was filled with spectators already well settled in compact clusters. I had never seen anything like this in my life! But all was not lost, the Stones had been announced for the end of the afternoon. I had eight hours left to get close to the stage.

Eight hours to cross the wall of the crowd. Eight hours of patience, cunning, apologetic smiles, and trickery to advance. I would not drink, eat, pee, or do anything else for eight hours – just stare at the stage and advance towards it. Centimeter by centimeter, apologizing for a stolen shoulder, a foot that stepped between two spread-out legs. Ten miserable centimeters of free space, and there I was. People were snarling or laughing at seeing me crawl. The Stones' concert was not Woodstock's peace and love and company. Here, everyone defended their territory. It was noon and it had become extremely sunny! My black shirt – that's what I found that looked the most "Stones" in my high-school suitcase – was sticking to my skin, but I was only a hundred meters away from the stage.

A little later, Alexis Korner, Third Ear Band, King Crimson, Screw, Family, and Pete Brown's Battered Ornaments, no less, did everything to make us forget the heat and the tense atmosphere. But every time a song ended, everyone continued, in a moment of mad hope, to fight to gain ground. I let them argue among themselves and I took advantage of the slightest opportunity to move forward in front of my closest opponents. One centimeter, two. It was long, it was hard, I was yelled at, jostled, pulled backward. However, when Pete sounded the withdrawal of his Ornaments, around 9:00 p.m., I was only fifteen meters from the stage. But that was it. I could not move forward, as the crowd in front of me was rammed solid. We just had to wait. And the next half hour would seem like an eternity. It was long, very long. I was very thirsty and I was famished, but my eyes were glued to the right side of the stage, where I had spotted the arrival of the musicians. They were already here, somewhere behind the stage, they were getting ready for US. For ME. I just had to wait a little longer, before the end of that feeling. Because of the wait that day, I learned what it meant. The stress that came with it was immense. My heart was pounding, a vice gripped my lungs, my throat was dry, my stomach hurt more than ever before. At the same time, I knew that I was living a unique moment: In a few minutes, I would see the ROLLING STONES and my life would be changed forever. I would become a fan of the Rolling Stones in the real world.

I would go on to see them often in various exceptional circumstances. At the Palais des Sports in 1970, in Brussels in 1973, at the Abattoirs in 1976, in East Berlin and in Rome in 1990, at Shea Stadium in 1994 for three nights in a row, in the rain of Longchamps in 1995, in the slush of Werchter and as a VIP at Madison Square Garden in 1998, in a front-row seat in the Olympia in 2003, in the masterful O2 Arena in 2006. But even though those concerts are transcendent memories, that Saturday, July 5, 1969, will remain forever the most beautiful day of my life. Even the Trabendo club show in 2012, where I lived in a dream, with my new wife who had just become a fan too, and surrounded by all my Stones friends, cannot compare to that day of pure happiness. You can only be a virgin once . . .

∗∗∗

Everybody Got to Go, or the Fantasy World of the Fans

So, what does it mean to be a Rolling Stones fan? How are we different from those fans of Madonna or Springsteen? The main factor is that even though it was not really intended, this common love of the Stones has generated a world that is parallel to them, a fantasy society, but at the same time very real, that enables us to both communicate and sometimes even meet with each other. Virtual fantasy and desire become reality thanks to the internet and the Stones.

Each fan has his or her own thoughts, special relationship with the Stones, concerts, encounters, favorite records, etc., and then there is the universal thought, the one that brings us together, the common denominator that whatever our particular loves (there are, for example, the pro-Mick and the pro-Keith fans), we always come back to the main point: If the Stones play somewhere, we want to be there and nowhere else. *When you call my name, I salivate like Pavlov's dog* . . .

So, we spend a lot of money and time to satisfy these irrepressible desires. With luck and often thanks to friends at the top of the Stonian news, we sometimes get there. To go to a Stones concert is the Holy Grail (to travel to Olympus, to meet the gods).

We want to be where *life* is – there, among our peers, when the room is only a voice, a single vibration, where we would like communion to be total, where we can express everything: our desires, our anxieties, our doubts, our hopes. It is there where, for a few moments, we know why we came into the world.

That makes us live two lives: the official life, the one that was assigned to us by our parents, which leads us from kindergarten to high-school graduation, an internship at the head office, even unemployment, our first grandchild; and then ours, the unofficial life, the one that totally belongs to us since it was invented by us – the life of a fan of the Rolling Stones.

Some live it alone, although they are few today. Most share it with some friends, a partner or children. Still others want to participate more actively and create fan clubs, curate sites, share online content, publish fanzines, and write blogs.

Still others, known to fans around the world, become a type of self-proclaimed Druid. Doug and his *Shidoobee* site organize cover band concerts in the USA.[2] The "superfan" Bjornulf uses his famous IORR site in the Netherlands to have a chance to approach the band from time to time.[3] Marcelo Tejera, in Argentina, keeps the South American world in suspense with the *Stones Please Don't Stop* website.[4] Meanwhile, Serge of the now-defunct TWIS fan club (*The World Is Stones*) told the world about his latest Stonian adventures in real time on his blog from his home near Montpellier.

In Germany, Wolfgang and Mary have opened their own museum dedicated to rock and the Rolling Stones. Martin, having set up a website with his friend Bob in London, wrote a 600-page book, the Bible of all self-respecting fans, in which he describes song by song all the recording sessions ever performed by the Stones. It is a book that he updates every five years.

Yoko, who lives in Nagasaki, has had her tongue tattooed with the Stones, so as to be one with her idols and carry them in her constantly. Her Japanese compatriots Sonoko and Mikiko follow the Stones all over the world, spending a fortune. Branko, a Serbian with no money to see his idols, managed to be hired as a bouncer and thus attend all the concerts of the 2003 tour. In Germany, Monika and Peter fill their house with Rolling Stones memorabilia and, as husband and wife, have followed them on the European tours for thirty years.

Terri, an Englishwoman, has seen them nearly 350 times since 1963, when she spied on them on the corner of Edith Grove in London, where with her friends she waited for hours hoping that Brian, Mick or Keith would go out to buy a bottle of milk or look out their window. Émilie queues all night in front of a door of the Stade de France to be in the front row and leave behind 89,999 other spectators.

Thirty Swedes and Norwegians gathered under the name Nordic Stones Vikings, a horde of happy folk almost controlled by the imposing Vilhelm and the friendly Barbro, were in love with Brian from an early age. In 2007, they took advantage of concerts in London to visit the grave of their idol in Cheltenham.

Blue Lena, self-titled after the name Keith had given his Bentley in the seventies, a name that was itself a tribute to jazz singer Lena Horne, has been one of the most active American bloggers for two decades. Cindy "Ilovemickjagger.com" Kasmar made a work of art primarily dedicated to Mick. Matt the Brit becomes a record store during conventions to keep satisfying his passion for Stones design and increase his collection of posters, album covers, and flyers of the *Pierres qui roulent*.

The world of Rolling Stones fans is indeed very large and diverse, spreading over the entire planet for over fifty years. As Keith says so well: "There has always been the sun, the moon . . . and the Rolling Stones!" For my part, it was in 2002, with the imminent announcement of their next tour, that the dice of my life rolled on the carpet of Stonian time and stopped on an obvious fact: On the one hand I am a filmmaker, on the other a fan of the Rolling Stones. I have to combine both to make a film about this "fanlife." Why had I not thought of this sooner? Thus was born *Vers l'Olympe [Towards Olympus]: Being a Rolling Stones Fan*, my contribution to their legend, thrown into the world as a documentary. For five years, the fans I met at their homes, on the road, or at pre-concert tailgates welcomed me and gave me their secrets.

The concluding words are theirs.

***

The Word from the Fans

You can't always get what you want but if you try, sometimes you might find you get what you need.

I am looking for seats at the Olympia and I offer €3000 for two seats.   ANONYMOUS

The children of our generation, the children who are now around 60, the post-war grandparents, have needed to cling to values that no longer existed. And we found these new values with rock bands. If you're in religion with the Stones, then your age doesn't matter. 2007 tour. I'm like on the first day, on the Internet, searching for information, looking for seats; I'm ageless. In fact, I think that with the Stones we touch the timeless.   JEAN-PIERRE LESCHER, FRANCE

I was always in a place where I was the most dedicated Stones fan when I was in India, then in Puerto Rico. And in some ways initially I felt isolated, so, I tried to create a Stones atmosphere around me and tried to bring everyone into my way of thinking. And for me that's what it was until the Internet, where a lot of things changed. Then, I realized I wasn't the only one!   NANDITA, PUERTO RICO

I was lucky enough to go to Jajouka, where Brian Jones recorded the Master Musicians of Jajouka. It is a very closed village; it is really a kingdom within the kingdom of Morocco. With Bachir Attar, who is the head of the Master Musicians, we made a very deep connection, and one evening, to make me happy, he allowed me to sleep in a room where Brian Jones had slept. There, Bachir told me his childhood memories. One day, when he was 11 years old, he was at the entrance of the village and he saw Brian Jones dressed as an English psychedelic dandy, in this village where sheep run everywhere, where there is no running water or electricity.

He ran to his father: "Daddy, daddy, weird guys are coming! What is it?" They were like aliens to him!

Brian Jones was quickly accepted, however. They smoked grass, they feasted, and then Brian was allowed to record the Master Musicians. And for me, sitting on the bed where Brian had slept, the fact that Bachir told me that, it was really cult worship, because it's really a transmission, a transmission from father to son, and from the son to the little French journalist who hung out in Jajouka. It was fabulous. An extraordinary experience. It was delirium, but if you could scatter my ashes at Jajouka, I think my soul could rest in peace. The loop would be complete. *FRÉDÉRIC LECOMTE, FRANCE*

Rock music is a kind of Esperanto, but not only for people coming from different countries; it is also a common language between the generations, now, you know, and this is particularly true in the case of the Rolling Stones. *SERGIO DAGRADI, ITALY*

They are outside of time; they are not affected by fashion. *JEAN-CHARLES DE CASTELBAJAC, FRANCE*

Are the Stones gods? Maybe to some people they are. To me they're me. And I'm them. We are a family, we're connected, we're so interconnected that I don't even see where the separation is anymore. *MARILOU, USA*

This decadent image of the Stones version '73; that's why I fantasized in punk rocker. It's not even that I fantasized; I did not think for one second to do anything other than to be Keith Richards in life. *PATRICK EUDELINE, FRANCE*

The first time I saw Mick Jagger was in Senegal, Africa. He was there on vacation and seemed very excited. So for me, this curiosity to go to Others, this curiosity to go and search for Others, shows the magnitude of this gentleman and the perspective of the group. And that's where he's really strong, you know, he can shake his behind like an African, he has humor and at the same time he has class. And he received a medal from the Queen! In sneakers at Buckingham Palace, let's not forget! I don't know, it's a gift from God. Mick is a gift from God. *MOKO, SENEGAL*

When *Let It Bleed* came out, I rushed to the Fnac. At the time, there were good speakers in the booths and I asked to listen to "Gimme Shelter." And there, this intro took me away. I was no longer in the booth, I was no longer on Earth. Because this guitar, I don't know, there is a precision, there is a sweetness at the same time. And then the choirs that come and ... well, for the kid that I was, it was like a sky suddenly filled with stars. You are under a black sky and suddenly you see a Milky Way. It was magical ... *JEAN-LOUIS BERTIGNAC, FRANCE*

Ciao! I'm from Rome, Italy. I'm the voice of Le Pietre Rotolanti, tribute band of the Rolling Stones. Io ho cercato de seguirli di ascoltarli sempre con in qualsiasi momento della mia vita. Sono stati la colonna Sonora della mia vita. The soundtrack of my life. Riesco a sentire in ogni riff di Keith Richards qualcosa che mi appartiene, che é mio.[5] *FABIO HOTSTUFF, ITALY*

I'm a tax inspector, so I'm a bit of a villain in the story; I make adjustments, I perform checks. So how can one be both a representative of the law and a fan of a group that was totally outlawed? One must be bold and at the same time show a certain nonconformity, because, contrary to what one might think, when one makes a tax inspection, it is always a dialogue. It can be done with a certain lack of conventionality, with a certain vision of the world, a little like a Stonian approach. That is to say a little detached. When someone has a very conformist life like me, when we work for the government, with strict schedules, with strict behaviors, we cannot be deviant, we need an outlet. And the Stones are this outlet for me. Whenever I see them, I am no longer myself, I push the envelope. I have a hard time imagining people who are at the same time conformist in their social behavior, at work, etc., and at home! I don't know how they live! *JEAN-LUC, FRANCE*

In the USSR during the seventies, people who listened to the Stones were considered dissident and blacklisted. And since I was a child then, I dreamed of looking at vinyl records in the Melody store window. That's why I became a rock guitarist, to get out of this intellectual ghetto. I survived, and I became who I am thanks to the Rolling Stones. *NIKOLAI, MOSCOW*

I am not married to Erwan, I am married to Erwan and the Rolling Stones! *PATRICIA, FRANCE*

That's something the Rolling Stones probably won't realize: they create so much community sense among fans, something that creates friendship. That's what makes the world go 'round, isn't it? People talking, communicating, and now the Internet is a great help. Well, [now everyone wants to stay with you]; he sends me an email and he will be always welcome to stay. *PAULINE, AMSTERDAM*

A Rolling Stones concert is a huge party. It is at the same time the biggest and the simplest party we can afford. They can offer it to us but we offer them that party too. We are not together to celebrate gods. We celebrate ourselves. We celebrate them and they celebrate us. We celebrate each other. It's a sublimation of life! *TESSA, A ROMANIAN LIVING IN PARIS*

What would we have done without them? *PHILIPPE MANOEUVRE, FRANCE*

Notes

1 *Editor's note*: A character in François Rabelais' *Gargantua and Pantagruel*, "Panurge" is evoked in French to represent someone who blindly, uncritically, follows the actions or path of another or a group.
2 www.tapatalk.com/groups/shidoobeewithstonesdoug/ (accessed February 28, 2019).
3 www.iorr.org/travel/ (accessed February 28, 2019).
4 stonespleasedontstop.blogspot.com (accessed February 28, 2019).
5 "I've tried to follow [the Stones] by always listening to them in every moment of my life. It was the soundtrack of my life. I'm able to hear in every Keith Richards riff something that belongs to me, that is mine." (trans. Victor Coelho).

Bibliography

See www.timeisonourside.com/references.html for a useful, detailed, and updated bibliography of writings about the Rolling Stones.

Autobiographies and Biographies; Historical and Eyewitness Accounts

Booth, Stanley. *The True Adventures of the Rolling Stones*. New York, 1984.

Brocken, Michael. *The British Folk Revival, 1944–2002*. Farnham, Surrey and Burlington, VT, 2003.

Cohen, Rich. "Inside Mick Jagger and Keith Richards's Five-Decade Bromance." *Vanity Fair*, April 1, 2016.

Covach, John. *What's That Sound: An Introduction to Rock and its History*. New York, 2006.

Dalton, David, ed. *The Rolling Stones: The First Twenty Years*. New York, 1981. ed. Rolling Stones. New York and London, 1972.

Davis, Stephen. *Old Gods Almost Dead: The 40-Year Odyssey of the Rolling Stones*. New York, 2001.

Dawson, Julian. *And on Piano . . . Nicky Hopkins: The Extraordinary Life of Rock's Greatest Session Man*. San Francisco, 2011.

Everett, Walter. *The Beatles as Musicians: The Quarry Men through* Rubber Soul. New York, 2001.

Faithfull, Marianne with David Dalton. *Faithfull: An Autobiography*. New York, 1994.

Greenfield, Robert. *S.T.P.* [Stones Touring Party]: *A Journey through America with the Rolling Stones*. New York, 1974.

Hagan, Joe. *Sticky Fingers: The Life and Times of Jann Wenner and* Rolling Stone *Magazine*. New York, 2017.

Jackson, Laura. *Brian Jones: The Untold Life and Mysterious Death of a Rock Legend*. London, 2009.

Jones, Brian. Liner notes for *Brian Jones Presents the Pipes of Pan at Jajouka*. Polygram CD, 1995.

Loewenstein, Dora and Philip Dodd, eds. *According to the Rolling Stones*. San Francisco, 2009.

Lydon, Michael. "The Rolling Stones Discover America." In Michael Lydon, *Flashbacks: Eyewitness Accounts of the Rock Revolution*. New York, 2003, 123–86.

Marcus, Greil. *Mystery Train: Images of America in Rock 'n' Roll*. 6th edn. New York, 2015.

McDevitt, Chas. *Skiffle: The Definitive Inside Story*. London, 2012.

Norman, Philip. *The Stones: The Acclaimed Biography*. London, 2002. *Mick Jagger*. New York, 2012.

Oldham, Andrew Loog. *Rolling Stoned*. Vancouver, 2013. *Stoned: A Memoir of London in the 1960s*. New York, 2000.

2Stoned. London, 2003.

Richards, Keith and James Fox. *Life*. New York, 2010.

Selvin, Joel. *Altamont: The Rolling Stones, the Hells Angels, and the Inside Story of Rock's Darkest Day*. New York, 2016.

Serwer, Andrew. "Inside the Rolling Stones, Inc." *Fortune*, September 30, 2002.

Shapiro, Harry. *Alexis Korner: The Biography*. London, 1997.

Spitz, Mark. *Jagger: Rebel, Rock Star, Rambler, Rogue*. New York, 2011.

Trynka, Paul. *Brian Jones: The Making of the Rolling Stones*. New York, 2014.

Wicke, Peter. *Rock Music: Culture, Aesthetics, and Sociology*. Trans. Rachel Fogg. Cambridge, 1990.

Wood, Ronnie. *Ronnie: The Autobiography*. New York, 2007.

Wyman, Bill. *Rolling with the Stones*. New York, 2002.

Stone Alone: The Story of a Rock 'n' Roll Band. New York, 1990.

Reference Books; Album, Gear, and Song Guides

Appleford, Steve. *The Rolling Stones – It's Only Rock and Roll: Song by Song*. New York, 1997.

Babiuk, Andy and Greg Prevost. *Rolling Stones Gear: All the Stones' Instruments from Stage to Studio*. Milwaukee, 2013.

Clayson, Alan. *The Rolling Stones – Beggars Banquet*. New York, 2008.

Elliott, Martin. *The Rolling Stones – Complete Recording Sessions 1962–2012: 50th Anniversary Edition*. London, 2012.

Janovitz, Bill. *Exile on Main Street*. New York, 2005.

Rocks Off: 50 Tracks that Tell the Story of the Rolling Stones. New York, 2013.

Karnbach, James and Carol Bernson. *It's Only Rock 'n' Roll: The Ultimate Guide to the Rolling Stones*. New York, 1997.

Margotin, Philippe and Jean-Michel Guesdon. *The Rolling Stones – All the Songs: The Story Behind Every Track*. New York, 2016.

Patel, Cyrus R. K. *Some Girls*. New York and London, 2011.

Interviews

Beckotube. "Rolling Stones: Keith Richards on *Blue and Lonesome* with Becko from Triple M," Sydney, December 6, 2016: www.youtube.com/watch?v= 0aHpFAujp7Y (accessed February 22, 2019).

Colothon, Scott. "LISTEN: Keith Richards Talks UK Tour, New Rolling Stones Album and Retirement." February, 2018: www.planetrock.com/news/rock-news/ listen-keith-richards-talks-uk-tour-new-rolling-stones-album-and-retirement/ (accessed February 22, 2019).

Cott, Jonathan. "Mick Jagger: The Rolling Stone Interview – The King Bee Talks About Rock's Longest Running Soap Opera." *RSt*, June 29, 1978.

Cott, Jonathan. and Sue Cox. "The Rolling Stone Interview: Mick Jagger." *RSt*, October 12, 1968. Reprinted in Dalton*RS*, 99–109.

Flippo, Chet. "Nothing Lasts Forever: Who Will Rescue the Rolling Stones?" *RSt*, August 21, 1980.

Fricke, David. "Jimmy Page Looks Back." *RSt*, December 6, 2012.

Greenfield, Robert. "The Rolling Stone Interview: Keith Richard." *RSt*, August 19, 1971.

Kent, Nick. "Mick Taylor: But I Still Love Him . . ." *NME*, October 12, 1974.

Nelson, Paul. "The Guys Can't Help It." Review of *Some Girls*. *RSt*, August 10, 1978.

Schulps, Dave. "The Unknown Stone: Four and a Half Years Later, Mick Taylor Makes his Move." *Trouser Press* 41, August 4, 1979.

Scoppa, Bud. "Gram Parsons Interview: Burrito Deluxe." In Sid Griffin, *Gram Parsons: A Music Biography*. Pasadena, 1985, 99–111.

Wenner, Jann. "Mick Jagger Remembers." *RSt*, December 14, 1995.

Reviews and Criticism

Note: album reviews from *Rolling Stone* are cited here with the original publication reference; citations to the same reviews archived at *rollingstone.com* can be confusing since the date given there is of the album release, not the original publication date of the review, and furthermore often deletes or alters the original review titles.

Bangs, Lester. "Dandelions in Still Air: The Withering Away of the Beatles." *Real Paper*, April 23, 1975. Reprinted in *Creem*, June, 1975; and in *Mainlines*, ed. Morthland, 39–46.

    Goats Head Soup. Creem, December, 1973. Reprinted in *Mainlines*, ed. Morthland, 152.

    "It's Only the Rolling Stones [review of *It's Only Rock 'n Roll*]." *Village Voice*, October 31, 1974.

    "The Rolling Stones: *Black and Blue*." *Creem*, July, 1976.

    "State of the Art: Bland on Bland [review of *Black and Blue*]." *Creem*, July, 1976.

    "1973 Nervous Breakdown: The Ol' Fey Outlaws Ain't What They Used to Be – Are You?" *Creem*, December, 1973. Reprinted in *Mainlines*, ed. Morthland, 143.

Bonici, Ray. "Mick Jagger Starts It Up! Hanging Fire Where the Boys All Go." *Creem*, January, 1982.

Brazier, Chris. "More Meat from the Stones." Review of *Some Girls*. *MM*, June 10, 1978.

Christgau, Robert. *Any Old Way You Choose It: Rock and Other Pop Music, 1967–1973*. Expanded edn. New York, 2000.

Cohen, Debra Rae. "The Politics of Sin [review of *Tattoo You*]." *RSt*, October 15, 1981.

Crowley, Allen. "Mellow Stones: Contradiction in Terms? [review of *Goats Head Soup*]." *Creem*, December, 1973.

Dalton, David. "Let it Bleed." In Dalton*RS*, 332–5.

DeCurtis, Anthony. "Love and Hope and Sex and Dreams: Punk Rock, Disco, New York City & the Triumph of the Rolling Stones' *Some Girls*." Liner notes to 2011 reissue of *Some Girls*. Reprinted in Lethem, Jonathan and Kevin Dettmar, *Shake it Up: Great American Writing on Rock and Roll and Pop from Elvis to Jay Z*. New York, 2017, 530–5.

DeCurtis, Anthony, ed. *Blues and Chaos: The Music Writing of Robert Palmer*. New York, 2009.

Hilburn, Robert. [Review of Stones' 1975 Tour of the Americas] *Los Angeles Times*, June 3, 1975.

Kaye, Lenny. "'Tumbling Dice' Puts the Cherry on the First Side of 'Main Street'." *RSt*, July 6, 1972.

Landau, Jon. "Beggars Banquet: Music, The Sword and The Stones." *RSt*, January 4, 1969. Reprinted in Dalton*RS*, 328–31: www.rollingstone.com/music/music-news/review-the-rolling-stones-beggars-banquet-186424 (accessed February 28, 2019).

Loder, Kurt. "The Stones: Rock and Roll Without Apologies [review of *Undercover*]." *RSt*, December 8, 1983.

Marcus, Greil. "Sticky Fingers." *Creem*, August, 1971. Reprinted in Dalton*RS*, 342–7.

Morthland, John, ed. *Mainlines, Blood Feasts, and Bad Taste: A Lester Bangs Reader.* New York, 2003.

Palmer, Robert. "The Rolling Stones: Once Adolescent, They've Grown Up [review of *Tattoo You*]." *NYT*, August 26, 1981.

"The Stones Gather Strength [review and interview about *Emotional Rescue*]." *NYT*, June 29, 1980.

Rockwell, John. "The Stones at Palladium [concert review]." *NYT*, June 21, 1978.

Swartley, Ariel. "The Rolling Stones: What Kind of a 'Rescue' is This?" *RSt*, August 21, 1980.

Watts, Michael. "An Institution Strikes Back [review of *Emotional Rescue*]." *MM*, June 28, 1980.

Welch, Chris. "Miss You [concert review]." *MM*, July 1, 1978.

Wenner, Jann. "Love in Vain: Dylan and the Stones in the 70s [review of *Some Girls*]." *RSt*, September 21, 1978.

Recording/Sound

Cherry J. F., K. Ryzewski, and L. J. Pecoraro. "'A Kind of Sacred Place': The Rock-and-Roll Ruins of AIR Studios, Montserrat." In *Archaeologies of Mobility and Movement: Contributions to Global Historical Archaeology.* Ed. M. Beaudry and T. Parno. New York, 2013, 181–98.

Cleveland, Barry. *Joe Meek's Bold Techniques.* Los Angeles, 2011.

Frith, Simon and Simon Zagorski, eds. *The Art of Record Production: An Introductory Reader for a New Academic Field.* Farnham, 2012.

Frost, Matt. "Keith Grant: The Story of Olympic Studios." *Sound On Sound*, August, 2012, 146–53.

Johns, Glyn. *Sound Man.* New York, 2014.

Lacasse, Serge. "'Listen to My Voice': The Evocative Power of Voice in Recorded Rock Music and Other Forms of Vocal Expression." Ph.D. diss., University of Liverpool, 2000.

Lewisohn, Mark. *The Beatles Recording Sessions.* New York, 1988.

Moore, Allan. "Beyond a Musicology of Production." In *The Art of Record Production.* Ed. Simon Frith and Simon Zagorski-Thomas, 99–111.

Moylan, William. "Considering Space in Recorded Music." In *The Art of Record Production.* Ed. Simon Frith and Simon Zagorski-Thomas, 163–88.

Repsch, John. *The Legendary Joe Meek: The Telstar Man.* London, 2000.

Zak III, Albin J. *The Poetics of Rock: Cutting Tracks, Making Records.* Berkeley and Los Angeles, 2001.

Race, Politics, Sexuality

Bertrand, Michael. *Race, Rock, and Elvis*. Urbana, 2000.

Burley, Leo. "Jagger vs Lennon: London's Riots of 1968 Provided the Backdrop to a Rock 'n' Roll Battle Royale." *The Independent*, March 9, 2008: www.independent .co.uk/arts-entertainment/music/features/jagger-vs-lennon-londons-riots-of-1968-provided-the-backdrop-to-a-rocknroll-battle-royale-792450.html (accessed February 22, 2019).

Guralnick, Peter. *Sweet Soul Music: Rhythm and Blues and the Southern Dream of Freedom*. New York, 1986.

Hamilton, Jack. "How Rock and Roll Became White." *Slate Magazine*, October 6, 2016: www.slate.com/articles/arts/music_box/2016/10/race_rock_and_the_rolling_stones_how_the_rock_and_roll_became_white.html (accessed February 15, 2019).

"Just Around Midnight: The Rolling Stones and the End of the Sixties." In Jack Hamilton, *Just Around Midnight: Rock and Roll and the Racial Imagination*. Cambridge, MA, 2016, 246–76.

Hellman, Jr., John M. "'I'm a Monkey': The Influence of the Black American Blues Argot on the Rolling Stones." *Journal of American Folklore* 86 (1973), 367–73.

Peraino, Judith. "Mick Jagger as Mother." *Social Text* 124 (2015), 75–113.

Walser, Robert. *Running with the Devil: Power, Gender and Madness in Heavy Metal Music*. Middletown, CT, 1993.

Whiteley, Sheila. "Little Red Rooster v. The Honky Tonk Woman: Mick Jagger, Sexuality, Style and Image." In *Sexing the Groove: Popular Music and Gender*. Ed. Sheila Whiteley. New York, 1997, 67–99.

Film Studies and Literature

Baker, Michael Brendan. "Martin Scorsese and the Music Documentary." In *A Companion to Martin Scorsese*. Ed. Aaron Baker. Hoboken, 2014, 239–58.

"Rockumentary: Style, Performance, and Sound in a Documentary Genre." Ph.D. diss., McGill University, 2011.

Bulgakov, Mikhail. *The Master and Margarita*. London, 1967.

Burke, Patrick. "Rock, Race, and Radicalism in the 1960s: The Rolling Stones, Black Power, and Godard's *One Plus One*." *Journal of Musicological Research* 29 (2010), 275–94.

Coelho, Victor. "Through the Lens, Darkly: Peter Whitehead and The Rolling Stones." *Framework: The Journal of Cinema and Media* 52 (2011), 174–91.

Gleiberman, Owen. "The Rolling Stones in 'C—sucker Blues': A Verité Gas, Gas, Gas." *Variety*, July 21, 2016: variety.com/2016/film/columns/the-rolling-stones-robert-frank-1201819197/ (accessed February 27, 2019).

Havers, Richard. *Rolling Stones On Air in the Sixties: TV and Radio as it Happened*. New York, 2017.

Inouye, Shaun. "Indicting Truth: Jean-Luc Godard's *Sympathy for the Devil* and 1960s Documentary Cinema." *Studies in Documentary Film* 7 (2013), 147–60.

Nichols, Bill. *Representing Reality: Issues and Concepts in Documentary*. Bloomington, 1991.

Whitehead, Peter. "Those Crazy, Joyous Days." *The Guardian*. November 22, 2002:
    www.theguardian.com/culture/2002/nov/22/artsfeatures7 (accessed February 27,
    2019).

Wolfe, Tom. *The Kandy-Kolored Tangerine-Flake Streamline Baby*. New York, 1965.

Films and Documentaries (listed by producer/director)

Ashby, Hal. *Let's Spend the Night Together*. USA (1983).

Binder, Steve. *T.A.M.I. Show*. USA (1964).

Binzer, Rollin. *Ladies and Gentlemen: The Rolling Stones*. USA (1974).

Dugdale, Paul. *Olé Olé Olé!: A Trip Across Latin America*. USA (2017).
    The Rolling Stones: Havana Moon. USA (2016).
    Sticky Fingers Live at the Fonda Theatre. [UK] (2015).
    Sweet Summer Sun: Hyde Park Live. [UK] (2013).

Frank, Robert. *Cocksucker Blues*. USA (1972).

Gable, Jim. *Stripped*. USA (1995).

Godard, Jean-Luc. *Sympathy for the Devil [One Plus One]*. UK/FRA (1968).

Gowers, Bruce. *The Rolling Stones Bridges to Babylon Tour, '97–98: Live in Concert*.
    USA (1998).

Kijak, Stephen. *Stones in Exile*. USA (2010).

Kroitor, Roman, Noel Archambault, David Douglas, and Julien Temple. *Rolling
    Stones: Live at the Max*. IRE/CAN/USA (1991).

Lenau Calmes, Lynn. *Some Girls: Live in Texas '78*. USA (1981).

Lindsay-Hogg, Michael. *The Rolling Stones Rock and Roll Circus*. UK (1968).

Longfellow, Matthew. *Classic Albums – Never Mind the Bollocks: Here's the Sex
    Pistols*. USA (2002).

Maysles, Albert, David Maysles, and Charlotte Mitchell-Zwerin. *Gimme Shelter*.
    USA (1970).

Michaels, Lorne. *25 × 5: The Continuing Adventures of the Rolling Stones*. USA
    (1989).

Morgen, Brett. *Crossfire Hurricane*. USA (2013).

Scorsese, Martin. *Shine A Light*. USA (2007).

Whitehead, Peter. *Charlie Is My Darling*. UK (1966).
    Tonite Let's All Make Love in London: Pop Concerto for Film. UK (1967).

Woodhead, Leslie. *The Stones in the Park*. UK (1969).

Musicology, Ethnomusicology, Theory; Philosophy

Coelho, Victor. "Picking through Cultures: A Guitarist's Music History." In *The
    Cambridge Companion to the Guitar*. Ed. Victor Coelho. Cambridge, 2002,
    1–14.

Covach, John. "From Craft to Art: Formal Structure in the Music of the Beatles." In
    Reading the Beatles: Cultural Studies, Literary Criticism, and the Fab Four. Ed.
    Kenneth Womack and Todd K. Davis. Albany, NY, 2006, 37–53.

Dick, Luke and George A. Reisch, eds. *The Rolling Stones and Philosophy: It's Just a
    Thought Away*. Chicago, 2011.

Dinello, Dan. "Lucifer Rising and Falling." In *The Rolling Stones and Philosophy: It's Just
    a Thought Away*. Ed. Luke Dick and George A. Reisch. Chicago, 2011, 251–64.

Foy, Joseph J. "How Come You're So Wrong, My Sweet Neo-Con?" In *The Rolling Stones and Philosophy: It's Just a Thought Away*. Ed. Luke Dick and George A. Reisch. Chicago, 2011, 201–9.

Heimarck, Brita Renée. *Balinese Gender Wayang (Shadow Play) Music of Bapak I Wayan Loceng, from Sukawati, Bali, Indonesia: A Musical Biography, Musical Ethnography, and Critical Edition*. Middleton, WI, 2015.

Khalfa, Jean, ed. *An Introduction to the Philosophy of Gilles Deleuze*. London, 2003.

Kristiansen, Lars J., Joseph R. Blaney, Philip J. Chidester, and Brent K. Simonds. *Screaming for Change: Articulating a Unifying Philosophy of Punk Rock*. Lanham, MD, 2010.

Marcus, George E and Erkan Saka. "Assemblage." *Theory, Culture & Society* 23 (2006), 101–6.

Peattie, Thomas. *Gustav Mahler's Symphonic Landscapes*. Cambridge, 2015.

Waksman, Steve. *Instruments of Desire: The Electric Guitar and the Shaping of Musical Experience*. Cambridge, MA, 1999.

Wise, J. Macgregor. "Assemblage." In *Gilles Deleuze: Key Concepts*. 2nd edn. Ed. Charles J. Stivale. Montreal and Kingston, 2011, 91–102.

General (specific studies of musicians, groups, and genres)

Adams, Ruth. "The Englishness of English Punk: Sex Pistols, Subcultures, and Nostalgia." *Popular Music and Society* 31 (2008), 469–88.

Clark, Rick. "Mark Knopfler – Best of Old and New." *Mix Magazine Online*. May 1, 2005. https://www.mixonline.com/recording/mark-knopfler-375278 (accessed March 5, 2019).

Covach, John. "Afterword." In *Part of Everything: The Beatles' White Album at Fifty*. Ed. Mark Osteen. Ann Arbor, MI, 2019, 263–9.

  "George Harrison, Songwriter." In *Part of Everything: The Beatles' White Album at Fifty*. Ed. Mark Osteen. Ann Arbor, MI, 2019, 177–96.

  "The Hippie Aesthetic: Cultural Positioning and Musical Ambition in Early Progressive Rock." In *Composition and Experimentation in British Rock 1966–1976*, a special issue of *Philomusica Online* (2007). Reprinted in *The Ashgate Library of Essays on Popular Music: Rock*. Ed. Mark Spicer. Burlington, VT, 2012, 65–75.

  "Yes, the Psychedelic-Symphonic Cover, and 'Every Little Thing.'" In *The Routledge Companion to Popular Music Analysis: Expanding Approaches*. Ed. Ciro Scotto, Kenneth Smith, and John Brackett. New York, 2019, 279–92.

DeRogotis, Jim. *Turn On Your Mind: Four Decades of Great Psychedelic Rock*. Milwaukee, WI, 2003.

Exhibitionism: The Rolling Stones. N.p. [2016].

Gregory, Georgina. *Send in the Clones: A Cultural Study of the Tribute Band*. Sheffield, UK and Bristol, CT, 2012.

Harrison, Daniel. "After Sundown: The Beach Boys' Experimental Music." In *Understanding Rock: Essays in Musical Analysis*. Ed. John Covach and Graeme Boone. New York, 1997, 33–57.

Heckstall-Smith, Dick and Pete Grant. *Blowin' the Blues: Fifty Years of Playing the British Blues*. Bath, 2004.

Henke, James and Parke Puterbaugh. *I Want to Take You Higher: The Psychedelic Era, 1965–1969.* San Francisco, 1997.

Heylin, Clinton. *Babylon's Burning: From Punk to Grunge.* New York, 2007.

Hill, Sarah. *San Francisco and the Long 60s.* London, 2016.

Hoskyns, Barney. *Hotel California: The True-Life Adventures of Crosby, Stills, Nash, Young, Mitchell, Taylor, Browne, Ronstadt, Geffen, the Eagles, and Their Many Friends.* Hoboken, 2007.

Humphries, Patrick. *Lonnie Donegan and the Birth of British Rock & Roll.* London, 2012.

Kellett, Andrew. *The British Blues Network: Adoption, Emulation, and Creativity.* Ann Arbor, MI, 2017.

Kurutz, Steven. *Like a Rolling Stone: The Strange Life of a Tribute Band.* New York, 2008.

McCarty, Jim with Dave Thompson. *Nobody Told Me! The Yardbirds, Renaissance, and Other Stories.* N.p., 2018.

Meyer, David N. *Twenty Thousand Roads: The Ballad of Gram Parsons and His Cosmic American Music.* New York, 2007.

Myers, Paul. *It Ain't Easy: Long John Baldry and the Birth of the British Blues.* Vancouver, 2007.

Powers, Michael. "The Rolling Stones: Danceable Mythic Satire." *Popular Music and Society* 10 (2008), 43–50.

Proehl, Bob. *The Gilded Palace of Sin.* New York, 2008.

Reising, Russell and Jim LeBlanc. "Within and Without: *Sgt. Pepper's Lonely Hearts Club Band* and Psychedelic Insight." In *Sgt. Pepper and the Beatles: It Was Forty Years Ago Today.* Ed. Olivier Julien. New York, 2016, 103–20.

Index of Songs, Albums, and Visual Media Cited in the Text

Note: Album and visual media titles appear in *italics*. For all non-Stones songs and albums listed in this index, the original recording artist (which is not always the song's author) is listed after the song title, followed by, if applicable, the earliest Stones version.

General Index

Printed in Great Britain
by Amazon